ALFRED A. KNOPF

1915 · 100 YEARS · 2015

Women *of* Will

Women *of* Will

Following the Feminine in Shakespeare's Plays

Tina Packer

ALFRED A. KNOPF · NEW YORK 2015

THIS IS A BORZOI BOOK
PUBLISHED BY ALFRED A. KNOPF

www.aaknopf.com

Grateful acknowledgment is made to the following for permission to reprint previously published material:
    Faber and Faber Ltd: "To My Wife" by Harold Pinter, copyright © 2004 by Harold Pinter. Reprinted by permission of Faber and Faber Ltd, London.
    Carcanet Press Limited: "Beware Madam" from *Robert Graves: The Complete Poems in One Volume* by Robert Graves, edited by Beryl Graves and Dunstan Ward (Carcanet Press Limited: Manchester UK, 2000). Reprinted by permission of Carcanet Press Limited.

Library of Congress Cataloging-in-Publication Data
Packer, Tina, date.- author.
    Women of will : following the feminine in Shakespeare's plays / Tina Packer. – First edition.
        pages cm
    "This is a Borzoi book."
    Includes bibliographical references.
    ISBN 978-0-307-70039-1 (hardcover : alk. paper) –
ISBN 978-0-385-35326-7 (eBook)   1. Shakespeare, William, 1564–1616–
Characters–Women.   2. Women in literature.   I. Title.
    PR2991.P16 2015
    822.3'3–dc23
                                                        2014012321

Jacket images: (center) *Lady MacBeth* by Henri Fuseli/SuperStock/ Getty Images; (background) E+/wepix/Getty Images; (crack) Michael Betts/Getty Images
Jacket design by Abby Weintraub

Manufactured in the United States of America

First Edition

To Elayne Bernstein, whose spirit
and family carried us through so much;

and Sarah Hancock, who continues the journey

CONTENTS

PROLOGUE

Somewhere in the midst of my forty years of directing Shakespeare's plays, acting in quite a few of them (never at the same time—directing and acting occupy different parts of the brain, and I find it impossible to be in both states at once), somewhere in the midst of this I realized that the Shakespeare who wrote *The Taming of the Shrew* was not the same Shakespeare who wrote *The Tempest;* that the Shakespeare of *Henry IV Part 1* was very different from the Shakespeare of *Coriolanus;* and where a principal difference lay was in Shakespeare's relationship to his women. The callow youth who penned *Shrew* undertook a long, arduous, always-seeking journey to become the playwright who wrote *The Winter's Tale.*

The development in Shakespeare's relationship to women was always there in front of me, hidden in plain sight. I wasn't looking for a pattern to emerge; it came of its own accord. It came because I had done so many of the plays over and over again as actor, director, teacher, and writer. It came because I am a woman, and the women's parts had always been so alive to me, even one-line servant parts. It came because I often felt antipathy to the women in Shakespeare's early comedies, I was electrified by the women of the middle plays, and I responded gently to the women of the mature plays. It came because a pattern is there, written into the very fabric of all his work, plays and poems. What happens to the women, how Shakespeare thought about them, what he had them do, what they represented to him, and, finally, how he became one of them, is there. It is written on the page, but it lives principally in performance; it is there to be understood, breathing, alive through the minds and hearts of other people now embodying the scenes.

Over the years, I have struggled with the fate of Kate in *The Taming of the Shrew*. Each time I have directed it, I have tried to work out an ending that says the words that are in the text but does not send the message to the audience that I think the only way to draw the play to a close is by her happy, willing submission. Shakespeare was compassionate toward Kate, gave her a voice to say how it was for her: "My tongue will tell the anger of my heart, or else my heart concealing it will break." And yet . . . and yet I can never reconcile myself to the way in which Petruchio forces her into surrender—starving her, taking her clothes away from her; worse, taking her language away from her, making her lie about what she sees and knows. Living with a man who would do that kills the spirit. Was I supposed to think that their marriage could be a happy one? And, yes, I think the very young Will Shakespeare thought it was a happy ending.

I have plunged into despair as I directed *Coriolanus* because of the manipulative, relentless bullying of Volumnia, who sends her son to war when he is but a child—and is deeply proud of it. "If my son were my husband," she says to the wife of her son, "I should freelier rejoice in that absence wherein he won honour than in the embracements of his bed where he would show most love. When yet he was but tender-bodied and the only son of my womb, when youth with comeliness plucked all gaze his way . . . I, considering how honour would become such a person . . . was pleased to let him seek danger where he was like to find fame. To a cruel war I sent him. . . ." And she did, and he returned triumphant, a national hero, and now a killing machine. The depiction of Volumnia, written toward the end of Shakespeare's writing life, is complex, detailed, and accurate, totally without sentiment. And the actions of the play flow seamlessly from the actions of her mind and the upbringing of her son.

One day I was watching a performance of *The Tempest* from the lawn of Edith Wharton's home, The Mount, where Shakespeare & Company—the company we founded in 1978—had lived for a couple of decades. I was pulling up the grass on either side of me, watching the actors, catching the nuance of their thoughts, feeling how it was reflected in their words. A courageous, distinctive actor called Midori

Nakamura was playing Ariel, naked except for a brief loincloth, with the ability to make herself physically and vocally into either a man or a woman or something else. She had started the performance way above the audience, on the chimney top of The Mount, throwing down thunderbolts from the sky, while The Mount itself became a great ship, cracking in two, sails torn, sailors leaping for their lives, a soundscape of a tempest created by Roger Reynolds which tore into our ears in rending shrieks. And Ariel Midori leapt in ecstasy as she created this magic, mesmerizing the six hundred people watching below. Here was a spirit who should be free, if ever there was one.

At the end of the play, after she has persuaded Prospero not to take revenge upon his enemies but to forgive them, redeem them, when she yet again requests her freedom and finally Prospero keeps his word (having broken it so many times before) and she is freed, she starts her journey away from the audience and the simple stage, and recedes into the woods, huge white pines that Edith Wharton had planted a hundred years ago, and that now stretch into darkness as far as the eye can see.

As Ariel makes this journey, she passes Miranda, Prospero's daughter, newly in love, newly betrothed, another wild spirit of the island, growing up among nature with only the spirits and Caliban, child of Sycorax, the witch, as playmates. Miranda, too, is making a journey, but in the opposite direction. She is going with her new husband and kings and princes back to civilization, a place she barely remembers. Miranda is also skimpily dressed, but her body, unlike Ariel's, is covered. Her life will soon change beyond anything she could imagine, as she encounters all the embedded ideas surrounding status, race, class, gender, religion, in a culture that will make her heir apparent to two Italian kingdoms.

When these two women cross each other onstage—one the creative force that allowed Prospero to work all his magic; the other Prospero's blood, nature's creative force, the daughter who will now inhabit the power world of princes—I sat there tugging at the grass and scattering it in my lap, listening and watching. I knew I was sensing Shakespeare's own creative reality under this scene, for nowhere is it in the written text. The women pause for a moment and look back at each other: two halves of one whole, connected yet separate, a moment not recorded anywhere in the words on the page of *The Tempest* (indeed, they never speak to each other in the play), but alive here, in this present moment of actors on a stage, this particular performance in these particular grounds of Wharton's house, watched by six hundred, a world that comes out of the dramatic imagination of William Shakespeare, born 450 years ago.

If you are a director or an actor of his works, you start listening for, looking into, allowing the unwritten alchemy of how human beings behave in one another's presence to be part of your knowledge of who William Shakespeare is; and why he has lived and is living and will live, as long as human beings are on this planet. This unwritten dramatic alchemy is engendered every time actors and directors create their world of the play. The alchemy lies in the energy and spirits of those artists, how they infect and affect each other, and this collective power spreads out to the audience, and they, too, become a part of it. Nowhere is it written in the text. It is created in the rehearsal space over several weeks, like ripples in a pond, disturbing layers of meaning, churning up pain and laughter, to make a presentation of life. Shakespeare wrote plays that demand an active participation of all the people involved; the way in which he wrote has as a prerequisite the creativity of others. Without the truth of others, the plays do not exist. And every single performance of every single production is a unique collaborative act. Shakespeare's writing demands and triggers play from the players in the playhouse. This collaborative play is the energy that forms the world the characters live in; Shakespeare's words are the piercing shafts to drill deep, penetrating the conscious and unconscious minds of the players, the characters, and the audience.

It was somewhere in the midst of watching the world of this particular *Tempest,* sitting on the lawn, that I thought, "Oh, the Shakespeare who wrote at the end of his life found a way to make the world come into harmony, make it all come right—not simply right, but complexly right, as life is complex, for there are few simple answers in the daily task of living. He made it all come right, and he made it come right through the women." For when those two women turned and looked at each other, they both knew that they had even larger tasks in front of them, and they had the strength and creativity to do the work, at this moment when they were in touch with their own power.

So different from the Kate in *The Taming of the Shrew*, written by the youthful Shakespeare, blind to what he didn't know.

I applied for a Guggenheim so I could take a little time off from running a theatre company full-time and spend some hours in contemplation. Those hours were fifteen years ago—and that year I worked my way through the whole canon in the chronological order in which we think he wrote the plays. I found the title of this book. Or, rather, my husband, Dennis Krausnick, suggested it as we were discussing themes. *Following the Feminine in Shakespeare's Plays* was my idea. And we merged the two.

Obviously, I was studying the women of Will Shakespeare; I was also understanding their own will to power, the myriad ways they expressed their desires for and fears of power, how they went underground, how they subverted or directly opposed power. Finally, I understood why "will" in Elizabethan English means sexuality or sexual desire, the sexual parts themselves, and how this kind of will played a major part in the actions of the plays, the power or destruction of the women, and why it is, even in this day and age, vitally important that women own their own sexuality on their own terms, that it not be the possession of any other person, culture, or king.

I turned that knowledge first into a performance piece that I could act in myself, then with one other actor; then into five plays; and finally into this book. I see Shakespeare not just as a theatre person who part-owned, acted, and wrote for a company (not unlike my own) but as an artist who underwent a spiritual journey in which the women became vessels for the truth, one way or another.

From that moment of realization, when I watched the crossing of Ariel and Miranda onstage—an event that occurred spontaneously once in rehearsal and then was officially directed by me, enacted by others—my own perspective shifted. In the rehearsal of *The Tempest* I had understood something dimly; I had then put it into practice; now I was watching its execution; and from that progression a much larger meaning emerged. It inspired me. I felt a deep desire to chase that meaning, investigate it, follow it, ask other people to discuss its meaning, start looking at it from multiple points of view, let it drop into my own psyche again and again, and see what came up. A thought emerged; a stage action was born. "Ariel and Miranda, they know each other, they have always known each other, they have lived with the sense of each other's presence for fifteen years on this island. But it is only in this moment of parting that they acknowledge each other. They'll never see each other again, but they will always travel with each other, take strength from each other. They are vulnerability and the desire to take on the world. They are the manifestation of Shakespeare's reason for living." This began my long journey to discover the truth that lay below the surface of the women in Shakespeare—a path that allowed me to see my own life. Eventually, it became the journey of my acting partner, Nigel Gore, and to some extent of our director, Eric Tucker; it also reflected the journey of our theatre company, Shakespeare & Company, and the two people who have stood with me through its thirty-seven-year progression: Kevin Coleman, director of education, and Dennis Krausnick, director of training.

The story of this book is a simple one. It follows the progression of the women in Shakespeare's plays. Then, from the way in which Shakespeare wrote about women, we follow his spiritual growth. And I have a hope that understanding the spiritual growth of an artist of Shakespeare's magnitude may provide a road map for the kind of creative action and understanding we need to alter the dangerous course the world is on—for Shakespeare pulled back from the apocalypse of *Lear, Coriolanus,* and *Macbeth* and found a way to the regeneration and rebirth of *The Winter's Tale* and *The Tempest.*

It's a huge canvas; but, then, Shakespeare is a huge soul. He's played in every part of the world, because he reflects back to people their inner state of knowing. There are usually only two to four women in each of the plays—as opposed to ten to twenty men; women are always the minority, always "other" in some way. I counted. Depending on whether you think fairies are male or female, witches are human or nonhuman (Is Hymen a god or a man? Does the goddess Diana exist, or is she a dream? Is Ariel a man or a woman?), there are nearly a thousand men in the canon, to 160 or thereabouts women and girls. And because the women are never assumed to be the apex of political power (except Cleopatra, of course), the women are always looking *at* power: either how to acquire some or how to avoid its worst violence, how to circumvent it or how to acquiesce to it, but they must watch it all the time. It is not a neutral subject to them. And of course they never just assume it's theirs to organize and exploit, as many of the men do. This means that women become skilled observers of power. And often the thoughtlessness of power is visited upon the women, so you can see what a society values by its power structures: if women do not have any overt power, their voices will not be heard, nor what they value in the raising of children, even though they may be the chief caregivers. In these cases, the will to power is very alive to women, because there is no accepted course for them to exert influence. They have to find a way to make an impact on the world of family politics and status. And, ultimately, Shakespeare knew the world would not find proper harmony if the qualities of women and men did not come into balance.

Women have been alive in the minds of writers and actors (until relatively recently, all male, of course) for the two thousand–plus years during which those professions have existed. Women did not get to portray themselves onstage or by pen until 350 years ago, and then only the feisty few who would not be put down. So women as the expression in the unconscious and conscious minds of male artists have been vibrantly alive in the center of most dramatic action; living women rarely had that privilege. This has had several consequences.

Because women are such potent ingredients of men's imaginations, we see how much power men feel women have over them, and how women must be suppressed, defanged, or idealized in one way or another. How, with Eve, they are often thought to be the root of the evil in the world—which says more about the man or men who wrote that story than about Eve herself. Eve is curious and wants knowledge, not power over others. The other consequence affects the women themselves: both onstage and offstage. Women have two levels of understanding concerning how to behave—one, to behave the way men want them to behave and forget that what they want might be different; two, to find out how they really feel and decide whether or not they are going to act on it! It has taken hundreds of years for women's voices to be heard and affect the course of human events. In order for the world to find its healthy balance, all women's voices need to be heard. I do believe artists of depth can portray both sexes—but as far as the history of theatre is concerned, it has been men writing, acting, producing, with women coming late into the game.

Shakespeare broke a mold. After about five years of writing, he saw women as women, *including* the bind they had been put into. No other playwright, writing before Shakespeare or at the same time as Shakespeare, had ever seen women as women.

You may question whether it is useful to ask why or how Shakespeare was able to do this; that he did it, and that the plays are still spreading their influence, is the most important factor. But the "why" and the "how" do throw light onto the source of Shakespeare's creativity, and are a major perspective of this book.

Shakespeare was an actor. He used the whole of his body, his voice, his spirit, his sexuality, when onstage. So he wrote as an actor—this is viscerally clear, especially once he hit his stride, from *Romeo and Juliet* onward. His words are embodied words. He was making plays with the whole of his being. What I hope to do in this book is to write as an actor, as a maker of theatre, as a player in the playhouse.

The scholarship around Shakespeare is awe-inspiring. In many ways, the commentary on his plays, taking place in academia in China, Australia, Japan, South America, India, every university in the United States, to say nothing of England and Europe, shows that the desire to understand human nature and decipher great art is palpable in the academy. In fact, the great intellectual tradition to explore the *perfectibility of man* is alive and well in Shakespeare studies everywhere. But the studier of the play only has one facet of the play to work with—the close reading of the text from an intellectual perspective. The performer of the play wallows in many different textures of psychic mud. And because it is mud, it has a mixture of sounds, smells, touch, unconscious leaps, actions, silences, feelings, that are hard to name. I would not know half the things I know about Shakespeare without my academic brethren; I am forever grateful to them. But it is playing in the playhouse that allows me to go to the depths. I believe Shakespeare's power came from a whole knowing of body, mind, spirit, and sound, developed through his acting. And, if I am honest, I think it's knowing him on this level that could really make a difference to our understanding of the world. We try to understand others and live in the world with only part of ourselves present. We develop systems where "profit" is narrowly defined. The whole Shakespeare may wallow, wail, and splat—but it is a body of work that informs the whole human being, and awakens dormant perspectives in our interaction with one another as members of the human race. If the way we know life is too narrow, our satisfaction is too narrow, and thus we are always looking mistakenly for satisfaction elsewhere.

I have directed most of the plays in the canon, but have only performed in seven of them—until we came to put the *Women of Will* cycle onto the stage. In the cycle (five parts, of course, like this book), we perform chunks of twenty-five of the plays, but touch on thirty-seven in all. Therefore, it is Nigel Gore whom you will hear about most often when I talk about my experience of acting the scenes. Both of us are transplanted Brits, went to theatre schools, and had early careers in Britain before coming to America. We met in 2006, when Nigel joined Shakespeare & Company as an actor.

Though I tell the story of Shakespeare's development through his writing of women, I will also follow tangents, and underpinnings, and subtexts, reporting on responses from many actors I have directed, my fellow actor in the play version of *Women of Will,* and the director and designers of *Women of Will,* creating an associative pattern that will, I hope, get closer to the truth of how Shakespeare created those worlds,* where the essence of life could be revealed—and how women's voices were essential to the revelation.

Note: Act, scene, and line numbers refer to *The RSC Complete Works.*

Women *of* Will

THE WARRIOR WOMEN:
VIOLENCE TO NEGOTIATION

SCENE I: Understanding the Structure—Form and Content

The ways in which Shakespeare wrote about women fall roughly into five cycles. I call them five acts because, odd as it may seem, the five cycles resemble the five-act structure in Shakespeare's plays. This leads me to ask, Do our psyches develop over our lifetimes in five different movements (our minds, not our bodies: our bodies travel through the seven ages of man)—and is that why stories often have five phases?

The five-act structure that Shakespeare used was copied from the Roman plays; it is also the structure followed by most Hollywood film scripts. Try applying what I say to the *Alien* movies or *Star Wars* and you will see what I mean.

In Shakespeare's plays, the first act is always the introduction to the central characters and the basic dilemma they face. This holds true for all his plays, early to late. The earliest plays of Shakespeare come in two categories—English-history plays in the form of *Henry VI Parts 1, 2, 3, Richard III,* and then three comedies, *The Taming of the Shrew, The Comedy of Errors,* and *The Two Gentlemen of Verona.* And then there's one oddball—*Titus Andronicus*—a Roman history play that is also a *very* black comedy, and a tragedy.

In these early plays, history or comedy, the women belong to roughly two types. They are either ferocious, overbearingly assertive, or they are idealized virgins-on-the-pedestal.

In all of the stories, histories and comedies, a constant leitmotif is that our hero has to deal with the harridan, finding a way to neutralize her. Or he has to find his way to woo and win the sweet young thing. The women fight ferociously. Or they learn to hide their true feelings and manipulate, using their attractiveness and modesty. How to deal with the virago women and pursue a proper man's agenda is the basic dynamic Shakespeare set up in these early plays. You notice how the material breaks down into binaries: It can be this or that. They are like this or that. Not a lot of subtlety here.

So, in *Women of Will: Following the Feminine in Shakespeare's Plays*, we establish the principles of our story in the first act, and then the ground changes. Swiftly and dramatically, we are in Act 2. Act 2 in a Shakespeare play is the first testing of our protagonist. Act 2 in *Women of Will* is a shift in the way the story is told. Our hero no longer sees women as adversaries—he falls deeply and irrevocably in love with them. And the women are no longer projections of a man's imagination; they are full human beings. In fact, both men and women fall in love so profoundly that they understand love as the great sexual/spiritual merging, out of which a new world order could appear. This story, beginning with *Love's Labour's Lost*, finds its full expression in *Romeo and Juliet*, its comic version in *A Midsummer Night's Dream*, its kabbalistic form in *The Merchant of Venice*, and its expression between everyday middle-aged, middle-class lovers in *Much Ado About Nothing*. It's a theme that never leaves the canon: it gets smashed up in *Troilus and Cressida*. *Antony and Cleopatra* is its last full-blown expression.

What is clear in this sexual/spiritual merging is that women and men can only love each other to this profound depth if there is absolute parity between them. I don't mean in worldly terms: I mean in inner, psychic terms. If there is an inequality of status in the lovers' minds, then true love is not possible.

But, of course, in real life, in the outside world, women do not have equality. They have been judged inferior to men—Adam's rib, his helpmate—with no soul of their own. This has been so since the beginning of Western civilization. Women may have been potent characters in plays by Aeschylus, Euripides, and Sophocles, but in classical Greek life, women were not allowed to leave their houses (except to go to the well or on certain feast days). Their names on all legal documents appear as "the daughter of so and so" or "the wife of so and so." They had almost no rights—"She is my goods, my chattels," as Petruchio says of Kate two thousand years later (*Taming of the Shrew*, 3.2, 220). And with the advent of Christianity we began the debate as to whether women had souls in their own right or whether they were an "add-on" to their husbands or fathers. What is clear is that the mother of Jesus had to be both a virgin and totally lacking in sexual desire. And she is the model for all women.

By the time we get to Shakespeare's era, a widow would automatically inherit a third of her husband's possessions if he died (but those possessions became her new husband's if she remarried). Women probably had souls (but it was still being debated), and a woman was a monarch. But in neither classical Greece nor Elizabethan England could a woman portray a woman onstage. So for Shakespeare to declare that men and women are equal, both have souls, those souls merge in passionate sexual bonding, and out of that a new order can appear, was a radical statement. It leads to the huge turmoil of the third act of our cycle.

It also means that the playwright hero of *Women of Will* had actually changed, both in his thinking and in his ability as an artist. He was no longer the thoughtless man inhabiting the early plays—but a man who now had the courage to fall in love *and* to point to the frame within which women are forced to live. Whether he was writing as Romeo or Benedick or Antony, the fact is that Shakespeare himself was brave enough to change, to undergo an internal journey that means his heroes have the capacity for self-reflection as well as for fighting a battle or giving pleasure to others. And the women are full partners with the men. The artist Shakespeare inhabited the women's world with as much depth as he did the men's.

If women have full agency, if they speak, they feel, their intelligence is keenly aware, then what happens as they come up against the institutional structures that deny that this is true? If the church, the government, the educational system, the law, the money-wielding people, even the theatre maintain that women have no rights, what do the women do?

Well, in the middle section of Shakespeare's writing life, Act 3, they take it on: all endeavor to tell the truth about what they see and hear. They are courageous. Sooner or later, they step out. We are talking about the women in *As You Like It, Julius Caesar, Hamlet, Measure for Measure, Othello, Twelfth Night.* If they stay in their frocks and tell the truth, they are killed or kill themselves. If they disguise themselves as men, they are responded to as men; they can own their voices and authority, and others respond to their ideas and influence. This is also true if they are nuns or have to be respected because they are in deep mourning—and have no male relatives to whom they must answer! But whichever way you look at it, telling the truth about what they see and hear is an extreme journey. Act 3 in a Shakespeare play is always where the opposing forces line up against one another, with the threat of great violence, inner and outer. And you could say that the hero of our journey was pushing his writing imagination to extremes in order to understand the gravity of the situation these women find themselves in. It looks as if salvation may be at hand—but as in all good scripts, just as you think it can work out (the evil force has been killed), then all your assumptions are smashed. And we come to the fourth act. And, as in all fourth acts, all hell breaks loose.

The women in the *Women of Will* fourth act are not interested in truth; they are interested in power. They stay in their frocks and they take what they want, just as the men do. They want power, status, respect, economic wealth. I am talking about the eldest daughters in *Lear*, Lady Macbeth, Volumnia in *Coriolanus.* And the result is horrendous, for everyone. The country is engulfed in war, love has very little voice, and suffering abounds. It is a dark, dark picture. The absence of women to express compassion, care, the binding ties of relationships, alternate viewpoints, tips a society into fascism, repression, and despair. Our writer of these stories is also questioning the efficacy of acting, one of his two art forms.

Always Act 4 of a Shakespeare play is a cliffhanger. Will the forces of good or evil prevail? In Act 4 in the development of Shakespeare's women, the answer is obvious. If we stay on this course, with both men and women grabbing for themselves, then the whole world will be destroyed by greed, desire for dominance, love of status, suppression of others.

Shakespeare went to the brink and saw that the future was not good. In the fifth act, he changed the story completely. The same desire for dominance—the my-way-or-the-highway energy—of our male protagonists is still present at the top of the play, but then a different tale is told. Shakespeare found a way out. (In the fifth act of a Shakespeare play, one of two things happens: everyone either gets killed—a tragedy—or married—a comedy.) But in *Women of Will* Act 5, the daughters redeem the father's mistakes. The women once again seek a way to counteract the mostly male drive to power—and this time they succeed. They succeed by strengthening women's ways of knowing; they succeed by working with one another and with a few good men; they succeed because in the end the artist is on their side. They are the power of Ariel and Miranda, acknowledging each other and going forward to a new world in *The Tempest*. The insight of the artist is matched with the tenacious vulnerability of the women and a willingness to change in the men, and, finally, the story comes right. It gives a map to balance the forces of power and love, to find true satisfaction and surrender to life. It takes two generations to do it—but it can be done.

The through-line of the story of the five acts is of course the struggle in Shakespeare's psyche and his relationship to women: what they meant to him in his imagination, how much they took over his creative mind, where they guided him in the end.

It is the story of a man who lived, acted, wrote, part-owned a theatre, who put his body and mind through every atrocity and ecstasy, every embarrassing, humiliating situation; who used language to make clear what he understood, but also language that expands the mind and triggers creative energy for other people (actors, yes, but anyone who takes on the plays with an open mind and a sensitive body), a language that actively generates the ability to think and feel, and generates thoughts and feelings in others. A creator of individual and collective knowledge, sourced by Shakespeare and built by and through the imaginations of many participants.

Of course, the theme of man/woman relationship wasn't the only theme Shakespeare was exploring. There are many others. While he was in the midst of following the sexual and the spiritual, for example, he wrote three plays deeply concerned with the very male idea of honor—especially honor in battle—*Henry IV Part 1*, *Henry V*, and *King John*. Later in the canon, honor as a theme vies with the mother/son struggle for power in *Coriolanus*. Lamentation—a way of expressing grief about death, and the psychic integration of the death of loved ones—makes strong appearances in *Richard III, King John, Hamlet, Winter's Tale*. The nature of government, the "right" of kings, dominates *Richard II, Henry IV Part 2, Julius Caesar, Macbeth, Hamlet* (*Hamlet* is about almost everything). A shifting world paradigm lives in *Hamlet, Cymbeline, As You Like It,* and so on. I am not claiming that the developing relationship between men and women (or the masculine and feminine, if you prefer it that way—for it is about balancing, matching, and developing masculine and feminine qualities) is the only worthy theme in the plays and poems—that would be ridiculous. If you look at the whole canon, a pattern can be perceived through the man/woman relationships which gives us a sense of Will Shakespeare's consciousness, and a consciousness of how women have been regarded by those with overt power, how they are regarded now, and how possibly we might change for the good of all in the future.

If I am talking about a play and I have left out what is to you the most important aspect of that play, I apologize in advance. My firsthand experience of why a certain point (beyond the man/woman relationships) is the most important revelation in that particular play is alive to me. Shakespeare's ability to reveal us to ourselves in hundreds of different ways is staggering. I am not saying a different theme doesn't exist; it simply isn't relevant to the thread I am following.

We live in a world of right/wrong, good/bad, dominance/submission, mine/not mine, me/other, have/have not. We stumble upon a world where that is no longer true, and through active love we find we *are* the other. That knowledge recasts the story that has been told since 800 B.C., and the women endeavor to break through the power structures. For a short interlude, women want the same kind of power as the men, and this results in a decimated world. Finally, the artist and the young women join together with the witch and a few good men and point the way to a new order.

Or, in semi-haiku form:

> Blindness, ecstatic love,
> Fighting the fight
> Unending misery, light.

Or:

To be or not to be: that is the question.

SCENE 2: Which Came First

We don't really know exactly which plays Shakespeare wrote first—and it only matters to us in this story because we are trying to map his relationship to women and how it progresses. Did he write the history plays first, slotting the odd comedy in between? Did the comedies come first, because he was mostly stealing the plots from other well-known sources, and he knocked them off pretty quickly, before attempting the larger task of four successive history plays, the events and stories taken from Edward Hall's and Raphael Holinshed's chronicles and Thomas More's *Richard III*?

Several scholars think that he wrote *Henry VI Parts 2* and *3* before he wrote *Part 1*. The plays originally had different titles, and it was only later, when he wrote *Part 1*, that they were put under the rubric of *Henry VI* and thus became a trilogy. From a theatrical point of view, that idea doesn't make much sense, because the development of the character and plot starts in *Part 1* and clearly builds upon the earliest work. To which the response is "Oh well, he went back and amended the scripts later so they would make a coherent whole." For much of his life, Shakespeare reworked his plays.

I think it's good to learn what we can from these early plays as a whole and not bother too much about exact order. That said, through doing the plays many times, I have gotten the idea that Shakespeare began *Henry VI Part 1* while he was still in school. It is stuffed full of fights, and the dialogue between the men is all bombast and pontificating, very little actual human interaction—that only happens when the women appear. I think he liked writing orations and speeches over dead bodies—as he had been taught in school—and he loved the battles and deeds of derring-do! He acted them out with all his schoolmates. These plays then became his workbook—this was how he learned to write plays. And the skill and structure of *Parts 2* and *3* are so superior to *Part 1* that, though they may have been performed in the London theatre before *Part 1*, I intuitively feel he wrote them consecutively. And *Richard III* is superior to them all *not* because of the structure of the play, but because his ability to draw character in all the protagonists had grown so immensely. In the characters of Richard and Margaret, he was truly beginning to understand the darker forces in the human soul—and probably perceiving them in himself.

SCENE 3: The Comedies

The Taming of the Shrew, The Comedy of Errors, The Two Gentlemen of Verona

The plot of *The Taming of the Shrew* is relatively straightforward: There are two sisters; the older, Kate, is a whirling dervish, a harridan, and a shrew. And her younger sister, Bianca, is a sweet, pretty thing. They both have generous dowries, and their father is keen to marry them off. (No mother is ever mentioned.) Problem is, no one wants to marry Kate. And Baptista, their father, has said he won't allow Bianca to marry until Kate is safely settled. He doesn't want to be stuck at home with her. Many men are vying for Bianca's hand, and they are all terrified of Kate. Enter impecunious Petruchio, looking for a rich wife. He's not frightened of a woman; he's fought in battle and knows how to tame the enemy. Bianca's suitors give him money to woo Kate, which he willingly agrees to do. Before he even sees her, he tells the audience directly how he's going to deal with her.

> I'll attend her here,
> And woo her with some spirit when she comes.
> Say that she rail, why then I'll tell her plain
> She sings as sweetly as a nightingale.
> Say that she frown, I'll say she looks as clear
> As morning roses newly washed with dew.
> Say she be mute and will not speak a word,
> Then I'll commend her volubility,
> And say she uttereth piercing eloquence.
> If she do bid me pack, I'll give her thanks,
> As though she bid me stay by her a week.

If she deny to wed, I'll crave the day
When I shall ask the banns, and when be married.
But here she comes, and now, Petruchio, speak.

THE TAMING OF THE SHREW (2.1, 166–79)

They meet. Perhaps they are attracted to each other—most productions set it up that way; otherwise what follows is too hard to swallow. (I still find it hard to swallow no matter how you play it.) Verbally, they are evenly matched. Petruchio doesn't run away from Kate, which most other men do. At one point Kate gets fed up with the sparring and tries to leave. Petruchio insults her with sexual innuendo. She socks him. They fight more ferociously. Her father is returning, and Petruchio tells Kate he's going to marry her, no matter what she wants. (You can see why Burton and Taylor had such success with these roles.)

Baptista betroths his daughter. Kate seems to want to do it. (Shakespeare doesn't give her any words at this point; the actor playing Kate has to decide what makes most sense. In my first production, forty years ago, the actor playing Kate—the scrappy, honest Susan Kingsley—screamed, but Petruchio slapped his hand over her mouth, and everyone else onstage laughed in delight.) When the marriage party gets to the church, it seems as if Petruchio isn't coming. Then, when he eventually turns up, he's dressed outrageously, drags Kate into the church, abuses the clergy; when they come out, he refuses to go to the reception but drags her off to his house, a day or two's horse ride away. Once there, he starves her of food, won't let her sleep, slashes her clothes, and generally treats her like an animal whose spirit he is determined to break. Which he does.

She ate no meat today, nor none shall eat.
Last night she slept not, nor tonight she shall not.
As with the meat, some undeservèd fault
I'll find about the making of the bed,
And here I'll fling the pillow, there the bolster,
This way the coverlet, another way the sheets.
Ay, and amid this hurly I intend
That all is done in reverend care of her,
And in conclusion she shall watch all night,

And if she chance to nod I'll rail and brawl
And with the clamour keep her still awake.
This is a way to kill a wife with kindness,
And thus I'll curb her mad and headstrong humour.

THE TAMING OF THE SHREW (3.3, 160–72)

Then he turns to the audience and says:

He that knows better how to tame a shrew,
Now let him speak. 'Tis charity to show.

THE TAMING OF THE SHREW (3.3, 173–74)

So we all become culpable in his taming.

When they are on their way back to the father's house, he tells her the sun is the moon, and when she finally acquiesces, he says she's lying. Then Petruchio's friend advises her to "say as he says, or we will never go." Most productions let this be a game between Kate and Petruchio; she is finally able to get with the program: "I will pretend to be what he wants." This has never sat well with me, for it is the strategy of every conqueror to take away the language of the conquered. And as we all know, if you don't have language, you have a difficult time knowing who you are. When Nigel and I play this scene, he drags me around with his belt around my neck as a dog collar. Nigel says he feels a great surge of testosterone—an "Aren't any of you going to stop me?" attitude toward the audience.

Bianca, in the meantime, has identified the man she wants, has abandoned all the others, and secretly marries her love. She long ago learned how to use language to manipulate her father, her suitors, and even herself.

At the end of the play, the shrew is tamed, and the sweet young thing has got her way. All good fun. Under the guise of comedy, the most horrible acts are perpetrated on a woman. It's a nightmare, because the sexism is so completely accepted—it is simply "the way it is." Nowhere is it questioned.

The Comedy of Errors, written maybe a year later, breaks down into the same kind of pattern. Adriana, the elder sister, married to Antipholus of Ephesus, is tormented by jealousy, because she thinks her husband is off with another woman (he is), and she yells and screams about it. Her younger sister, Luciana, tut-tuts, tells her sister to be sweet and mild and to obey her husband, because women's obeying men is the natural order of the world.

> Why, headstrong liberty is lashed with woe.
> There's nothing situate under heaven's eye
> But hath his bound in earth, in sea, in sky.
> The beasts, the fishes, and the wingèd fowls
> Are their males' subjects and at their controls.
> Man, more divine, the master of all these,
> Lord of the wide world and wild wat'ry seas,
> Indued with intellectual sense and souls,
> Of more pre-eminence than fish and fowls,
> Are masters to their females, and their lords.
> Then let your will attend on their accords.
>
> THE COMEDY OF ERRORS (2.1, 15–25)

Now, the plot of *The Comedy of Errors* is taken from a Roman play, the *Menaechmi* by Plautus, which Shakespeare probably performed in Latin in grammar school. But the character of Luciana is Shakespeare's own invention, and the words he put in her mouth depict the accepted power structure. It is the "natural" order of things, ordained by God, and so any woman who thinks otherwise is disobeying divine law. Men have intellectual sense; women don't. Men have souls; women don't. In the animal kingdom, all females obey the males. Humans should follow suit.

Shakespeare himself must have thought this. We know his early life was conventional. He got married at eighteen; his wife, Anne, was twenty-six. She became pregnant during their trothplight. They married and had three children. But we never hear one thing about her. She's a blank. His wife clearly was meant to follow the rules. We have to assume that she did—or certainly did nothing that would attract public attention to her.

The Comedy of Errors is obviously a comedy, so it all works out: Adriana promises to shut up and is rewarded with a jewel for being good, and Luciana falls in love with Antipholus's twin brother (the soaps were not the first to discover how useful identical twins are in drama). It is a tightly structured play, delightful to perform; it always earns good box office, and is over in about two hours. It shows Shakespeare as a master of form—form that uses the idea that women are either harridans or sweet young things.

The Two Gentlemen of Verona is a little different. Our heroine, Julia, dresses up as a boy to follow her love, only to find her betrothed has fallen for another woman and has abandoned her entirely. Julia is not as ferocious as either Kate or Adriana, but she does have to be "dealt with." Silvia, in the meantime, is not quite the virgin-on-the-pedestal that either Bianca or Luciana is—but she is literally locked up at the top of a tower so she can be worshipped only from below! The main theme of *Two Gentlemen* is the friendship between men, and the real shocker comes at the end of the play. Proteus has betrayed his friend Valentine by doing everything in his power to steal Silvia from him. (Meanwhile, the women perform a couple of real acts of friendship toward each other.) When the men reconcile at the end of the play, as an act of friendship Valentine offers Silvia to Proteus. And the women are right there onstage. It's a staggering act of arrogance and insensitivity—no director ever knows what to do with it. What it shows about Will Shakespeare is that he was deeply interested in the friendship between men (an idea much alive in ancient Greece, medieval literature, and Paul Newman–and–Robert Redford movies; maybe such friendship existed between Shakespeare and the actor Richard Burbage, or Shakespeare and Richard Field, the publisher). But women he saw as chattels, something that could be offered in the quest for a "higher" good, the friendship between men.

All three plays are extreme in their treatment of women—and show how women should be treated by fathers and lovers, the backbone of the plot.

Shakespeare ameliorated the violence of *The Taming of the Shrew* a little by making it a play within a play. He set the "real" event in a pub just outside Stratford. For both Shakespeare and Burbage, who was also born in Stratford and was playing Petruchio, this could have been a frat-boy in-joke—the pub was probably notorious in life, one where the teenage lads liked to hang out and tease the local drunk. (Did Shakespeare write this even *before* he got to London?) The lord of the manor and his men come in; then a troupe of players turn up and are hired to play a practical joke on the drunk. *The Taming of the Shrew* is the lord's idea of having fun with inebriated Christopher Sly. Let's make him think he is a lord, and the real lord's page can be his lady. There's much presenting of painting (a Burbage idea?–he was a painter as well as an actor in real life), and questions about what is reality, who is what sex, and other silly goings-on. All this reminds me very much of teenage high energy, but not too much deep think-ing taking place here. Similarly, *The Comedy of Errors* has a frame of a father trying to find his lost son and one son trying to find his twin brother. And the mother and wife of this family appears as the Abbess at the end–and she sorts it all out.

These plays, with their farcical humor, crude jokes, and simplistic attitudes about sex and relationships between men and women, have endured, *Shrew* and *Comedy* more than *Two Gents*. When I was just beginning in the theatre, I played Luciana for about a year–and I loved it. I didn't think much about it, either. And wherever we went, audiences loved it. Ian Richardson was my Antipholus, and I secretly loved him, too. It's only with age that I see the play differently. And, with age, Shakespeare wrote a very different play about twins: *Twelfth Night.* In *The Comedy of Errors,* all the twins are the same sex–an excuse for sex with the wrong person, beating the wrong servant. In *Twelfth Night,* the twins are of opposite sexes (as Shakespeare's own twins, Hamnet and Judith, were), and Shakespeare's depth of understanding fed into insights about love and sexuality that are profoundly moving.

What we can say about the young Shakespeare is that he was a terrific comedy writer, high-spirited and unapologetic. And he knew hardly anything about women. There's a glimpse of his treating them like real human beings here and there, but that didn't particularly interest him. He was more interested in jokes and verbal games and violence, whether men hitting women, or masters hitting slaves.

SCENE 4: Joan

Violence, of course, is the backbone of all the *Henry VI* plays and culminates in a huge bloodbath in *Richard III.* So let's turn to the

English histories now. He probably wrote the history cycle and the comedies in the same time frame—though if I had to put money on it, my theatrical self says *Henry VI Part 1* was indeed the first play he ever wrote. As I said before, it feels to me as if he started writing it when he was still a schoolboy, or perhaps shortly after he left school. He borrowed the form from the *Iliad* or Caesar's *Gallic Wars* (which he would have studied in school, in Latin). The plays have a huge idea behind them—the founding of England—but very little stagecraft. He introduced and dismissed characters almost at random; he loved the big fights and individual outbreaks of violence, of which there are something like thirty-six just in *Part 1;* and people declaim ideas or take actions with little buildup or motivation other than the obvious.

The story of the *Henry VI* plays comes mostly from Edward Hall's chronicle, *The Union of the Two Noble and Illustre Families of Lancastre and York,* published about fourteen years before Shakespeare's birth. The story of Joan of Arc, the first woman to appear in the canon (if indeed *Henry VI Part 1* is Shakespeare's first play), comes from Holinshed's *Chronicles of England,* a version of which appeared in 1577 (when Shakespeare was thirteen years old), and the full-blown thing in 1587—the year Shakespeare could have been working on it in hope of its first professional production. Ideas are years in the making, wandering around in the unconscious mind, looking for a local habitation and a name, until, suddenly, they come out in a concrete form. (I wrote my first play when I was eleven years old—about a woman highwayman, and how she got away by leaping off the stage. No one had ever leapt off the stage in my school; how she fooled everyone and was doing good really. I have been living a comic version of that story ever since.) In the story of *Part 1,* the noble English are trying to hold on to their rightfully owned territory of France. But the perfidious French think up many cunning ways to defeat them. They never fight honorably. Mostly it's this cunning witch called Joan who leads the fight on behalf of the French. Eventually, the noble Duke of York burns her at the stake—but she curses him and his country, and the curse comes true, and that's the story of the next two *Henry VI* plays.

When you write for the theatre, the play gets embodied in its first concrete form by an actor, and the writer and actor rework and reembellish the idea and find its dramatic tension. The ideas, interpreted by audiences invited specifically to test out the play, gain life and vitality and insight with each new iteration. Today in the United States we go through draft after draft of a play before it reaches its final form—readings, workshops, invited audiences, maybe twelve to twenty reworkings before it's pronounced ready for production. The extent to which actors and playwrights collaborated, writers co-wrote, actors were writers, ideas were stolen and made into new plays—all this leads me to believe the Elizabethans built plays through the same kind of practice (which is why "newly worked and amended" appears often on title pages).

Back to our story of the *Henry VI* plays. The English think they own France. This is how it happened. The two countries have been kind of united since 1066, when the Duke of Normandy, William, conquered England. He made London the headquarters for himself and his heirs, and they ruled both countries from there. Aristocratic Englishmen quickly learned to speak French, the English legal system became French, and the English and Norman aristocracy intermarried. Ordinary folks talked about eating "lamb," but the posh folks said "mutton," and gradually everyone forgot that it was France (well, a part of what became France) that had conquered England: instead, England now believed it owned France. Fast-forward eighty-six years from the Conquest: Henry II of England married Eleanor of Aquitaine (Peter O'Toole and Katharine Hepburn in the movie *The Lion in Winter*). Now England owned even more of the Continent, in the form of Aquitaine. Europe was involved in a load of disastrous crusades, Christian kings going to fight the Muslim infidel, of whom one English king, Richard the Lionheart (Henry II's son), is the best-known example. However, Richard was never in England, or maybe once. He was usurped by his youngest brother. John was the bad king reigning while Robin Hood lived in Sherwood Forest and the basis of democracy, the Magna Carta, was signed. *King John* was a later Shakespeare play. John was succeeded by his son Henry III, who had a long, dull reign. Henry III's great-great-great-grandson was Richard II (a Shakespeare play again), who was usurped by his cousin Henry Bolingbroke (we've skipped over three Edwards and the Black Prince). Bolingbroke became Henry IV (and worthy of two plays by Shakespeare). His son Henry V stopped civil war in England by going to France and getting back all the lands once owned by the descendants of William the Conqueror, at the Battle of Agincourt. Then Henry V died. His baby son inherited when he was a few months old—and the English were desperately trying to hold on to France. This royal family was called the Plantagenets. There were now two branches of the family, the House of York and the House of Lancaster. Sometimes they supported each other and sometimes they didn't—but they were all agreed that they were the kings of England and France. And the French no longer agreed.

Now you are caught up. In Shakespeare's time, the literate subjects of England would know this story, because they would have read the chronicles. Most people would know the general gist—a bit better or a bit worse than American teenagers know the story of the Founding Fathers, or European teenagers know the causes of the First World War.

Shakespeare started the play *Henry the Sixth Part 1* with the death of the great English warrior hero Henry V. France is getting restless again. The French king who was defeated at Agincourt handed his daughter Katherine over to Henry V in marriage, which means the Dauphin has been denied his heritage. Henry VI, Henry V's heir, is a teenager at this point (in Shakespeare's story—in life, he was twenty-three), simple, spiritual, but with no "manly man" qualities.

England is being led by valiant Bedford and valiant Talbot. The French are an effete lot who normally would not have a chance against the English, but a young woman has appeared who says she's from God and is going to lead them to victory.

I like to think Joan of Arc was the first woman Shakespeare ever wrote about, partly because Shakespeare's depiction of her changes so much over the course of the play, and we see Shakespeare himself more clearly because of that. In the first scene in which she appears, she is just like a young Warwickshire girl—she looks after sheep, is forthright, knows her business, and is full of spiritual inspiration. In fact, she's wonderful—and Shakespeare appeared to think so, too! She is the most interesting, least clichéd character so far. The Dauphin plays a trick on her when she first appears, making Reignier, King of Naples, Duke of Anjou (more of him later), pretend to be Dauphin in his stead. Joan isn't in the least fooled. She calls the Dauphin out, and tells him what she wants.

> Dauphin, I am by birth a shepherd's daughter,
> My wit untrained in any kind of art.
> Heaven and our Lady gracious hath it pleased
> To shine on my contemptible estate.
> Lo, whilst I waited on my tender lambs,
> And to sun's parching heat displayed my cheeks,
> God's mother deignèd to appear to me,
> And in a vision full of majesty,
> Willed me to leave my base vocation
> And free my country from calamity.
> Her aid she promised, and assured success. . . .
> My courage try by combat, if thou dar'st,
> And thou shalt find that I exceed my sex.
> Resolve on this: thou shalt be fortunate,
> If thou receive me for thy warlike mate.
> HENRY VI PART I (1.2, 72–82, 89–92)

She inspires the Dauphin, too. They buckle in single combat, she beats him, and he instantly falls in love with her.

> Was Mahomet inspirèd with a dove?
> Thou with an eagle art inspirèd then . . .
> Bright star of Venus, fall'n down on the earth,
> How may I reverently worship thee enough?
> HENRY VI PART I (1.2, 140–41, 144–45)

You see he calls her "Bright star of Venus"—so, like Psyche in Apuleius's *Cupid and Psyche* story, she is the human incarnation of Venus, fallen from above, the stuff of which souls are made. And at first, Joan is successful. She's courageous and she speaks in spiritual terms; everything about her is charming.

Then, suddenly, Shakespeare changed his attitude toward her. It's as if he suddenly saw his terrible mistake—she's not charming at all, she's a French woman, a foreigner, who is beating all our valiant

Englishmen! So within a few scenes he had her seducing the Duke of Burgundy, persuading him to change sides. Then he had her juggling wicked spirits, and asking the devil to take her soul in exchange for victory in battle. He hinted that she's sexually promiscuous and definitely sleeping with the Dauphin (they run naked across stage). Obviously, she must be captured and burned at the stake. Which is exactly what Richard Plantagenet, the Duke of York, does! The Duke of York is the most recent valiant English hero now that Bedford and Talbot are dead through the tricks of this perfidious French woman (actually, the English get a bit of blame for it, because they wouldn't bring up reinforcements). The Duke of York becomes the leader of the English forces in France—and, once he gets back to England, the leader of the Yorkist forces against the Lancasters in the War of the Roses. It's in *Henry VI Part 1* that the red rose and the white rose are picked in the garden to become the symbols of the House of York and the House of Lancaster. There is incessant tedious wrangling between all the powerful men in England, jockeying for position under a weak king. It is only when Joan is onstage that it's dramatically interesting. (In one scene, the French Countess of Auvergne pretends to seduce Talbot in order to capture him; it is the most dull, awkward scene in the play.)

Shakespeare's first impulse toward Joan was a generous one. He was actually very taken with her. He liked that she dressed as a man, had visions from God and God's mother, wielded a sword, and was a good fighter; he wrote a sweetly erotic swordfight. This is Shakespeare at his most natural. It's only when he followed Holinshed's story that he turned: she can't be good; she has to be evil and unnatural; and of course she has to be burned at the stake for a witch.

> The regent conquers, and the Frenchmen fly.
> Now help, ye charming spells and periapts,
> And ye choice spirits that admonish me
> And give me signs of future accidents.
> *Thunder*
> You speedy helpers, that are substitutes
> Under the lordly monarch of the north,
> Appear, and aid me in this enterprise.

Enter Fiends
This speed and quick appearance argues proof
Of your accustomed diligence to me.

HENRY VI PART I (5.3, 1–9)

She's into blood sacrifice. What bit of her body will she lop off
and give to the devil?

> Where I was wont to feed you with my blood,
> I'll lop a member off and give it you
> In earnest of a further benefit,
> So you do condescend to help me now.
> *They hang their heads*
> No hope to have redress? My body shall
> Pay recompense if you will grant my suit.
> *They shake their heads*
> Cannot my body nor blood-sacrifice
> Entreat you to your wonted furtherance?
> Then take my soul—my body, soul, and all—
> Before that England give the French the foil.

HENRY VI PART I (5.3, 14–23)

This is not the same woman who had a vision, whom the Virgin
Mary blessed and made beautiful.

The Duke of York captures her while she's conjuring the devil. He
is unafraid of her: "Fell banning hag, enchantress, hold thy tongue!"
York then becomes her judge and jury and orders her to be burned at
the stake. She renounces her father, a simple shepherd. She proclaims
her blessedness from God and her royal ancestors. She tries to avoid
execution by saying she's pregnant—first by the Dauphin, then Alen-
çon, then Reignier, King of Naples. The last thing she does is curse
England and York:

> Then lead me hence; with whom I leave my curse.
> May never glorious sun reflex his beams
> Upon the country where you make abode,
> But darkness and the gloomy shade of death

Environ you till mischief and despair
Drive you to break your necks or hang yourselves.

HENRY VI PART I (5.4, 86–91)

The curse comes true.

In Joan, we have a salient picture of young Shakespeare's psyche. His first impulse was to be sympathetic toward women. The moment he came up against the traditional story (and this is true of the comedies as well as the histories), he was unwilling to go out on a limb. If he emphasized certain qualities in a woman—she's a great fighter, courageous, inventive, a leader—it would look as if he were devaluing the men. And at this point he was not going to do that. So in Joan we see first Shakespeare's openness toward women, and then a turning away, adopting a more traditional stance. This double standard plays out in various ways in the women who follow Joan. But all the time, as he wrote about women, he was deepening his relationship and understanding of them—though it was hard for him to give up the clichéd pictures of how women should be!

In his portrait of Margaret, the woman who follows Joan, we get a picture of a woman who grows, deepens, find layers of meaning, takes on governments, armies, church officials, escapes death, gives birth, has a lover as well as a husband, and is a full player in every sense of the word. She stayed in Shakespeare's imagination longer than any other person (four plays in all), and in the process of writing her Shakespeare had time to really think and feel with her, and through her all women.

She is one of the great challenges for an actor, if the actor gets the opportunity to play Margaret through the three parts of *Henry VI* and into *Richard III*. I haven't been able to do that, but I have had the opportunity to play chunks of it—and watching Peggy Ashcroft do the whole thing at Stratford in the 1960s was one of the great experiences of my theatrical life. Peggy Ashcroft had come to fame playing Desdemona to Paul Robeson's Othello and Juliet to both Laurence Olivier and John Gielgud, who were switching roles as Romeo and Mercutio. Now, well into her middle years, she bounded onto the stage as the teenage Margaret of Anjou, positively luring the Earl of Suffolk to capture her. She then galvanized the men, those that loved her and those that hated her, and made them understand she was a player in this dangerous game of politics and war, the magnet of attention in all four plays, still cursing her enemies as she finally returns to France at the end of *Richard III*. Peggy Ashcroft never let up for a minute, always assumed onstage that she was the center of the action, her voice as resonant as any of the men's, her movements fast, fluid, and still. In that moment, she (Peggy/Margaret) inspired me to always be courageous in my own work.

Shakespeare wasn't able to stay empathetic to Joan during her existence in *Henry VI Part 1*, but he grew with Margaret. The longer she stayed around, the better he wrote her, and the more he was able to track the passages of her life—deepening his understanding of people who are not like him, using his actor's empathy to divine psychologically what she is about. And my own exploration of Margaret has deepened my creative life. Through her, I understand the passage of time, what remains important, what falls away. I understand how love and hate can reside side by side, one person being the focus of both. As archenemies, on opposing sides of York and Lancaster, the Duke of York and Queen Margaret do everything in their power to destroy each other—and eventually she wins. But the Duke of York may be the only man who could have replaced Suffolk for Margaret; killing him is a tragedy for both. I go through this killing ritual each night with Nigel Gore, the actor who plays him in the dramatic version of *Women of Will*. Our bodies push into each other, and then we tear away. There are so many layers of meaning in a single dramatic action: and if you are playing it, not just writing it for others to play, the possibility of human knowledge is an ever-changing, ever-enriching exploration.

With Margaret, I understand the nuance and development of Shakespeare's creativity: for her life is a complete artistic journey.

SCENE 5: Margaret

Margaret of Anjou was the first woman in the canon I ever passionately wanted to play. The "molehill" speech (as it's called), when she taunts and then executes the Duke of York, was the speech I used to audition for the Royal Shakespeare—and after ten auditions over one week I got in, so I must have been doing something right with it, even back then.

She's found running around on the battlefield toward the end of *Henry VI Part 1*, in between the moments in which Joan of Arc is captured by the Duke of York and then York puts Joan on trial and burns her as a witch. As York is getting rid of one foul French woman, the next one appears. You think you can get rid of a problem by suppressing it? Just wait.

What is Margaret doing on the battlefield? She is by herself. She's dressed in no armor, she has no protection—she must have slipped out from her father's castle and gone to where the action is! Why? Because she's bored being holed up in a castle? Because she wants to watch men fighting? Because she wants to find some young English earl to fall in love with her? (That is actually what happens.) Whatever the reason, for sheer guts and adventurous behavior, she takes some beating—it's an extraordinary action for a woman of that age and place. The Earl of Suffolk captures her. He's enthralled by her. Shakespeare used a soliloquy for Suffolk to work out how he feels about Margaret—possibly the first time a soliloquy was used to follow the development of an idea for the audience to ponder on with the character—an early Hamlet.

He wants her to be his love, but he can't marry her, because he's already married. So he comes up with a brilliant idea. He arranges for her to marry the King of England, even though her father has no money for a dowry, not much political clout, and demands the return of his lands in Anjou and Maine from England as part of the marriage deal. Her father is that Reignier, King of Naples, Duke of Anjou, who stood in for the Dauphin when he was trying to fool Joan in the first scene. It's a great coup for Margaret, which she instigates and pulls off all by herself. She is amazing. I love her ability to take her own life in her own hands—not waiting for any of the usual channels to be negotiated, just gambling on her own inventiveness and fearlessness, and believing she can overcome all obstacles.

These qualities hold her in good stead when she gets to England. She finds that the man she has married, Henry VI, is more interested in saying his prayers and in his relationship with God than he is in her. She married him in Rheims Cathedral by proxy—a common practice in those days, by which one or the other of the royal partners is represented by a third person (in this case, Henry VI was represented by Suffolk). She has a child (got to get the heir in place first–is it Henry's?–Henry certainly accepts it as such), and then Suffolk becomes her lover, and is hardly ever far from her side. In fact, *Henry VI Part 1* ends with a soliloquy by Suffolk telling the audience he's going to rule England through Margaret.

The Duke of York, of course, is so angry he is fit to be tied–he got rid of one French woman and now he's got another–and this one becomes queen of England, for God's sake. He decides he'd better become king himself, so, backed up by his sons, he challenges Henry. The country is plunged into civil war, and Joan's prophecy of darkness and the gloomy shades of death comes true. The Duke of York is doing well: he's a warrior, which Henry is not; he has three grown sons who fight on his side, which Henry has not; he has "the Kingmaker," the Earl of Warwick, with his mighty fighting force, on his side. So Henry, in agony about the turmoil in the country and actually unsure himself about his own right to be king, agrees in Parliament to let the Duke of York inherit the throne after his, Henry's, death, and the Duke of York's sons after him. Thus Henry disinherits his own son. Margaret is devastated. Then the Earl of Warwick maneuvers to get the Earl of Suffolk banished. This is a turning point both for Margaret in her life and for Shakespeare in his poetic writing.

We are now at about the halfway point in *Henry VI Part 2*. The farewell scene between Margaret and Suffolk contains not only great poetry, but nuanced character studies of Suffolk and particularly Margaret. Up until this time, there have been all kinds of twists and turns in the struggle for power and the loss of France. All the male characters–York, Warwick, Bedford, Somerset, Salisbury, the Cardinal, and so on–bluster, threaten, do devious things behind one another's backs in their desire to be on the winning side. The good Protector Gloucester has been undermined by his proud wife, Eleanor, who conjures wicked spirits to try and get the crown. (I'll talk briefly about her later.) When casting the play, it's necessary to cast actors of very different physical types and delivery, so the audience can tell them apart–and the actors must work hard to make their causes seem sympathetic, authentic, and different from anyone else's; otherwise, it all seems more of the same. However, there was a shift in Shakespeare's writing at this point—and it shifted because of the material he was dealing with.

The farewell between Margaret and Suffolk contains the most beautiful poetry in the canon up to this point. The bookends of the scene are a little clunky, but then there are twenty lines that are sublime, not only tender and erotic but viscerally alive, so that the physical expression of Margaret and Suffolk's connection is transmitted to every audience member: the idea of the breath of the lover entering the body of the beloved, there to live in bliss.

SUFFOLK If I depart from thee, I cannot live.
  And in thy sight to die, what were it else
  But like a pleasant slumber in thy lap?
  Here could I breathe my soul into the air,
  As mild and gentle as the cradle-babe
  Dying with mother's dug between its lips;
  Where, from thy sight, I should be raging mad,
  And cry out for thee to close up mine eyes,
  To have thee with thy lips to stop my mouth,
  So shouldst thou either turn my flying soul
  Or I should breathe it, so, into thy body—
  [he kisseth her]
  And then it lived in sweet Elysium.
  To die by thee were but to die in jest;
  From thee to die were torture more than death.
  O, let me stay, befall what may befall!
QUEEN MARGARET Away. Though parting be a fretful
  corrosive,
  It is applièd to a deathful wound.
  To France, sweet Suffolk. Let me hear from thee.
  For wheresoe'er thou art in this world's globe
  I'll have an Iris that shall find thee out.
SUFFOLK I go.
QUEEN MARGARET And take my heart with thee.
  [She kisseth him]
SUFFOLK A jewel, locked into the woefull'st cask
  That ever did contain a thing of worth.

Even as a splitted bark, so sunder we—
This way fall I to death.
QUEEN MARGARET This way for me.
[Exeunt severally]

HENRY VI PART 2 (3.2, 389–415)

It's as if Shakespeare found a deeper level of writing because he could actually feel the love between these two.

And the difference in character between the two is likewise clearly illuminated. Margaret is more practical, thinking of the future; Suffolk wants to stay in the present moment and connects their love to childhood, the erotic mother and child, and spiritual life. The image of Suffolk's soul entering Margaret's body is exquisite, the ending abrupt. It comes after so many images within images of messages, flowers, ships, the world, wounds which must be cauterized—all layers of love that fold into one another.

Suffolk is killed by pirates as he crosses the Channel, and his head and severed body are sent back to Margaret. The next time we see her, she is carting the head around, cradling it in her lap, holding it in the same place where he had said, "Here could I breathe my soul into the air, / As mild and gentle as the cradle-babe / Dying with mother's dug between its lips." Then she drags the head over her body, as if the lovemaking is continuing. It's a stunning moment in theatre—horrific, but with a gruesome poetic form.

Hath this lovely face
Ruled, like a wandering planet, over me . . .

HENRY VI PART 2 (4.4, 14–15)

It is after this that Margaret gets physically violent and personally takes up arms. We are now into *Part 3*. She aligns herself with two northern lords, Clifford and Northumberland, and goes after the Duke of York. She captures him on the battlefield at Wakefield (just outside York) and there taunts him and beheads him. (Her husband, of course, has put himself into the Tower in order to avoid the whole issue.) This is the famous "molehill" scene.

She captures him. She makes him stand upon a molehill. She asks him where his sons are. She shows him the hankie Clifford has dipped in the blood of his youngest child, and she smears it over his face. Then she puts a paper crown on his head, declares he's broken his oath by becoming king while Henry is still alive, and orders the crown and his head to be taken off together. She orders he should be executed, while she remains exultantly alive.

York responds with a diatribe against her unfeminine qualities: whereas Margaret rails against York for his treachery, breaking his oath to the King, York's invective is all based on Margaret's gender—how she ought to behave, and how disgraceful it is that a women is behaving as she is.

> She-wolf of France, but worse than wolves of France,
> Whose tongue more poisons than the adder's tooth—
> How ill-beseeming is it in thy sex
> To triumph like an Amazonian trull
> Upon their woes whom fortune captivates!
> But that thy face is vizard-like, unchanging,
> Made impudent with use of evil deeds,
> I would essay, proud queen, to make thee blush.
> HENRY VI PART 3 (1.4, 111–18)

But he does go on, putting up images of "true" womanhood and how unnatural she is.

> 'Tis beauty that doth oft make women proud—
> But, God he knows, thy share thereof is small;
> 'Tis virtue that doth make them most admired;
> The contrary doth make thee wondered at;
> 'Tis government that makes them seem divine—
> The want thereof makes thee abominable.
> Thou are as opposite to every good
> As the Antipodes are unto us . . .
> O tiger's heart wrapped in a woman's hide!
> HENRY VI PART 3 (1.4, 128–35, 137)

How much of this gets to Margaret is not clear in Shakespeare's writing. When I play it, I find that he does get to me—which is why I don't kill him immediately but let him continue.

Women are soft, mild, pitiful, and flexible—
Thou stern, obdurate, flinty, rough, remorseless.
Bidd'st thou me rage? Why, now thou hast thy wish.
Wouldst have me weep? Why, now thou hast thy will.

HENRY VI PART 3 (1.4, 141–44)

It's after he starts to weep that my defenses really crumble, and it becomes unbearable. I have to kill him, because I cannot bear what I've done.

A mixture of grief, rage, and unresolved pains consumes Margaret. Joined by Clifford, she stabs York through and commands his head be cut off and stuck on his gate (which is indeed what happens—it stays there until the next round of fighting, when Clifford gets killed and his head replaces York's on York Gate).

It was through doing the molehill scene that I realized I, Tina, was capable of great violence. The adrenaline of fighting the battle, the blind fury of knowing I would be killed if I did not kill first, the ecstasy of capturing the man who would take away my son's right to the crown, the fear of being annihilated if I paused for one moment—each of these emotions electrified my body. Knowing that this powerful man, this man who led the occupation of my birth land, France, whose very presence humiliates my husband, and who despised my lover, is now at my mercy, I want his blood. I want him to see me wanting it. I want to see his agony about the slaughter of his youngest. I want him to die more slowly than Suffolk had done. I want to pour every piece of my misery into the act of killing him.

Then he speaks, and for a few moments I hear him, I see him as a father, as a lover, a brave man, and I feel his scorn for me, his lack of understanding of what he has done to me—and I can't bear it, so I kill him, stand over him straddled across his body. He will never rise again.

It staggers me that I could so enjoy to do this—and that I could use the loathing I see in my acting partner Nigel's eyes as a mark of how far I had succeeded. I don't have to acquiesce to his loathing; I am in charge; I can annihilate him so he will be no more.

In life I am never physically violent. I was brought up by gentle pacifist parents, and I went to a Quaker school. And yet I know this violent creature lives in me, not too far below the surface.

Nigel is even more explicit about what goes on for him as he plays York. Usually after we have done the scene in performance, he tells the audience how deeply I repulse him, and it is closely tied up with my being a woman. If I were a man, it would be bad enough, but he would not feel the same level of shame. And Nigel sees the double standard. Henry V at Harfleur threatens to rape the women, smash the old men's heads in, and spit the babies on pikes—and we regard Henry V as the great English warrior hero. He warns the citizens of Harfleur that if they don't surrender they should

> . . . look to see
> The blind and bloody soldier with foul hand
> Defile the locks of your shrill-shrieking daughters;
> Your fathers taken by the silver beards,
> And their most reverend heads dashed to the walls;
> Your naked infants spitted upon pikes,
> Whiles the mad mothers with their howls confused
> Do break the clouds . . .
>
> HENRY V (3.3, 33–40)

When I directed the molehill scene, decades earlier, I had Margaret cut off York's balls. When I was playing it myself, his balls interested me not at all—it was his heart I wanted. (I later connected this with Beatrice's "I would eat his heart in the market-place" in *Much Ado About Nothing*.) I don't know what to make of this.

Doing this scene together gave Nigel and me a place where we could allow violence to flow safely, in life and art. As a young actress auditioning with *only* Margaret's speech, I could understand the triumph, but I never understood how deeply symbiotic the scene is. As I worked on it with Nigel, I began to understand how much the violence was caused by the lack of love—love that had been there once (a long time ago, way before the Duke of York had ever come into Margaret's life), but at the earliest age it had been denigrated in some way, humiliated: I want people to love me but I can't let them have power over me. Briefly, with the Earl of Suffolk, as he leaves, I know I love him but also know we are saying goodbye—and then the inevitable happens, love is removed, torn away, with a dead head sent to represent that loss. I take my son, Edward, out to the battlefield when he is still a child to teach him about war—to make sure he knows that might makes right, that behaving as his father does (absenting himself from battle) will not only cause you to be despised by everyone in the kingdom, but will keep you from ever understanding this salve for pain, killing someone before he kills you or killing to avenge a killing.

The violation perpetrated upon Margaret gives her two choices: she can shut down all feeling, or she can allow it to take her into whatever actions come up. Her husband, Henry VI, tries to remove himself from the fray. He doesn't want to be either a zombie or a revenge killer, but removing himself doesn't work, either: the country is plunged into more violence because he is so weak. (I have to say, in Henry VI's defense, that historically he did do some good in life: by setting up many schools and colleges, which became the backbone of our education system, he did contribute to a more civilized world.)

But back to the scene itself. As I felt Nigel loathe me every night, a kind of peace settled over our personal relationship—he could truly allow himself to feel the suffocating, overwhelming presence of a woman who was never going to let him go until he was dead. And encountering those emotions offered a kind of direct truth about his own life.

York and Margaret are a deeply connected dyad, known ultimately only to themselves. Opposites who uniquely play for life and death, making sure their children inherit the consequences of their rage.

Because, of course, York's sons will kill Margaret's son, Edward. Richard the Crookback will kill Henry VI. Edward, York's eldest son, becomes King of England—and Margaret lives out her days hanging around the edges of his palace, living in the battlements somewhere, using her voice to tell anyone who will listen about what happened and what she can see will happen. This is where she is in the final play of the tetralogy, *Richard III*. The last thing she does is teach the women how to lament.

> Forbear to sleep the night, and fast the day;
> Compare dead happiness with living woe;
> Think that thy babes were sweeter than they were,

And he that slew them fouler than he is.
Bett'ring thy loss makes the bad causer worse.
Revolving this will teach thee how to curse.

RICHARD III (4.4, 117–22)

But back to the molehill scene one more time. It brings up something else, a sensation of overwhelming closeness; I'm not sure I'd call it love, but it is a deep, deep knowledge. This man Margaret so hates is the man with whom she goes through a most intimate act. Killing someone can be as intimate as lovemaking, in some ways more so, because this is the ultimate act and both of you know it. And I kill him close up—he's next to me, my arm around his chest, as I thrust the knife into his back. I can smell his body. We lock in an embrace; I struggle to get free as I pull the dagger out; the breath is tearing through my body as I shove him to the floor, using all my strength not to go with him; and, finally, we are separated, and the life is going out of him, and I want to bathe in it. I don't want anyone to know how I grieve as well as triumph over his death and I will smash his body to smithereens for making me suffer so much and I will tell the world how I won. Let no one else think they can annihilate me. Decapitation: the ultimate violation. "Off with his head and set it on York Gates, so York may overlook the town of York."

Through writing Margaret, Shakespeare was living moment by moment with a woman, her natural abilities, her loves, her ferocity, her innocence. He learned from her.

The other person who really comes alive in these plays is a man: Richard, York's third son, the hunchback, the great outsider. Margaret has a greater development of character from her entrance to her exit; her capacity to love is much greater than Richard's. But I can feel Shakespeare's personal connection to both of them.

What we have not commented upon is Margaret's relationship with her husband, Henry VI, but it does merit some study and speculation. They are an ill-matched couple. Henry's emotional and physical absence perhaps has a resonance with Shakespeare's marriage to Anne Hathaway. We don't know what Anne thought. Perhaps she was glad to be rid of Shakespeare for years on end. But assuming she did want a sex life (as most women do) and did want someone to discuss the events of the day with (as most women do) and did want to think through the large issues of raising children, doing commerce, dealing with the in-laws (as most women do), then she would be pretty fed up with her husband, who was living in the thick of things in London, coming home perhaps once a year, for a couple of weeks. Perhaps she was happy enough to be her own boss. Perhaps she found a different kind of partner. But if she did want the companionship of her husband, she didn't get it. And if she wanted the passion of her husband, she didn't get it. That was poured into his poems and his plays, and perhaps other lovers. In Shakespeare's plays, the good wife who stays at home minding the hearth (like Penelope waiting for Odysseus's return) doesn't get much airtime. At one point Margaret says to Henry:

> I here divorce myself
> Both from thy table, Henry, and thy bed,
> Until that act of parliament be repealed
> Whereby my son is disinherited.
>
> HENRY VI PART 3 (I.I, 250–53)

If you look at the casting of the plays, it is far more likely that Burbage played Talbot and Richard III. Shakespeare would be playing Henry VI, letting his wife run the kingdom.

What we do know about Anne is that she must have been a capable woman. She looked after her father's affairs before she married Shakespeare, and for twenty-five years she looked after his. So maybe Anne was happy living in Stratford, living a sexless life. Margaret isn't.

The next powerful woman, who moves onto the stage at the end of *Henry VI Part 3,* is definitely not happy living that life.

SCENE 6: Elizabeth

With the advent of Elizabeth Woodville, we get a portrait of a different kind of woman. First, she's not a virgin. She already has three children by her husband, a minor knight called Sir Richard Grey (not necessarily bad; it means she's a good breeder). She doesn't burst into a room, much less a battlefield. She waits submissively without until invited in; she doesn't open her mouth until she's given permission to speak. She does use language remarkably well. And she does happen to be stunningly beautiful, so obviously she knows she'll be invited in and spoken to by some man in power fairly soon. She doesn't take up arms to get her own way. But she is just as resolute as either Joan or Margaret about getting what she wants. What does she use instead? She uses sexuality.

You may ask, what is wrong with that? Women have been using their sexuality to get what they want since time immemorial, and still are. And if there is no other way to exert power, then to use your will to procure your will is probably a good idea.

However, if what you are implicitly promising (a good time in the sack) is not actually what you want to do, and in order to deliver you must separate yourself from yourself, then it does have its shortcomings as a negotiating tool. You pay a price; you separate yourself from your body. I say this from a woman's point of view. Men, I think, don't have the same problem. And, as some of my young feminist friends have pointed out, you cannot change a corrupt system by using its own tools. Ah, the joy of being able to say that. But Elizabeth Woodville lived over five hundred years ago. She doesn't have much choice, she's in a bind, she is ambitious, and she's got to fix it. As she steps onto the stage, toward the end of *Henry VI Part 3*, she faces a newly triumphant Yorkist faction, now headed by the Duke of York's eldest son, recently crowned as Edward IV. Margaret was right when she taunted the Duke of York on the battlefield; she called the eldest son the "wanton Edward," and wanton he certainly is; he is famous for the number of women he has sex with, and Elizabeth Woodville would know this. Both of his brothers are aware of it, and they spy on Edward's first meeting with Elizabeth with much glee and foulmouthed banter.

Elizabeth's husband, Richard Grey, was killed in the fighting between the clans York and Lancaster. Whichever side you're on, if you die your lands and goods are confiscated by the conqueror—in this case Edward. However, as Richard Grey died fighting for the Yorkists (at least, that is true in *Henry VI Part 3;* in *Richard III,* he's reported as fighting on the Lancastrian side. And his real name was

John, but Shakespeare always called him Richard), it would be gracious of Edward to give the land back. Edward, true to his lascivious form, decides to get something for his benevolence.

Elizabeth must win this negotiation. Without her husband's lands, she has no way to support herself and her children. If she becomes the King's mistress, the family may still not be secure. There may be more rounds of the fighting between Yorkists and Lancastrians, and she could end up on the wrong side; Edward will tire of her, as he has of hundreds before her; she would have no established power as his mistress. How soon in the scene Elizabeth decides she is going to use her sexual and considerable verbal powers to get him to marry her is unclear. Perhaps she always knew that was her goal, before she even got to the court—it's a choice the actor playing Elizabeth has to make. But, whatever the choice, somewhere along the way she decides to go for the top prize, to become the Queen of England. And so she uses seductive words ("please," "resolve," "pleasure," "satisfy") that could be interpreted as a come-on.

> Right gracious lord, I cannot brook delay.
> May it please your highness to resolve me now,
> And what your pleasure is shall satisfy me.
> HENRY VI PART 3 (3.2, 18–20)

And then, when Edward comes on, she rejects him by feigning moral outrage.

KING EDWARD *(to Lady Grey)* But stay thee—'tis the fruits of
    love I mean.
LADY GREY The fruits of love *I* mean, my loving liege.
KING EDWARD Ay, but, I fear me, in another sense.
    What love, think'st thou, I sue so much to get?
LADY GREY My love till death, my humble thanks, my
    prayers—
    That love which virtue begs and virtue grants.
KING EDWARD No, by my troth, I did not mean such love.
LADY GREY Why, then, you mean not as I thought you did.
KING EDWARD But now you partly may perceive my mind.

LADY GREY My mind will never grant what I perceive
  Your highness aims at, if I aim aright.
KING EDWARD To tell thee plain, I aim to lie with thee.
LADY GREY To tell *you* plain, I had rather lie in prison.
KING EDWARD Why, then thou shalt not have thy
    husband's lands.
LADY GREY Why, then, mine honesty shall be my dower;
  For by that loss I will not purchase them.
KING EDWARD Therein thou wrong'st thy children mightily.
LADY GREY Herein your highness wrongs both them and
    me.
  But, mighty lord, this merry inclination
  Accords not with the sadness of my suit.
  Please you dismiss me either with ay or no.
KING EDWARD Ay, if thou wilt say "ay" to my request;
  No, if thou dost say "no" to my demand.
LADY GREY Then, no, my lord—my suit is at an end.

HENRY VI PART 3 (3.2, 58–81)

She echoes and copies his words. (Shakespeare understood this repeating and mirroring—it's a figure of speech called anaphora in the art of rhetoric. Repeating the words of someone you want to align yourself with is a tool that has been used for centuries.) In any case, within fifteen minutes Edward is so full of desire that he is not going to be satisfied unless they do sleep together, and that clearly means marriage, so he proposes and she agrees.

This marriage comes at a price for Edward. His father's great ally, the Earl of Warwick, is in France, arranging a dynastic marriage for him, one that would strengthen his position as king and gain a great ally. When Warwick discovers that Edward has frivolously married a commoner, when he could have had a French princess, Warwick is humiliated. He immediately abandons Edward, changes sides, and supports Margaret and Henry VI in their struggle. He then strengthens this alliance by marrying one of his daughters, Anne, to young Edward, heir to Henry VI and Margaret. It happens fast, because, shortly thereafter, this Edward (that so many people have the same name is only one of the irritating factors in English history; the other is that their behavior is so predictable) is killed, in the next battle, by Edward, George, and Richard, thus making young Anne a widow at a very early age. And then, of course, Richard nips off and kills Henry in the Tower.

In any case, Elizabeth Grey née Woodville becomes Queen of England, and in a very short space of time, Edward and Elizabeth have seven girls and three boys. They are very happy, but he can't help womanizing, and so, at the beginning of the play *Richard III,* he dies of syphilis.

Elizabeth does not rest on her laurels when she becomes queen. Wisely, over the next nineteen years she builds a large power base, a faction that becomes known as the Woodville clan. She has also moved the three children from her former marriage into pivotal positions; likewise her brother, and others close to them. She automatically has influence, because she is the mother of the King's ten legitimate children. (There are umpteen illegitimate ones by other women, but they don't count in terms of inheriting the crown, the ultimate cash prize.) And, even more important, three of the ten are males. She is a queen bee with a rather large hive.

When her husband, Edward IV, dies, it is necessary to get his eldest son, Edward (sorry), crowned as soon as possible. Edward IV's brother Richard of Gloucester organizes this. However, he also organizes for the two boys (the third one disappears; Shakespeare never brings him onstage—two are enough for the dramatic point) to stay in the Tower— from which they never emerge. They become known as the Princes in the Tower and are very famous after their death.

Richard has them murdered—because he, Richard, intends to take the crown himself. He marries Warwick's daughter Anne (the one bartered and sold in the court of France), seducing her over Henry VI's dead body, as she sets him down in a public space and performs lamentation rituals over his corpse. Laurence Olivier, in his film, makes it the corpse of her husband, young Edward. Probably made more sense for the movie—but it does diminish somewhat the bravery of Anne's act. To cart around the dead body of the deposed king and lament his death in public is an act of treason. Obviously, Shakespeare wanted the audience to get this. It's not quite clear why Richard wants to marry Anne; dynastically, it doesn't strengthen his cause.

Does he really care for her? Is it simply a turn-on, after killing so many of her male relatives? Did I mention that he killed her father, Warwick, too?

Anne is spirited in her accusations against Richard—she, like Margaret and Elizabeth, attempts to tell the world what kind of man he is.

> For thou hast made the happy earth thy hell,
> Filled it with cursing cries and deep exclaims.
> If thou delight to view thy heinous deeds,
> Behold this pattern of thy butcheries.—
> O gentlemen, see, see! Dead Henry's wounds
> Ope their congealèd mouths and bleed afresh.—
> Blush, blush, thou lump of foul deformity,
> For 'tis thy presence that exhales this blood
> From cold and empty veins where no blood dwells.
> Thy deed, inhuman and unnatural,
> Provokes this deluge supernatural.
>
> RICHARD III (1.2, 51–61)

Anne's emotional turmoil, when she is parading her father-in-law's dead body in the streets, is a strong example of a woman attempting to tell the truth about what is going on, and its having no effect whatsoever. And then she completely crumbles before Richard's seduction. He swears he did all the killing for her, so that he could spend "one hour" in her bedchamber.

LADY ANNE I would I knew thy heart.
RICHARD GLOUCESTER 'Tis figured in my tongue.
LADY ANNE I fear me both are false.
RICHARD GLOUCESTER Then never man was true.
LADY ANNE Well, well, put up your sword.
RICHARD GLOUCESTER Say, then, my peace is made.
LADY ANNE That shalt thou know hereafter.
RICHARD GLOUCESTER But shall I live in hope?
LADY ANNE All men, I hope, live so.
RICHARD GLOUCESTER Vouchsafe to wear this ring.
LADY ANNE To take is not to give.

RICHARD GLOUCESTER Look how my ring encompasseth
    thy finger,
Even so thy breast encloseth my poor heart.
Wear both of them, for both of them are thine.
RICHARD III (1.2, 202-14)

She sees what is going on, yet she's helpless to resist him. Would it be different if she hadn't just lost her husband, her father, and her father-in-law? I do think this knowledge of having no support—financial, moral, social—puts Anne in such turmoil, she ends up accepting Richard's proposal. Once they are married, he begins to poison her slowly. For fun? So he can marry someone else? Or just because she's a woman and he hates women? Or because he loves her and can't bear to love anyone?

Previously, Elizabeth had joined with Anne and Richard's mother, the Dowager Duchess of York, to visit the Tower, where her young sons are lodged. The women are not allowed into the prison—and they prophesy what will happen to the country. Elizabeth tells her son Dorset, by Richard Grey, to flee the country.

QUEEN ELIZABETH O Dorset, speak not to me. Get thee
    gone.
Death and destruction dogs thee at thy heels.
Thy mother's name is ominous to children.
If thou wilt outstrip death, go cross the seas,
And live with Richmond, from the reach of hell.
Go, hie thee! Hie thee from this slaughterhouse,
Lest thou increase the number of the dead,
And make me die the thrall of Margaret's curse;
"Nor mother, wife, nor England's counted queen." . . .
DUCHESS OF YORK O ill-dispersing wind of misery!
O my accursèd womb, the bed of death!
A cockatrice hast thou hatched to the world,
Whose unavoided eye is murderous.
STANLEY *(to Anne)* Come, madam, come *[to be crowned queen*
    with Richard].
I in all haste was sent.

LADY ANNE And I with all unwillingness will go.
O would to God that the inclusive verge
Of golden metal that must round my brow
Were red-hot steel, to sear me to the brains.
Anointed let me be with deadly venom,
And die ere men can say, "God save the queen."
RICHARD III (4.1, 40–48, 54–65)

As Richard kills his way to the throne, only the women show any public opposition. Margaret joins them to denounce Richard, and recount the whole story of the Wars of the Roses. Lancastrians and Yorkists find unity in their grief; together they tell the story of the dead. I talk more about this in the chapter called "Dealing with Loss: Lamentation Versus Honor," for acting to tell the truth publicly about what is happening is one of the ways women, and the feminine, can affect a society and change a culture.

The new head of the Lancastrian clan, a Welshman, Henry Tudor, Earl of Richmond, though not a direct descendant of Henry VI, makes the claim through two women: his mother, Margaret Beaufort (now married to Thomas Stanley, Earl of Derby), and his grandmother Catherine of France, and her second marriage, a love match to Owen Tudor. Because they are both women, this is not a strong claim—but it's the only claim the Lancastrians have, so they go for it.

Elizabeth now begins secret negotiations to marry her eldest daughter, Elizabeth (sorry), to this Henry Tudor, thereby uniting the House of York and the House of Lancaster. It is a brave and masterful move. And if she fails, they will probably all be killed.

Toward the end of *Richard III,* the Duchess of York and Elizabeth (Anne is now dead, and Margaret is going back to her homeland, France) waylay Richard with his army. He's off to fight Henry Tudor, Earl of Richmond, and the Duke of Buckingham (his former ally). First Richard's mother curses him and hopes the opposite side wins.

Either thou wilt die by God's just ordinance
Ere from this war thou turn a conqueror,
Or I with grief and extreme age shall perish,
And never more behold thy face again.

Therefore take with thee my most grievous curse,
Which in the day of battle tire thee more
Than all the complete armour that thou wear'st.
My prayers on the adverse party fight,
And there the little souls of Edward's children
Whisper the spirits of thine enemies,
And promise them success and victory.
Bloody thou art, bloody will be thy end:
Shame serves thy life and doth thy death attend.

RICHARD III (4.4, 186–98)

Then Elizabeth attempts to leave, but Richard stops her—and embarks on a mission to persuade her that he should marry her eldest daughter (i.e., his niece). Strengthened by the words of the women in the previous scene, and his mother, Elizabeth publicly rebuts every argument King Richard can put forward. This struggle between them is a battle royal—of survival, morality, and sexuality. Richard threatens death to the whole country if he does not get his way. At the end Elizabeth says yes, she'll think about it. Does she mean it? Is she just saying it to get out of there alive? Does she know that if Richard wins the battle she *will* marry her daughter to him, whether it is incest or not?

In any case, Henry Tudor wins the battle. And by marrying her daughter to him, Elizabeth strengthens his claim to the throne. Finally, the Houses of York and Lancaster are united—through the negotiating power of Elizabeth Woodville, using first her sexuality and then the power of motherhood—and peace finally comes to England. The Tudor dynasty begins in England. The Red Rose of Lancaster enfolds the White Rose of York and becomes the Tudor Rose. The Earl of Richmond becomes Henry VII—and he is the grandfather of Elizabeth I, who will sit on the throne for much of Will Shakespeare's life.

SCENE 7: The Drive to Make Plays

Why would Shakespeare write four plays with one storyline? Christopher Marlowe had two parts to *Tamburlaine the Great*, but four plays!

Writing a play is working out something; it's trying to hear many voices tell a story. To each voice the story looks different, and yet they end up in the same narrative. To write one play or even two plays on the same subject could be called youthful exuberance–but to write four is an obsession. Perhaps a healthy obsession, for each play is an improvement on the last, and each play gets closer to the heart of the matter.

Why do writers write? Or any artists practice their art form? It's difficult to articulate, because either you are doing it, in which case the "why" is irrelevant, or you are not doing it, in which case you are not at that moment in touch with the drive to create, and the question has importance only if it can lead back to the drive to create. The act of creating comes from the unconscious mind, some part of ourselves that does not know what or why it thinks the way it does. (Not journalism–that is a response to stimuli, and if one is skilled and has good technique, and if it is framed well, fresh insights come forth.) For the artist, the first idea appears by itself. You may have been ruminating about something for days, weeks, years, or maybe not at all.

It's the poem that comes unannounced, the doodling that becomes the Madonna and Child, the schoolboy scribble that becomes *Henry VI Part 1.*

That Shakespeare would write his first play about the English wars, the invasion and retreat from France, makes sense to me when I think about the tensions of everyday life that Shakespeare grew up with–the internal and external tensions. Similarly, when I think of what Shakespeare studied in school, and the extent to which dramatic presentation was part of the education system–acting out, making orations, copying Plautus and adding a twist or two to eventually construct *The Comedy of Errors,* reciting Ovid to the class–when I think of the oral teaching Shakespeare experienced, it points not just to why suddenly theatre came into being at this point in time, but also to why Shakespeare should use it as his artistic medium. He was a wordsmith who loved to act and to see things from many points of view. Taking a popular tale of a taming of the shrew and setting it in the taverns of Stratford with a troupe of players passing through also makes creative sense–though neither of these is as original or ambitious as writing four plays on the founding of England. I am aware of the mountain of commentary that has been written about *Henry VI Part 1*–it's so inferior it can't possibly be Shakespeare's; *Parts 2* and *3* came first, and then he and other writers put together *Part 1*. The answer, in my mind, is much simpler.

He was writing *Part 1* for years. He started messing with it when the first chronicle came out, when he was thirteen or thereabouts. It's about the English in France. He carried on reworking it on and off for years. He had absolutely no stagecraft when he began–he'd never been anywhere near a playhouse nor knew anything about theatre economics. He'd read some Roman plays. If one of the apocryphal tales is true, he would make up an oration before he slaughtered a calf for his father's business of glove-making. Maybe he listened to local storytellers, had been to the odd performance by traveling players, done plays in the classroom. The Bible he knew through and through, as did every child in England. Possibly he knew the *Iliad* in Latin. But (and this is the important point) he wrote a play because he was, by nature, a writer and as such responded to the tensions of his own daily life and his own internal story by putting words down on paper. He would be responding to events that he might not have remembered clearly–but that were held in his unconscious mind. He was an artist, and as with all artists the conflicts they hold beg for attention, so they can be examined, perceived, made whole, made use of!

Shakespeare was four when his father was elected bailiff (mayor) of Stratford, and during his tenure the Privy Council ordered that churches be stripped of images and painting, bringing them more in line with the thinking behind Protestantism rather than Catholicism. He was five when the northern lords' Catholic uprising was suppressed by Henry Carey, first Baron Hunsdon, later lord chamberlain to Elizabeth and one of Shakespeare's most important patrons. Both events must have been ardently discussed in the Catholic/Protestant home of the Shakespeare family.

Shakespeare was eight when the Saint Bartholomew's Day Massacre took place in Paris, probably the most horrific crime in the religious civil war. The good people of Stratford may not have heard about it until some weeks afterward, but they would have heard about it–not least because England and France were obsessed with each other, in something of the same way that America and Iran are obsessed with each other. Each always aware of what the other is doing. Always interfering with each other's economic and foreign policy. France had been England's enemy for centuries. As I said, it began in 1066, when England was invaded by the Normans. England dealt with the Conquest by embracing the conquerors and saying, Okay, England now owns France, London is the capital of this joint territory. And so the two countries became tied—suspiciously, awkwardly, always vying for superiority. When England finally lost France, the English monarch still kept "King of France" in his title, until 1801. What the French did reverberated in England, whether by competition with them or by the huge influx of French Huguenot refugees, fleeing religious persecution, which England accepted. (Shakespeare lived with one such family in London.)

Now, the Saint Bartholomew's Day Massacre was not about territory but about religion. And it didn't remain just one terrible overnight massacre, in which a thousand Protestants were killed in Paris in the space of a few hours. No, the event gradually spread all over France, repeated in towns from north to south; and then reprisals began, and Protestants slaughtered Catholics, and so on for the next thirty years. All the time Shakespeare was growing up, this slaughter for religion's sake was taking place across the Channel. It might subside for six months, but then it would start again, bringing with it the four horsemen of the Apocalypse: famine, disease, poverty, and war. It was the backdrop to all the religious dissension in England (and there was a lot): would the English end up like the French, in unstoppable, spasmodic, but seemingly continuous violence? We have examples of this kind of fighting now—Afghanistan chief among them, Iraq, various African countries, and the northern provinces of China.

And since Henry VIII's break with Rome in 1534, England had only narrowly avoided that kind of internal strife. Shakespeare's parents, John and Mary Shakespeare, witnessed Henry VIII dissolving the monasteries, executing twelve monastic leaders, and turning the monks and nuns out onto the streets to wander where they would, ransacking religious houses to provide money for the monarch and his nobles, destroying the old ways of the ordinary people's relationship with the land, changing the way the legal system worked. Henry's son Edward turned the country Protestant and ruled for six years.

There was an attempt to ensure that the country stayed Protestant at Edward's death with the Nine Days' Queen (Lady Jane Grey, who then was executed), because the Catholic Mary was next in line. She is known as Bloody Mary, given her perpetual burning of Protestant heretics. She took the country back into the bosom of Rome. During Mary's reign, the Calvinist John Knox published his scream of rage about the women monarchs of Europe in *The First Blast of the Trumpet Against the Monstrous Regiment of Women*. It was published the year Mary died. She reigned for five years.

Elizabeth came next, and the country returned to Protestantism. But Elizabeth, whose mother and stepmother had been executed by her father, made a concerted effort to rule not by a rigid belief system but by a milder Protestantism, whereby "we will not look into men's souls" providing Catholics kept a low profile and didn't thrust their Catholicism down other people's throats and were loyal nationalists. For many Catholics this was a godsend, and they served Elizabeth faithfully. Others, however, still wanted to return to Rome. There were repeated attempts on Elizabeth's life, principally by Catholics—plots hatched mainly around Mary, Queen of Scots, who was held captive in England for eighteen years, after she fled Scotland in danger of her life from her own people. Eventually, in 1587, she was executed, after one plot too many. Then there were ongoing threats of Spanish invasion. The Spanish Armada sailed in 1588; men from every town were mustered to meet the invasion, including eight from Stratford. Forcing England back into the Catholic fold was a major foreign-policy initiative of the papacy for fifty years—an initiative the Spanish and French forces were encouraged to lead. (Fortunately, they were not friends with each other—so never made a collaborative effort, which probably could have defeated England.) And of course Protestantism had taken hold in France, too, leading to religious wars. And all of Shakespeare's life, supporting the repulsion of Spain from the Netherlands was an ongoing task. This created a backdrop, which threatened to tip England into the same kind of civil wars that France suffered while Shakespeare was growing up.

So is it any surprise that the first place a young man with imagination would go in his work was the struggles in France? And does it not seem in some ways inevitable, perhaps even God's will, a divine providence, that England should have lost France a hundred years before Shakespeare was born? Thereafter, England had to deal with her own civil wars, the Wars of the Roses—not religious wars, it's true, but the kind of wars that keep every single "ordinary" person in the country aware that something awful could happen at any moment. It's a collective psychological unbalancing; though the people were calmed somewhat by the longevity of Elizabeth's reign, they could never feel completely safe. In heartrending scenes from *Henry VI*, the father mistakenly kills the son; the son, the father. Shakespeare expressed his fear of the mob throughout his writing life—watching the events in France, fearing Spain, hoping England would stay stable.

Beneath the account of these struggles between the Houses of York and Lancaster in the *Henry VI* plays lies an expression of the religious struggles manifested in France, and feared in England since Henry VIII's break with Rome. Religious difference is the ostensible cause of the outright hostility between England and Spain (though economic gain is its driving force). And, finally, there are religious tensions manifested in Shakespeare's family itself. His mother, Mary Arden, was probably a Catholic; that was difficult. His father was nominally Protestant. That the parents had rows, tensions, disagreements, distress when Arden relatives were executed for supporting Catholic plots—yes, these things would affect Shakespeare as he was growing up. But his genius lay in being able to see all sides of the argument. And that's where he stood, and that's what he wrote. The *Henry VI* plays are a good vehicle for a young man's imagination, motivated perhaps by something he often couldn't put a finger on. In all the modern controversy about whether Shakespeare was a Catholic or not, I say he wouldn't go near religion as a belief system with a barge pole.

We look back at wars to try and name pivotal forces, trying to make sense of what is going on today. The American Civil War took place 150 years ago—but it is alive in the American imagination in a way no other war is! We notice that many of the countries where America has troops today were or are involved in civil war. It took us years to bring our own Civil War to a close—why are we interfering in other people's? I was born during the Second World War, but I think much more about the First World War; my grandfather died in it, and it affected both of my parents' lives profoundly, as did the depression of the late 1920s and '30s that followed. I remember the sky lighting up in the night as Coventry burned. I can still hear a single-engine plane flying overhead one night, and remember how I wondered where it was going—and I was in a cradle. I absorbed that tension in my cells as I grew up. And yet it is the First World War I have studied, done plays about, read about, thought about, and tried to understand. I think Frank McGuinness's *Observe the Sons of Ulster Marching Towards the Somme* one of the great war plays of all time, and one of the productions I am most proud of! I don't connect directly with World War II. I need a metaphor.

Our children are growing up with the threat of terrorism, though most of them have never witnessed a terrorist act except on television: the Twin Towers coming down, killing three thousand; the Boston Marathon; and the unending list of school shootings. How is that ongoing dynamic functioning in their lives? What does it mean to grow up always thinking an enemy is going to get you?

I am suggesting it was the same for Shakespeare. He grew up under the tensions of potential religious war in England. His own family embodied those tensions, the more aristocratic Catholic Ardens on his mother's side and the very Protestant Stratford town fathers, including glover John Shakespeare. One of the ways Shakespeare deals with his dis-ease is to write about it, not directly but indirectly. The plays of *Henry VI* are episodic, like the religious wars in France in so many ways: this battle happened, and these people got mad about it; revenge spurred on that action, and those people got mad; all kinds of subplots were happening between people ostensibly on the same side; another reprisal happened; and so it went on. The plays are full of gratuitous violence, side adventures that are fun but do not necessarily contribute to a coherent whole; it's a mishmash, a young man's first attempt at dramatic literature, with a vague nod to the format of the well-made Roman play, or to the simplistic form of the miracle and mystery plays, with their stock biblical characters of good and evil. But just as the *Iliad* became the story that first Greece, and then Western civilization, recognized as its founding story, so the *Henry VI* plays became England's founding story. They eventually became a huge success, playing many, many times over the years, including at the Rose Playhouse when Shakespeare was part of Lord Strange's Men. Shakespeare wasn't the only playwright writing English history. In *The Queen's Men and Their Plays*, Scott McMillin and Sally-Beth MacLean posit the idea that the Queen's Men and the Earl of Leicester's Men were formed expressly to play material that offered the population the story about the founding of England and what it meant to be English. And provided a warning about civil war and its dangers. What makes these plays different from either the *Iliad* or Caesar's *Gallic Wars* is the women and the role they play in the action of the story.

The women in these plays (the *Henry VIs* and *Richard III*) not only break up the repetition and (after a while) tedium of the battle action and perfidious political plotting. Each woman shifts the balance of power—and breaks up the monotony of the way men fight. Often the only way we can distinguish one fight from another ("Yield" . . . "I will not yield" . . . "Oh God, I am dead, let me give a speech") is by what the women are doing, in the background as much as the foreground. Monty Python and "Pyramus and Thisbe" capture the tragedy well! "Lovers, make moan. / His eyes were green as leeks." Perhaps I exaggerate. I did enjoy inventing different battle after different battle—how to entertain the audience in a thousand ways. There is a repetitive stream of killing, revenge, plotting, and more killing, and it is the women who finally bring it to an end. Even though war is a man's story, Shakespeare found himself interested in the way the women were influencing the story.

So, having asserted that Shakespeare wrote to give voice to the tensions he and the country grew up with, I now offer the idea, possibly through studying Elizabeth I herself, that he was able, over a period of years, to perceive the structure of power and that women had qualities that allowed them to circumvent the normal paths. Sometimes this had tragic consequences, but nevertheless it offered the idea that it doesn't always have to be like this.

Consider the women in these four plays (a few of whom I didn't mention in the earlier narrative): Joan of Arc, the fighting virgin who doesn't stay a virgin long, but is condemned universally as a whore and a witch (and only five hundred years later is elevated to sainthood). The French Countess of Auvergne, who pretends to be honorable and nearly seduces our brave John Talbot, though he fortunately sees through her ruse. The seductive, young, impoverished French Princess Margaret, who marries the weak King of England and brings the enemy right into home territory; she becomes a fighting warrior (as Joan was), and later a loony bag lady living on the edge of the court. The vain, ambitious Protector's wife (Eleanor—we've only mentioned her, but she falls into the virago category), who does not know her place, juggles with wicked spirits (as Joan did), and must be led through the streets covered with papers telling of her crimes, humiliating both her husband and herself, and bringing them both down. The lowborn Elizabeth, the most beautiful woman in all England, who uses her sexuality to attract the Yorkist Edward IV, produces a prodigious number of children, creates her own power base by elevating her family, loses her sons before they can inherit the throne, and is finally able to bring the wars to a close by marrying her daughter to the heir of the Lancastrian clan.

Then there is a daughter of the kingmaker Warwick called Anne, who is used as a seal of dynastic alliances. In *Richard III* she is brave and is active in her opposition—but ineffective. She marries into both houses, York and Lancaster. First she is married to the son of Margaret and Henry VI. Richard kills him. Then Richard marries her himself—but poisons her when he doesn't want her anymore. Anne has a sister called Isabel, who is married to Clarence, the brother of Richard and Edward IV. We never see her. But we do see her ten-year-old daughter, who also bewails her father's death in public. Finally, there is the Duchess of York, wife to the Duke, mother to Edward, George, Duke of Clarence, Richard, and the youngest, Rutland. As Richard goes into the final battle, she publicly curses him, giving voice to the fears of a nation, doing what she can to bring the wars to an end.

Then there's the odd witch or concubine who helps move things along. But you can see from this description that women have a limited number of tools in their kit to garner power or wield influence. They are not on the big chessboard at all. They are standing in the wings (to change my metaphor), waiting for the moment when they can dart onto the stage, mix things up, throw in alternative moves, and then get out of there if they possibly can. They can use their sexuality or their ancestry (if it has any worth). If they are really brave, they will take up arms and lead men into battle—but they will be vilified for it. Otherwise, the devil is their only friend—even if the Virgin Mary and Saint Catherine smiled at first! And yet, by the time we get to *Richard III*, the women bury their differences, find common ground, and are looking for a way through the morass to stop the unending struggle for power. And this, I think, is what happened to Shakespeare. He wanted to find some way of shifting the picture—and the women in *Richard III* might mark one of the first times he registers that he has sympathy for and empathy with the women as a group. He draws a more complex picture of the ability and function of women in the history plays than of those in the early comedies. Elizabeth Woodville appears in two plays. The rest appear in only one each, except for Margaret. She is in the middle of the action in all four plays. And I suggest she so took hold of Shakespeare's imagination that she trained him to learn about women, in attraction and repulsion; eventually, she became a *whole* woman who would not go away!

The other thing Shakespeare learned in these war plays is that war and revenge are not very useful ways of furthering mankind. Men may win "honor" (but that's just a word, breath, as Falstaff says in a later war play). Nothing is ever solved or resolved in the long run by one side's triumphing over another if the winners still have to live with the people they have suppressed. If one side completely obliterates the other, the cycle of revenge takes generations—but it will come. Eventually, too, new schisms grow up within victors' ranks; over time they split into two, and as opposite sides they start to fight again. I think Shakespeare exhausted himself with this story. The bloodbath is unending, revenge unending, trying to maintain "honor" unending. Henry VI himself—that saintly man (and perhaps the part Shakespeare played)—could provide no answer.

I don't know at this point in time if Shakespeare thought that women might be able to solve the problem—but I do think he became deeply interested in the questions of power and government, and the possibility that the women stood outside it enough so they could look at it more clearly. As warrior women, they could take on the man's role, but they were never as successful at it as the men. And, ultimately, it didn't get them what they wanted. Even if it was a great emotional relief to pick up a sword and live in the midst of the action, it didn't promote those desires most important to them: long-lived children, security, relationships, and love.

It was by understanding the power structure and using subtler methods of persuasion, seduction, or just behind-the-scenes action that the women were most successful. Negotiating secretly brought more results; not always letting people know what you were up to was the cleverer way.

In any case, writing these plays was a rite of passage for Shakespeare–as an artist and as a human being. He learned to write on a large canvas, and by exploring the motives for why people did what they did, and how women can affect the course of history even when they have no overt power, the playwright and the women drew closer to each other. As outsiders who had common sympathies, they might be able to act as surrogates for each other in the thirty-odd plays still to come.

AN INTERLUDE: The Plague Years

After he wrote these early plays, something quite extraordinary happened to Shakespeare. His writing changed dramatically and substantially. He went from projecting onto women, stereotyping them, to groping his way toward some kind of understanding, to understanding them completely. He wrote as if he were a woman. Embodying them. Giving them full agency.

Why does this happen? How could it happen so swiftly, in just a few short years?

I think the answer is, he fell in love with someone who possessed qualities unimaginable to him previously. But once his passion for her filled his body and mind, his artistic self became the driving force of his life.

In order to understand better what happened to Shakespeare's writing of women, we need a context for his life between the years 1587 and 1594, concentrating particularly on the years 1591 to 1594. I don't know if everything is accurate in this account, but I am dealing with events in the way Shakespeare dealt with events—taking the events themselves and using them to stimulate the imagination so a story can be told.

I assume that Shakespeare left Stratford, Anne, and the three children in 1587. I am guessing (putting together all the trades others have suggested) that he was previously a law clerk at the Guild Hall, a glover, a butcher's apprentice, and a schoolteacher, often multitasking to make money, enjoying none of it. Once Anne got pregnant and they were married, his life crowded in on him. I am guessing that living in the house in Henley Street with his parents and their children, William's siblings, was hell on earth for someone aspiring to be a writer. Not only were his own three still toddlers, but his mother's youngest, Edmund, was only three when Shakespeare's eldest, Susannah, was born and Richard, his mother's fifth living child, was nine.

I am assuming that Shakespeare loved this great brood of children, but they also drove him crazy; it would have been hard to carve out any quiet time. (Also, the few times a brood of children occur in the plays, they get slaughtered.) I am assuming Shakespeare's mother dominated this household.

I am assuming that he joined an acting company, the Earl of Leicester's Men, as they passed through Stratford, a company that included actors Shakespeare would subsequently work with for much of his life. But he could have joined the Queen's Men. No fewer than five acting troupes performed in Stratford in 1587; even if Shakespeare did not join one of them, he would at least have realized that his talent was for acting and playwriting, not for clerking and glove-making. There is a tale that he substituted for William Knell, an actor with the Queen's Men who was killed at Thame, a village a few miles away from Stratford.

If so, Shakespeare, star pupil in the art of rhetoric at the Guild Hall, and in grammar school, a quick study, was able to step into Knell's place with little rehearsal. He seized the moment. I think he always seized the moment. All his life, both in his plays and in his personal actions, Shakespeare's timing was immaculate. Be aware of the need, and grab the brass ring without hesitation as it comes your way!

In another tale, he was caught, with several other likely lads, poaching deer from the local lord's estate. He was punished severely and in retaliation wrote a scurrilous poem and stuck it on Sir Thomas Lucy's entrance gate at Charlecote. Then he has to disappear in order to escape dire legal consequences.

However he left, he swore to send every penny he earned back to Anne and the kids; but he was grateful to be on the road, to leave his mother and be able finally to earn his living, however meager, doing what his talent demanded he do: to write and act.

Life on the road is hard. The spirit gets weary—too many people, too many places, too much new stimulus, totally dependent on your fellow actors for company, courage, and care. If you like and admire them, you can bond for life; if they irritate you, traveling with them is a kind of purgatory. And of course Shakespeare's troupe was probably traveling on foot, with perhaps one or two horses between them, and a cart for costumes and props. Perhaps you know where you are going; the troupe has played this circuit before, and people are looking forward to your visit. Or maybe not. Walk twelve to twenty miles. Seek permission from the town fathers to perform that afternoon and the next; permission denied, you push on to the next town; permission granted, you set up shop and announce your arrival. Some of the troupe parade through the streets, doing a bit of a dog-and-pony show on what you are going to perform, and at what time; the others find the performance place, unpack costumes and props, find out where you may stay that night, who'll feed you, and so on. Do the show. Perhaps be paid five shillings—maybe more, maybe less, depending on the generosity and wealth of the town and its elders. Divide that up between seven or eight of you—some getting more, some getting less—and set off for the next town, village, or lord's house.

As he traveled across the country, playing in different towns or great men's houses, Shakespeare would notice how Protestant or Catholic each place was: each would be different in gradation. Had the local church fervently embraced the edicts of the Privy Council, so there were no signs of popery anywhere? Did the town have a roster of Puritan preachers to speak there? Did the lord's house still have some signs and smells of the old faith? The events of the last fifty years had left the country in various states of flux: the farther away from London, the more likely it was that the edicts sent out from the Privy Council were ignored, or only half fulfilled. The north and west always remained closer to the old faith.

These things he would notice—together with the energy and bustle of the place, the freedom of the women, the education of the young, the relationship to the poor. Elizabeth's Poor Laws (whereby towns are held responsible for looking after their poor) were the beginning of "not-for-profit" legislation as we know it.

It was essential that everyone knew the players had the patronage of an aristocrat of the realm; otherwise, the town fathers could throw them into jail for being "sturdy beggars"—people who were *choosing* not to do a proper job but preferred instead to beg. Rogues and vagabonds were feared and frowned on; itinerant players came under that category. But Shakespeare didn't need to worry about this too much, because the Earl of Leicester was the most powerful peer in the land, the favorite and oldest friend of Queen Elizabeth, and he was the players' patron.

In fact, it is thought that Leicester and the Queen had both become patrons of companies of players, not just because they enjoyed the theatre themselves, but also because they wanted to encourage plays about the history of England, how the country had been wrecked with civil wars, how Yorkist faction versus Lancastrian faction had meant misery for everyone. They wanted plays that would go to every part of the country to encourage the idea of being "English." The Queen and Leicester wanted the theatre to help write England into existence, to create a sense of nationalism in the provinces, where there was often no sense of a collective larger good. So many of the plays the Queen's Men and Leicester's Men performed were about the founding of England, or a metaphor for it. And it just so happens that this moment in history was the very subject our young actor and would-be playwright was interested in. In fact, he'd been sketching out ideas for years on the very topic, and a new version of Holinshed's *Chronicles of England* had just come out, so he was able to familiarize himself more deeply with the subject even before he fled Henley Street and joined Leicester's Men.

So his first year on the road was grueling but promising. Occasionally, the troupe got to London, and that felt like hitting pay dirt. Not only could they stay in one place for a short period of time, but their income increased—they could each get paid as much as five shillings a performance for their work, infinitely better than provincial pay, even if lodging and food were more expensive, and the costumes for the plays had to be of a higher standard. Playwriting and professional acting were new professions. It looked as if they were going to last, but no one knew for sure.

In 1587, there was a massive funeral in London for Sir Philip Sidney, the greatest poet, soldier, and courtier of the age. Philip Sidney was everything poetical that Shakespeare wanted to be, everything aristocratic that Shakespeare's mother would have admired, and everything Protestant and soldierly that Shakespeare's father would have saluted. Sidney alive and dead had a huge influence on Shakespeare. He was the ideal courtier, a poet, a statesman, an intellectual, a soldier, and a lover, and he was killed leading a brave assault on the town of Zutphen in the Netherlands, trying to free it from Spanish and Catholic domination. The funeral was a huge outpouring of grief for the quintessential English aristocrat. The size of it, the furor it created in London, also conveniently counteracted any sympathy there might have been for Mary, Queen of Scots, who had been beheaded in Fotheringhay eight days before. She, of course, was, wittingly or unwittingly, the center of most of the Catholic plots against Elizabeth's life—plots that took place on a fairly regular basis. And of course in 1588 was the attack and failure of the Spanish Armada—an invasion intended to force England to return to Catholicism.

Sidney's funeral was paid for by Sir Francis Walsingham, Elizabeth's spymaster and principal secretary. He was Sidney's father-in-law, for Frances Walsingham was Sidney's wife.

Mary was beheaded on February 8, Sidney interred February 16. The Earl of Essex, Leicester's stepson and the Earl of Southampton's best friend, began his courtship of Frances Sidney née Walsingham. Shakespeare, however, was still on tour, and didn't know any of them personally—yet.

Did the twenty-three-year-old Shakespeare have a sex life as he toured the country or stayed for brief periods in London? Well, if he did, his heart was not engaged. He was saving what money he could and thinking up plays—even as he plodded along the country roads on Dobbin—because he could sell a play at five pounds a pop, and that would improve financial matters for him.

In 1588, Robert Dudley, Earl of Leicester, worn out by his service to the Queen, died. Leicester had represented a kind of steady Protestantism much admired by his colleagues—Walsingham, Burleigh (Elizabeth's chief minister), the Queen. He gave his name and encouragement not only to players but to many intellectuals and artists—poets, thinkers, musicians—people who used their talents to support the Protestant cause. They tended to lean slightly toward Puritanism, but were royalists all, Church of England stalwarts. Together, this group of artists, poets, musicians, intellectuals, and politicians had formed a mini-academy—with Philip Sidney their star.

The death of Leicester brought turmoil to the acting troupe Leicester's Men. They had either to identify another patron or to split up and join one of the other troupes of players; they seem to have done the latter. I think Shakespeare joined the Earl of Pembroke's Men—one of the oldest troupes, known originally for its tumblers, acrobats, and clowns, but more recently taking on plays. Pembroke's Men came to have possession of several of Shakespeare's scripts in the coming years, so his joining them makes the most sense.

After two more years on the road, Shakespeare was performing at the court at Christmas of 1590. To perform at the court was not only a privilege, a seal of approval by the monarch, but meant more money. Sir Walter Raleigh, one of the greatest explorers and thinkers of the age—but often in trouble because he wouldn't keep his mouth shut—was there at court, home from Ireland, where he had been awarded vast tracts of land taken from the indigenous Irish. He brought with him Edmund Spenser, an admirer of Sidney who was now being called the greatest poet of the age. His long poem *The Faerie Queene* deifies Queen Elizabeth, making her the symbol of enlightenment and bounty. We know Shakespeare deeply admired Spenser, as Spenser in turn had deeply admired Sir Philip Sidney. Spenser was a tailor's son, a scholarship kid at both the Merchant Taylors' School and later at Cambridge, and Shakespeare was a glover's son, so they had much in common, not least that each had to earn a living and support a family. Their passion for poetry was not the most lucrative profession on God's earth, so they needed to earn more money. Spenser almost hit it rich. Queen Elizabeth loved his work, and she granted him a most generous stipend so he could concentrate on his writing. Unfortunately, Burleigh was able to countermand the sum, reducing it to a much more modest amount; this forced Spenser back to his court-appointed job in the area around Kilcolman, North Cork. Raleigh, Spenser, and Shakespeare all met that Christmas at court. And though Leicester and Sidney were both dead, their influence was strong among this circle of artists at court.

Another huge event in Shakespeare's life was the two-part production of Christopher Marlowe's *Tamburlaine the Great*. Marlowe and Shakespeare were the same age, but Marlowe's star was burning far more brightly. *Tamburlaine* electrified London. The Rose Playhouse, built by Philip Henslowe among the brothels, pubs, and bear-baiting arenas on the south side of the Thames, outside the jurisdiction of the town fathers, had people flocking to it. In the part of Tamburlaine was

Edward Alleyn, the greatest actor of the age, married to Henslowe's stepdaughter. He was tall, commanding, athletic, and handsome, with a voice that thundered to the rafters.

Marlowe wrote in blank verse, a form that had come to England via the poets Thomas Wyatt and the Earl of Surrey some forty years earlier. But now their version of iambic pentameter morphed into "Marlowe's mighty line." His regular, heavily punctuated rhythms thundered from the playhouse, sweeping Tamburlaine across Asia and Europe, bringing death and destruction in his wake. Marlowe cared nothing for the classical form of confined time and place; he gave actors, and especially Alleyn, the kind of soaring part that can alter life forever. Blood, guts, savagery, every extreme of behavior catapulted onto the stage—and Shakespeare found his inspiration.

Shakespeare's plays about the wars between England and France and the Wars of the Roses followed *Tamburlaine* onto the stage. *Henry VI Parts 1, 2,* and *3* were all a great success, followed by *Richard III*, which boasted a villain almost as great as Tamburlaine. Marlowe followed his success with *Doctor Faustus* and *The Jew of Malta.* He wrote about the Saint Bartholomew's Day Massacre (Sir Philip Sidney had been in Paris that day for the marriage of Henry of Navarre [Protestant] and Marguerite de Valois [Catholic] and witnessed the atrocities firsthand. Walsingham, then Elizabeth's ambassador in Paris, sheltered Sidney and other English Protestants.) Previously, Marlowe had written *Dido, Queen of Carthage*, but now he pushed the envelope further and ventured into homosexuality and sodomy (both beheading offenses in Elizabethan England) with *Edward II.* Marlowe was the first "star" of the playwriting world, both adored and reviled. He and Raleigh and the Earl of Northumberland created their own little think tank, nicknamed the School of Night, to question accepted knowledge and investigate new ideas.

Shakespeare continued to write and act, but his own rising success came at a price. He was attacked in print by the university playwright Robert Greene, who thought Shakespeare was stealing the work of the properly educated playwrights like himself, Marlowe, and George Peele and wanted to expose his plagiarism. And he was right. Shakespeare was borrowing like mad—but I would call it being inspired by others, making old work new. Shakespeare's schooling had taught him to borrow the work of any writer he admired, copy his style, and then try to improve upon it. Greene's attack may also have had something to do with the fact that Shakespeare's play was earning six times as much as Greene's at the Rose Playhouse.

Another playwright, Thomas Kyd, was also having great success. A close friend of Marlowe's, he introduced the revenge tragedy as a genre into English playwriting. He wrote *The Spanish Tragedy*, probably a *King Leir*, a *Hamlet*. Shakespeare's *Henry VI Part 3* (in which revenge is everywhere) and *Richard III* were probably both influenced by Kyd as well as Marlowe. And certainly Shakespeare copied Kyd in what would become a jackpot, the masterpiece of comic/tragic blood and gore, *Titus Andronicus*. *Titus* contains a sexually aggressive warrior woman, Tamora, and a virgin, Lavinia, who is raped and mutilated, then killed, by her father, so he will not have to endure her pain and shame. Thomas Kyd's *Hamlet* was copied many years later by Shakespeare (and turned into one of the greatest plays of all time); likewise *King Leir*. How close personally Shakespeare was to Kyd and Marlowe is hard to tell, but even a decade later he was still putting allusions to them in his plays, so I would say he felt deeply connected to them; they probably frequented the same pubs, joined in the discussions and revelry around the Inns of Court, read one another's plays and poetry. Young playwrights and actors are greedy for one another's company—they perform in the same places, give one another credibility, bolster one another in a thousand ways, as well as compete and perhaps deride.

During this period Shakespeare also wrote three comedies, copying the style of Italian comedy in two—*Taming of the Shrew, Two Gentlemen of Verona*—and basing one on a Roman farce, *Comedy of Errors*.

He was still much on the road (he had to earn money), but coming into London more often now, to play at The Theatre (built in North London by James Burbage, Richard's father and leader of the Earl of Leicester's troupe) and the Rose for brief runs. His plays made him somewhat famous but not rich—maybe forty pounds spread over five years—nor did he own the rights. Whichever company bought the plays, whether Pembroke's Men, or Lord Strange's, or Sussex's (they all performed *Titus Andronicus*), or whether Philip Henslowe himself bought them and was renting them out to the other companies, the money no longer came to Shakespeare. Playwriting does not your fortune make, as Marlowe, Greene, and Kyd found out. Owning part of a company could make you rich. A share in Pembroke's company was being sold for eighty pounds at this time. (To put it in perspective, Shakespeare bought his first home, New Place—albeit maybe in poor repair—in Stratford for sixty pounds several years later.) The share meant a cut in all the box-office moneys, the fees from renting out plays, fees from the court, from the Inns of Court, and so on.

In order to make a decent living, support a wife and three children, and perhaps help repair the family fortunes, Shakespeare needed to put together the money to buy a share. He was beginning to get a reputation; the question was how to leverage that reputation into some substantial moneys. Finding a patron for himself—not as part of a company, but individually—would be a great advantage. He would have to have status higher than a common player, in this status-ridden age, and be someone who moved in important circles. For that to happen, he needed to be known not as a player but as a poet in his own right.

So a series of events happened that changed Shakespeare's life forever, and changed his relationship with women. This in turn led him to depths of understanding about all relationships, about sex, about power structures, the nature of the soul, and violence.

In 1591–92, the plague struck London. It had always been in the background, closing places of assembly for a week or two. (Rule of thumb: deaths from the plague under thirty per week, everything stayed open; over thirty, everything closed down.) Plague was well known to Shakespeare; his two elder sisters may have died from it in infancy, before he was born. But certainly Stratford was struck by it repeatedly. Friends and friends' children close to Shakespeare died. Like insurrection and religious tension, the plague was always hovering in the background of daily life; no one ever knew when and if it would break out.

But familiarity did not make it any less hard to bear. It was a horrible death—huge boils bursting out in the armpits, on the neck, fever, the skin turning black, and certain death within a few days. If a house was known to have the plague, the authorities boarded it up with everyone in it. (Shakespeare wrote about this in *Romeo and Juliet*.) All the playhouses were automatically closed down, and the troupes would take to the road. This time, the theatres in London were closed for most of two years. Residents of towns and villages were fearful that the players would bring the plague with them, so they were not always welcoming; uncertainty was everywhere.

There were two thoughts prevalent at the time about the causes of the plague. One was that it was a germ (though the Elizabethans would probably say it was a vapor carried in the air) and that it infected and spread through close contact with others. This meant that all those who could, left the town and went to live on their country estates, away from the epicenter. The second idea about the cause of the plague was that it was God's judgment, and that individual and/ or collective sin brought it about: God was angry and was punishing mankind. So plague victims were not treated particularly well, and only truly dedicated people, either in religious orders or responsible doctors, or poor destitute women who had no other means of earning a living, would stay to tend the sick.

And of course the tension about how long the plague would last was overwhelming to the players—always hoping they could get back into London within the next few weeks, having their hopes dashed, perhaps returning for the odd week or two, only to be sent out onto the road again. I have to tell you it is my idea of hell—doubtful venues, doubtful pay, doubtful health!

If Shakespeare hadn't been thinking of looking for a patron before, he must have done so now. And it happened that the Dowager Countess of Southampton was looking for someone to write some sonnets to her son, a poetry lover, to persuade him to get married. Perhaps Spenser or someone else who knew Shakespeare from his Christmas appearances at court recommended him. In any case, he wrote seventeen sonnets to a young man who was reluctant to get married and produce progeny so his line would go on after his demise. And we are fairly sure that that young man was the Earl of Southampton; his best friend was the Earl of Essex, now a leading light in Elizabeth's court, Leicester's stepson, the Queen's favorite. All important points in the story to follow.

The Dowager Countess of Southampton had reason to be worried about her teenage son, Henry. His father had died when he was seven, and so, like all underage sons who inherit the father's name, vast tracts of land, and huge fortune (earldoms were economic epicenters dotted all over the kingdom), he became a ward of the court. How earldoms were handled was of great importance to the monarch;

hence the law that any underage peer became a ward of the court. In this case, Southampton had been put directly in the charge of Lord Burleigh, Elizabeth's chief minister. Now Burleigh was proposing his own daughter as a suitable match (these alliances were always about property, inheritance, and power; if you liked the person, that was good luck, because you were certainly going to have to sleep together and, it was hoped, produce a large family). But Southampton wasn't having any; he didn't want to get married. This was a concern to many, because an enormous amount of economic, regional, and political interests were dependent upon his actions.

Southampton didn't seem to be particularly interested in women, which probably alarmed his mother even more, because he had turned eighteen in October 1591 and should have been interested. But his father had seemed to prefer his menservants to his wife and had left his steward a lot of money in his will. Added to which, Southampton was very beautiful, with feminine features and long golden locks.

But, whatever his looks, what he was most interested in was soldiering. Sir Philip Sidney was his hero, and he, too, was going to fight on behalf of English foreign policy. In 1591, he had crossed the Channel (without permission from the monarch) to join Henry of Navarre in his battle to occupy the French throne. Navarre was a staunch Huguenot. Though Southampton's family was nominally Catholic, they always put queen and country first, so Southampton would not find it a conflict to support Navarre against the Catholic League in its effort to prevent Navarre from taking up his rightful inheritance, the throne of France. Navarre himself was not a religious fanatic but a brave, honest man, a good leader, who cared about the people and their well-being, educated, worldly, and an ally of Elizabeth.

Southampton wanted to do as all great courtiers do: they are valiant in battle, they are civilized conversationalists and poets (or supporters of artists who will produce great literary works), leaders both in learning and on the battlefield.

Southampton wrote to his friend and mentor, the Earl of Essex, that he was already across the Channel and wanted to serve under him. Essex, who had by now married Philip Sidney's widow, petitioned the Queen to take an army to come to Navarre's aid. The Queen granted them permission, so Essex and Southampton, with a small army of English foot soldiers, joined Navarre and fought the Catholic League. It didn't come to much, though Essex's brother did get killed, and the friends returned home not quite as triumphantly as they had hoped.

Essex was indeed the rising star of Elizabeth's court. He had been at Philip Sidney's side when he died at Zutphen; he was the Earl of Leicester's stepson; he was highly educated (he was asked to be chancellor of Cambridge University); he was both dashing and introspective, paying constant courtship to the Queen. At the Accession Day tilts, he organized a dramatic homage to the Queen: Should he serve her as a soldier or as a statesman? Or should he retire from public life to follow the path of the ascetic, studying, writing poetry, following the arts?

In all Essex's actions, he was joined by his chief friend and acolyte, the Earl of Southampton. Essex was a meteor, Southampton a gentler soul.

Shakespeare's sonnets were proving ineffective in persuading Southampton to get married and procreate–Southampton was interested in finding honor on the battlefield–and Shakespeare needed to earn money.

Shakespeare knew Southampton and Essex by this time. He probably listened to their stories of fighting for Navarre. They all had a common love of learning and poetry; they loved the work and life of Philip Sidney. Shakespeare's assigned task in Southampton's life– inspiring him to look favorably upon marriage–was not working very well. But they could be friends because of their common interests, even though one was a peer of the realm and the other an actor, playwright, and now poet.

One of the things the King of Navarre accomplished, besides being a great soldier and politician, was to create an academy. All the French royal families (Protestant and Catholic) were keen on academies–gatherings of the best thinkers, artists of every persuasion but especially poets and musicians, philosophers and scientist/religious thinkers like Giordano Bruno–who would study and debate about the nature of man, God, knowledge, and how these were connected. Leicester's circle and the School of Night were the English equivalent of the French academies. I suppose our think tanks are the nearest modern equivalent, but most think tanks we set up are to prove a political point of view and are used as ammunition to change political ideas and university studies, and to buy politicians, rather than as genuine exchanges of knowledge. The French academies were genuine explorations, with the goal of finding the deepest connections in man's spirit. This did have a political purpose: everyone wanted the Wars of Religion to stop.

The French academies were of great importance because the royal leaders of both Catholic and Protestant sides wanted to find a way to curb fanaticism, to bring to an end the unending civil war—two decades of skirmishes and massacres, battles and bigotry. The goal of the academies was to find the connection between all the schools of religious thought and develop ideas profound enough to provide a path to unity. Frances Yates wrote a brilliant book, *The French Academies of the Sixteenth Century*, laying out the details of their thinking. Although out of print, it is a tour de force.

The wedding Philip Sidney had gone to Paris to celebrate, that of Henry of Navarre to Marguerite de Valois, Princess of France, was meant to bring Catholic/Protestant unity to the country. Instead, six days after the wedding, the great slaughter of the Huguenots visiting Paris for the wedding took place, defeating the intention of Catherine de' Medici, the queen mother, who had instituted the idea of the academies in France.

Catherine de' Medici was the mother of a great brood of Catholic kings: Francis II, Charles IX, and Henry III, as well as the aforesaid Marguerite de Valois; it is not surprising Catherine was a driving force for the academies because her great-great-great-grandfather was Cosimo de' Medici, who had set up the Florentine Academy in 1439; this in turn had been based on the original academy, founded by Plato in Greece around 387 B.C., both of which could be called pillars of Western thought.

When Essex and Southampton returned to England from fighting in France, I would like to suggest they set up a mini-academy. Inspired by Philip Sidney, they were following the way of the courtier. Now that they had come home from battle, it was time to write poetry, play music, and seek the meaning of life.

Mary Sidney, Philip's sister, now the Countess of Pembroke, wife to the patron of Shakespeare's current troupe of players, had taken over Sidney's literary work. She finished his translation of the Psalms (he got to 43; she completed the remaining 107). She was completing his *Arcadia.* Where would this group meet if not at the Countess's home, Wilton House? Or at Penshurst Place, the Sidney family home, inherited by Robert, Philip's younger brother—also with him at Zutphen, and a poet in his own right. The Sidney family had always welcomed artists and craftsmen into their midst, as Ben Jonson's "To Penshurst" extols years later.

> . . . of country stone,
> They're reared with no man's ruin, no man's groan;
> There's none that dwell about them wish them down;
> But all come in, the farmer and the clown . . .
>
> "TO PENSHURST"

Or the group may have met at Titchfield, Southampton's home in Hampshire, or Essex's London house by the Thames. Or all four. There were other driving forces besides Essex and his wife, Frances Walsingham Sidney: I believe Southampton was one, and his former tutor John Florio, who was now creating an Italian-English dictionary and translating Montaigne's *Essays;* George Chapman, playwright, who was then translating the *Iliad* and would later write an infamous play called *The Conspiracy of Charles, Duke of Byron* (about Navarre's right-hand man); Spenser when he was in town; Samuel Daniel, poet and tutor to the Countess of Pembroke's sons; Fulke Greville, Stratford native, close friend of Sidney's at school and the Inns of Court; Francis Meres, Cambridge graduate, minister, and schoolteacher, who wrote an essay referring to two versions of *Love's Labour's* (he highly approved of Shakespeare, Sidney, and Michael Drayton, disapproved of Marlowe, Peele, and Greene). Maybe the School of Night three were also part of the group, perhaps a little aloof, as Raleigh and Essex constantly vied for Elizabeth's attention; but Northumberland did marry one of Essex's sisters. Then there would be some musicians—maybe John Dowland, back from the French court, and the composer William Byrd—and other artists, including Richard Burbage, actor and painter, and actor/poet/playwright William Shakespeare. There may also have been a very callow youth called Richard Barnfield hanging around the edges, who stole everyone's first drafts, spied on relationships, and later published his goodies under the title *The Passionate Pilgrim*, claiming it all to be the work of the by-then famous playwright William Shakespeare.

Mary Sidney, Countess of Pembroke, may have begun her writing as her brother's literary executor, but she soon became known as a force in her own right: writing, thinking, translating, making scientific experiments, and supporting other women's efforts to attain literary eminence. So women would be welcomed into this mini-academy as poets and musicians. And so would builders of theatres, most particularly the Burbage family, who built their Theatre possibly with the help of John Dee, the alchemist, the Earl of Leicester's tutor, occasionally favored by the Queen herself. The science of numbers, the link between proportion, music, physical space—these are not divorced from poetry but integrated into it. Plays are poetry; poetry and music are expressions of the human voice; buildings are acoustical chambers to amplify the spirit, soul, and meaning. And these subjects are all fair game for the courtier, home from battle, looking to find the meaning of life.

If Southampton found he really admired Shakespeare and wanted to support him (despite those mediocre sonnets imploring Southampton to marry), then this was the chance Shakespeare had been looking for—to get off the road for a bit, settle down in one place, do some serious work (with some better sonnets and longer poems), read, read, read, strengthen relationships with friends in high places, and escape the plague. Their academy would be following in the footsteps of the circle of intellectuals and artists Leicester had supported and Philip Sidney had led. Sidney wrote a book that laid out much of his thinking about the role of art, and in particular poetry, which was printed after his death, in 1591, by Richard Field, Shakespeare's schoolmate from Stratford.

In *Defence of Poesy*, his seminal work, Philip Sidney declared three ideas that would affect Shakespeare permanently, and identified one that the French academies held but Sidney protested against.

The first precept was that poets were the greatest truth-tellers, and they were truth-tellers *because* their ability to write poetry lifted them to a level of perception others did not have. This idea of being a poetic truth-teller gave Shakespeare the agency he needed to know his work was important, and many lines in the sonnets certainly reflect this idea of enduring poetic art.

The second idea Sidney held to be true—together with both academies in France, Catholic and Protestant—was that music and poetry together could induce ever higher levels of knowledge and consciousness, and that consciousness opened perceptions to a greater understanding of how the world worked. I believe Shakespeare began his journey with music at this time. He probably did not play an instrument himself, but after this period his plays became filled with music. His verse also became almost self-consciously musical, seeking for ways to find a deeper truth which lay in sound, rhythm, "soul."

I further imagine that there was someone else who had music in every cell of her being, and who was his companion in this. Together they set sonnets to music, psalms to music, the Song of Songs to music, kabbalistic chants to music. *The Rape of Lucrece* and *Venus and Adonis,* Shakespeare's two long poems written in this period, would also be put to music, plus anything of Ovid's that lent itself to such practice.

An idea Sidney did *not* hold with but Spenser and most academies did was the idea of "poetic frenzy"—that poetry could and often was written in a kind of ecstatic trance, the poet communing with the gods (or archetypes, as the Jungians would have it) to create powerful pictures to hold ideas in the mind. Or, in Shakespeare's terms:

> Lovers and madmen have such seething brains,
> Such shaping fantasies, that apprehend
> More than cool reason ever comprehends.
> The lunatic, the lover, and the poet
> Are of imagination all compact.
>
> A MIDSUMMER NIGHT'S DREAM (5.1, 4–8)

Shakespeare not only held this to be true but had firsthand knowledge.

For the rest of his writing life, he wrote so many of his plays swiftly yet with almost perfect form (*Romeo and Juliet* in ten days) and instinctively used images that touch the core of our being, seemingly without effort. (Juxtaposing Gloucester's blinding with Lear's clarity of sight, for example; every storm hurling new knowledge ashore; love and death walking hand in hand.) In the years to come, I think Shakespeare the actor lived in a state of playwriting poetic frenzy, able to do so because he lived a daily life of theatrical intensity, returning evenings and mornings to a place of great simplicity in his lodgings. His artistic intensity was grounded and balanced both by solitude and by the practicalities of running a theatre! And very little personal life. I know of what I speak.

Philip Sidney also held that poetry is the art form that could bring ordinary people to a state of understanding, allowing them to experience a state of grace again (the Garden of Eden before Eve bit into the apple). From this, I think, Shakespeare drew strength. Not so good was that Sidney thought theatre was a very inferior art form and pandered to people's lower tastes. Occasionally when he was well into his writing life, Shakespeare may have feared Sidney was right—but mostly Shakespeare understood something about theatre that Sidney never grasped: that jokes about bodily functions and elementary sexual acts make people laugh, so they let go of themselves and un-self-consciously inhabit their bodies, and that this, combined with the most sublime poetry, allows the full spectrum of man's being. Theatre can do something poetry by itself could never do—it can give us all of humanity, all kinds of people standing side by side, building a community of understanding, empathetic understanding. And that connection in turn fosters the perception and language of God. Potent and regenerative! It was the purpose of the academies.

The Psalms in Sidney's world were inspired by the Holy Ghost; plays, in Shakespeare's world, revealed God through the actions of people themselves. These were experiences, not abstract ideas.

Sidney had one other effect on this circle he inspired posthumously—and which now Essex and Southampton took up with fervor. It was to know the role of the warrior, to encounter war, ride into death, to understand life through death. Shakespeare was an onlooker. The world of the warrior was not for him. He had responsibilities. "Why what would you have me do?" Bolt asks Mariana in *Pericles*. "Go to the wars, would you, where a man may serve seven years for the loss of a leg and have not money enough in the end to buy him a wooden one?" South Bank, where the playhouses stood, was filled with beggars without limbs, people incapacitated by sea battles, land wars, deforming diseases. Shakespeare was a year older than Essex and nine years older than Southampton; he had no money except what he earned. His health and ability to function were his wealth.

Southampton, as we have noted, fled to the Continent at an early age to fight for the King of Navarre. He was not interested in love; he must encounter death first. And Essex's brief life was about war—first serving at Philip Sidney's side in the Netherlands, receiving his sword in his dying moments, watching Sidney refuse water to give it to one of his wounded men (if it is true), dying because he (Sidney) was such a consummate courtier he had removed his leg armor to be equal with one of his fellow officers who had had his armor blown away.

Essex the soldier served Navarre in France, then against the Spanish, then in Ireland; and finally there was his rebellion against the Queen herself, which lost him his head at the age of thirty-five. Southampton was by his side for much of this—and was condemned to die with Essex, but his youth and friends were able to prevail on his side. (Once he was out of the Tower, when James I came to the throne, he became a wiser person; not only did he marry and have children, but he spent most of his time playing his part in the government of the land, supporting the arts and world explorers, and sending early settlers to America. For twenty years he was the mainstay of the Virginia Company, again and again finding ways of raising the capital to start new plantations and colonies in America. But I get ahead of myself.)

At this time, 1591–92, it was Southampton the warrior that Shakespeare tried to understand. If the Dark Lady of the sonnets (I know, we haven't got to her yet) catapulted Shakespeare to an understanding of love and music which he had never known before, it was Southampton who inspired him to look at war—and Shakespeare found that in extremis love and war went hand in hand. Not only did the three great love stories *(Romeo and Juliet, Troilus and Cressida, Antony and Cleopatra)* promise an ecstatic understanding of love in the world, all were set against the backdrop of violence and battle. Battle can give rise to a different kind of love. There is a passion some men have for battle that most of us do not understand. Where battle is, so a kind of love goes, and this love may be the most potent force in the world if the number of wars we fight is an indicator. The love of battle and violence and the love between men and women may not be related, but they have an intensity in common which can change people forever.

After *Romeo and Juliet*, Shakespeare wrote a series of lighter plays about love–*Midsummer Night's Dream, Merchant of Venice, Much Ado About Nothing*–but he also, concurrently, wrote plays about warriors and battle–*Henry IV Part 1, King John,* and eventually *Henry V.* I am sure Shakespeare never knew battle himself–he never committed himself to an ultimate truth about it, as he did about love between men and women–but his imagination and his male friendships led him into the aura of war, which enabled him to understand the connection men experience in battle, and that he wrote about. But this is in the future.

In 1591, Sidney's sonnet sequence *Astrophel and Stella* was published posthumously. Sonnet sequences become all the rage, especially among the literary wits at the Inns of Court. The Inns of Court was where law was taught–but the extracurricular activities of playmaking and sonneteering were the student body's joy and public spectacle. Sonnets were printed privately and passed around among friends, select groups of artists, aristocrats, and members of the law court. Shakespeare wrote a sonnet sequence, picking up after the first seventeen sonnets, those written to persuade (unsuccessfully) the young man to get married. The new sonnets were far more personal, and the writer of them was present at every moment, declaring his love, passion, friendship.

If this academy was taking place at the Countess of Pembroke's house, then Samuel Daniel would have been there, tutoring her children William and Philip (the brothers to whom the First Folio would be dedicated thirty years later), and he, too, wrote a famous sonnet sequence.

Writing sonnet sequences was high art, prestigious. Writing plays was not. Writing long poems about classical figures was prestigious. Marlowe writes a long poem, *Hero and Leander* (he didn't finish it). Shakespeare followed suit with *Venus and Adonis.*

Venus and Adonis is about a beautiful youth that Venus falls in love with–but the beautiful youth is not interested. He likes hunting the boar much better. What is unusual about *Venus and Adonis* is Shakespeare's exploration of Venus's sexuality. We get twenty-nine verses of her desire, then one of his disdain; she is frantic; he rushes off to get on his horse. The horse, we are happy to say, has just seen a mare—so we are given some powerful images of masculine desire at full throttle. This goes on for eleven verses, all something like this:

> Imperiously he leaps, he neighs, he bounds,
> And now his woven girths he breaks asunder.
> The bearing earth with his hard hoof he wounds,
> Whose hollow womb resounds like heaven's thunder.
>   The iron bit he crusheth 'tween his teeth,
>   Controlling what he was controllèd with.
>
> His ears up-pricked, his braided hanging mane
> Upon his compassed crest now stand on end;
> His nostrils drink the air, and forth again,
> As from a furnace, vapours doth he send.
>   His eye, which scornfully glisters like fire,
>   Shows his hot courage and his high desire.
>
> VENUS AND ADONIS (265–76)

The horses run off together, and Adonis sinks down on the ground, weary from trying to hold the stallion. Venus begins her seduction again, going on for another seven verses; he rejects her in one verse. She comes back. He declares:

> "I know not love," quoth he, "nor will not know it,
> Unless it be a boar and then I chase it. . . ."
> VENUS AND ADONIS (409–10)

Still Venus is not put off.

> "Had I no eyes but ears, my ears would love
> That inward beauty and invisible;
> Or were I deaf, thy outward parts would move
> Each part in me that were but sensible.
>   Though neither eyes nor ears, to hear nor see,
>   Yet should I be in love by touching thee.

"Say that the sense of feeling were bereft me,
And that I could not see, nor hear, nor touch,
And nothing but the very smell were left me,
Yet would my love to thee be still as much;
   Far from the stillitory *[distilling plant]* of thy face
     excelling
   Comes breath perfumed that breedeth love by smelling."
VENUS AND ADONIS (433–44)

However, all the poetry and Venus's desire put Adonis off even more. He won't respond. In the morning, Adonis is found dead, run through by a boar's tusk, and Venus is left to mourn.

Is there a moral to this tale? If there is, it would be that Adonis lost his life because the interests in his life were unbalanced. But it is more than that. For the first time, Shakespeare allowed his imagination to explore feminine desire. Was this because he had finally had some time to think about it? Because a woman was describing to him how it felt to be a woman? His poet's sensibility and curiosity naturally allowed him to be interested in this. And was *Venus and Adonis* so popular because young men had begun to be interested in "what women want"?

Shakespeare's dedication to Southampton at the front of the poem is respectful—in our terms, groveling, but common in Elizabethan terms when someone of a lower rank (Shakespeare) was addressing someone of a higher rank (Southampton) with whom he was anxious to curry favor.

So we have *Venus and Adonis* and the early sonnets. But the tone of the sonnets Shakespeare now wrote changes. A woman of unusual beauty comes on the scene. She has "black wires" on her head, her eyes are black, her skin is dun, and her breath is none too wholesome. She is not a conventional beauty in Elizabethan terms. But our poet is smitten.

My mistress' eyes are nothing like the sun;
Coral is far more red than her lips' red.
If snow be white, why then her breasts are dun;
If hairs be wires, black wires grow on her head.
I have seen roses damasked, red and white,

But no such roses see I in her cheeks;
And in some perfumes is there more delight
Than in the breath that from my mistress reeks.
I love to hear her speak, yet well I know
That music hath a far more pleasing sound.
I grant I never saw a goddess go:
My mistress when she walks treads on the ground.
   And yet, by heaven, I think my love as rare
   As any she belied with false compare.

SONNET 130

However, the lady seems to be holding out—or, wait a second, is she trying to seduce the young friend who doesn't want to marry? My God, she's succeeded. But now she's also sleeping with the poet. Now she's holding off from him. Now it's on again. Now he's so deeply in love with her, his whole life is changing. Can he really be in love with a woman who is the opposite of what women are meant to be: chaste, charming, demure, gentle?

In one sonnet, Shakespeare riffs on the word "will"—"will" meaning William Shakespeare, of course, but "will" also meaning the vagina and then the penis—and to top it off the mental "will" (in fact, the same three meanings of this book!):

Whoever hath her wish, thou hast thy Will,
And Will to boot, and Will in overplus.
More than enough am I that vex thee still,
To thy sweet will making addition thus.
Wilt thou, whose will is large and spacious,
Not once vouchsafe to hide my will in thine?
Shall will in others seem right gracious,
And in my will no fair acceptance shine?
The sea, all water, yet receives rain still,
And in abundance addeth to his store;
So thou, being rich in Will, add to thy Will
One will of mine to make thy large Will more.
   Let no unkind, no fair beseechers kill;
   Think all but one, and me in that one Will.

SONNET 135

Many people think these sonnets are conceits—all made up—there is no lover or beloved *in life,* only in the imagination. But I don't buy it. If Shakespeare were not writing about life, he wouldn't be connecting so passionately to what he's saying; his woman wouldn't be so mercurial, full of natural desire one moment, sleeping with other people the next; he wouldn't be waiting to see if he's contracted venereal disease, because then he would know for sure she's been sleeping around.

> Two loves I have, of comfort and despair,
> Which like two spirits do suggest me still.
> The better angel is a man right fair,
> The worser spirit a woman coloured ill.
> To win me soon to hell my female evil
> Tempteth my better angel from my side,
> And would corrupt my saint to be a devil,
> Wooing his purity with her foul pride;
> And whether that my angel be turned fiend
> Suspect I may, yet not directly tell;
> But being both from me, both to each friend,
> I guess one angel in another's hell.
>   Yet this shall I ne'er know, but live in doubt
>   Till my bad angel fire my good one out.
>
> SONNET 144

("Fire," of course, is venereal disease.)

I don't think this is the kind of stuff you'd make up—with all its grittiness and realism—if you were composing poems about idealized love. Perhaps the other poets creating sonnet sequences were doing that (and by now there was a veritable charge: Spenser, Drayton, Chapman, Samuel Daniel), but for Shakespeare it was the real stuff. Creativity and sexuality are deeply connected.

Shakespeare started to write a play at this time; it is the only plot in the whole canon that Shakespeare made up himself; it has no other source. It is crammed with incidents and characters from Shakespeare's own life—getting country girls pregnant, killing a deer (is it a pricket or a stag?), a precocious schoolboy who drives everyone mad with his word games, pedantic schoolteachers, kindly parsons. But principally it's about the King of Navarre and the Princess of France.

The King of Navarre, with his three friends, decides to set up an academy and study for three years. (The three friends are called Berowne [Biron], Longaville [Longueville], and Dumaine or Dumain—the actual names of the historical Navarre's closest supporters in life.) They will live very simply and dedicate themselves to learning the deeper truths in life. They vow they will see no women.

Enter four women: the Princess of France and her sidekicks, Rosaline, Maria, and Katherine.

Berowne has already expressed his doubt that it is wise to ban women from their company, or that knowledge can be learned without them, but he acquiesces, signing the edict along with the three other men.

Of course, it doesn't work. The four men fall in love with the four women and break their vows. Berowne, the character closest to Shakespeare, falls, very much against his will, in love with Rosaline. (She is the first of several women with "Rose" in her name. Rose appears in the sonnets, too. This may have significance!)

Rosaline is witty, has a good brain, and does not hold back from either expressing sexual jokes or in fact doing the deed.

> Ay, and, by heaven, one that will do the deed
> Though Argus were her eunuch and her guard.
> LOVE'S LABOUR'S LOST (3.1, 155–56)

But it is also her physical appearance that attracts Berowne—reluctant wooer though he is. She is surprising to him, both in how she conducts herself and how she looks.

> And among three to love the worst of all—
> A whitely wanton with a velvet brow,
> With two pitch-balls stuck in her face for eyes.
> LOVE'S LABOUR'S LOST (3.1, 152–54)

Each man sends the woman he's in love with a token of his passion—thereby breaking his vow. The women decide to trick the men: they change tokens and wear masks, and each man declares his love to the wrong woman. Berowne, who is witness to all this, exposes the men, but then is exposed himself; they all decide that the true way to knowledge is to become serious suitors to their women. There are other entertainments—the men dress up as Muscovites, do ridiculous dances, and so forth—but the central, pivotal point of the play is love, and what men can learn from women (instead of cutting out their tongues, which is suggested earlier). Berowne—speaking, I believe, in Shakespeare's voice—says:

> From women's eyes this doctrine I derive:
> They sparkle still the right Promethean fire.
> They are the books, the arts, the academes
> That show, contain, and nourish all the world. . . .
> LOVE'S LABOUR'S LOST (4.3, 352-55)

Now, all this has certain parallels to the academies in France, but, frankly, it is not a profound piece of work, except for some moments in the verse and in various symbolic ways. One of the explorations the historic academies concern themselves with is *how* to tell a story— that the truth should be hidden and devices used to make the story a myth or a parable, as Christ used parables to reveal truths to the people. I think *Love's Labour's Lost* was Shakespeare's first, rather clumsy attempt to do that. (Fifteen years later, Ben Jonson and Inigo Jones brought this art form to astounding levels: Masque—something the church has always known about, but new in playwriting.)

In fact, Shakespeare might have been retelling the courtship between the real Navarre and the real Princess of France. The real match became forever a scar on the psyche of France (though many bigots hailed the massacre as a great heroic act), and at no time was the marriage between Navarre and Marguerite a happy one. It was eventually dissolved in 1599, and Henry married Marie de' Medici. But in Shakespeare's play, the possible marriage between Navarre and the Princess of France offers the hope of unity of purpose and strength, which can be resolved by hard work and realistic thinking.

In any case, I would like to suggest that Shakespeare began writing the play when he was psychologically in one place and finished it when he was in another.

When he began *Love's Labour's Lost,* he was writing a comedy somewhat in the manner of *Taming of the Shrew* or *Two Gentlemen of Verona.* When he finished writing it, his world had been turned upside down, and he was groping toward a depth of understanding he had not known before.

In the first version Shakespeare wrote of the play, he had the men proposing to the women and the women accepting—a conventional ending. That play is called *Love's Labour's Won,* and early on it played to a small circle of friends, academics, and courtiers surrounding Southampton and Essex.

Then Shakespeare, through his deepening relationship with the Dark Lady, saw the superficial imbecility of this. He changed the ending.

> Our wooing doth not end like an old play.
> Jack hath not Jill.
>
> LOVE'S LABOUR'S LOST (5.2, 873–74)

The men propose. And the women say *no.* The conventional ending is not good enough for them—they want something more profound.

If the men will go away for a year and truly serve those in need (make the sick laugh) or deeply study the meaning of life, the purpose of the academies—if they will serve "the feminine," as do knights in medieval tales—then, at the end of the year, the men can ask again; if the love is true, the women will say yes. This version Shakespeare calls *Love's Labour's Lost*—and that is the play he has handed down to us; that is the one worth performing. Many years later Frances Meres mentions both plays. He saw both versions. And liked both versions. But for Shakespeare, *Love's Labour's Lost* is the play he stands behind.

Shakespeare's youthful sexual drive led him to become a dad and a husband before he really knew himself, certainly before he had devised a way to become an actor and playwright, his calling in life. He left the wife and children behind in the family home, and though he kept in close touch with them all, he just didn't see them much. He went through several years of apprenticeship as an actor and would-be playwright, finding friends and colleagues in the theatre community; he was influenced by the poetic, political, spiritual thinking of the age. He performed at court and began to interact with the aristocracy, the people who had power in the country. He now knew people on every rung of the social scale; leaving Stratford made him free to engage where his talent and intellect took him. His imagination now expanded exponentially; there was no time in history, no political system, no relationship, no adventure, no religion that he could not delve into, if he so pleased. He always needed to earn money, so he was not going to shove outrageous ideas into people's faces, but that was his choice. He knew he had the brains and talent to achieve mastery in his chosen profession.

It was in this expanded state of awareness that Shakespeare fell in love. The advent of the Dark Lady was signaled and recorded in the sonnets. Her full impact came into play when he was in the midst of writing *Love's Labour's Won,* and caused him to alter the ending and call it *Love's Labour's Lost.*

Who was the Dark Lady, and why did she have such an impact on Shakespeare? What made her different from the other women he had slept with out on the road (and I think we have to assume he did, here and there), or the ladies-in-waiting at court, or the wives of his fellow actors?

I join with A. L. Rowse and numerous others and say this woman was Aemilia Bassano, later called Lanyer, a musician, poet, and one of the first women ever to declare herself a feminist.

Aemilia Bassano would be an extraordinary woman in any age, but for a woman in the Elizabethan age she is without parallel. She is the daughter of Baptiste Bassano, the youngest of five brothers brought over from Venice by Henry VIII in 1538 to create a world-class orchestra. (Four Bassano brothers visited London in 1531–the same year Henry VIII invited the Venetian apostate Mark Raphael to give evidence in court when Henry VIII hoped to prove his marriage to Katherine of Aragon illegal.) Henry, anxious to be known as the most civilized prince in Europe, invited the Bassano brothers, who led the orchestra in Saint Mark's in Venice, to decamp, one and all, to London; here they put together Henry's orchestra and became the center of his musical endeavors. Henry was, as all courtiers were meant to be, a good musician in his own right–he wrote and sang his own songs (mostly about love)–and his choice of musicians was a strong one, for the Bassanos not only played many instruments but also made instruments, of which we think there are many still spread across Europe today!

The Bassanos were a fascinating family. The earliest record of them is in North Africa, where they kept silk farms. They were successful. They had a coat of arms, three silkworms on a half-scutcheon of a mulberry tree. They were Jews. So, at some point—perhaps during one of the great exoduses of Jews from North Africa, or maybe just making an individual choice—the family moved from North Africa up the east coast of Italy and settled in Bassano, just north of Venice. This is the first sighting of them as musicians, but obviously they were exceptionally talented, because they were hired by the most important orchestra in Christendom, the orchestra of Saint Mark's. Did they become Christians in order to take up their positions, or had they turned Christian when they had arrived in Italy, for safety and professional reasons?

In any case, they were now Christianized Jews living in Venice and doing extremely well, in spite of the odd pogrom; they were leaders in their field. Perhaps the Inquisition was threatening to come to town at the time Henry VIII offered them a job—the Inquisition always wanted to find out if Christianized Jews were *really* Christian or secretly practiced their Jewish faith at home. In any case, in England there was no Inquisition, mostly because of Henry's hatred of Spain, and deep suspicion of the Pope, but also because Jews had been banned officially in 1290, so supposedly no Jews lived in England. In his brilliant book *Shakespeare and the Jews,* James Shapiro shows that indeed there were Jews in England—about two hundred in London alone—and those that lived there led a fairly integrated life, going to church on Sundays, and probably worshipping in their homes on Saturdays. Hector Nuñez, the leader of the Portuguese Jewish community, attended the same church as Augustine Bassano—Saint Olave Hart Street.

The Bassano brothers were given homes and places to work in the Charterhouse, the dissolved monastery, for the first few years, and they were at court (whichever of his five palaces in London the king presided at—Greenwich, Windsor, Westminster, Richmond, or Hampton Court) every day, traveling by boat up and down the Thames.

The orchestra became famous. Besides Italian musicians, talent was gathered from Holland and France. It wasn't until 1593 that the first Englishman played in the royal recorder consort, finally replacing one of the Bassano clan.

Baptiste Bassano didn't continue to live with his brothers, but eventually set up household with an Englishwoman, Margaret Johnson. I believe that Margaret Johnson was also a musician, part of the Johnson family who also served Elizabeth I. John Johnson was a lutenist (c. 1545–94); his son Robert Johnson (c. 1583–c. 1634), the only composer who we know for certain collaborated with Shakespeare. He wrote songs for *Cymbeline* and *The Tempest*. After John Johnson died, Robert went into the household of George Carey, Lord Hunsdon, son of the lord chamberlain (the same lord chamberlain who was patron of Shakespeare's players and later Aemilia Bassano's protector). His son, Lord Hunsdon, also eventually became lord chamberlain, too, also a patron of the players. The Johnson family lived in Blackfriars, another converted monastery, where Shakespeare eventually bought a house.

When Henry VIII died, the Bassano brothers held on to their positions in court through the reigns of Edward VI and Bloody Mary— meaning they were really good at their jobs and religiously neutral. Under Elizabeth, they flourished. She loved music and dancing.

In any case, Aemilia was born to Margaret and Baptiste in 1569, so she was almost five years younger than Shakespeare. When she was seven, her father died—not surprisingly, for he must have been old by that time. The family was obviously well enough placed, because Margaret was able to send her daughter to the household of the Dowager Countess of Kent, a staunch Protestant whose mother, the Duchess of Suffolk, had taken her children and fled to the Continent during Bloody Mary's reign and the country's brief return to Catholicism. (Actually, she lived at The Hague for much of the time—the meeting place for the intellectuals of Europe, especially the Protestants and Jews, and eventually the home of Spinoza, among others.) Aemilia spent a lot of time during her formative years at Cookham, in Berkshire, receiving a thorough education, as the Dowager Countess of Kent and her mother would have insisted. Perhaps Aemilia played for them. The harpsichord was her instrument, and Shakespeare has a sexy line about jacks (keys of the instrument) touching her fingers.

How oft, when thou, my music, music play'st
Upon that blessèd wood whose motion sounds
With thy sweet fingers when thou gently sway'st
The wiry concord that mine ear confounds,
Do I envy those jacks that nimble leap
To kiss the tender inward of thy hand,
Whilst my poor lips, which should that harvest reap,
At the wood's boldness by thee blushing stand!
To be so tickled, they would change their state
And situation with those dancing chips,
O'er whom thy fingers walk with gentle gait,
Making dead wood more blest than living lips.
   Since saucy jacks so happy are in this,
   Give them thy fingers, me thy lips to kiss.

SONNET 128

At sixteen or seventeen, Aemilia was back in London and seems to have been a favorite with the Queen—at least, her cousins must have introduced her into the court, but as a musician, of course, for her birth and lack of aristocratic blood would not allow her to be anything other than a paid employee. (She couldn't be a lady-in-waiting, for example.) When she was eighteen, her mother died. She had no immediate family—only cousins and very elderly uncles who were court musicians—a position similar to the one in which Cressida finds herself in Shakespeare's *Troilus and Cressida.* The following year, she became the mistress to the lord chamberlain, Henry Carey, first Baron Hunsdon, a man old enough to be her father and then some (the one who had put down the rebellion of the northern lords in 1570). His son, in turn, was patron to Robert Johnson and John Dowland—leading composers of the age.

We know much of Aemilia's story from Simon Forman, an astrologer she would consult, whose diaries we still have.

The lord chamberlain controls the Queen's household. Nothing whatever happens in her palaces without his knowledge—and certainly all poets, musicians, playwrights, actors, anyone who may entertain the Queen, comes under his jurisdiction. So, for instance, in the year 1590, Spenser had offered a dedicatory sonnet to the lord chamberlain in the publication of *The Faerie Queene.* To be the lord chamberlain's mistress and be kept in high style by him was also a position of power—but one dependent upon sustaining his affection, attraction, and good will. And his being forty-five years older might have meant the sex was not piping hot—or maybe it was!

Shakespeare was still writing his sonnet sequence, which he had begun around 1592 (or perhaps begun before Southampton dashed off to be a soldier for Navarre in 1591). Somewhere in 1592, Aemilia got pregnant. Everyone assumed the baby was the lord chamberlain's—and to make everything look right she was married to a man dependent on the Bassano family, Alphonso Lanyer, a musician of French descent who was the first non-Bassano in the recorder consort at court. They were married in October, and in early 1593 she had a baby boy who was christened Henry. Everyone, including Alphonso, assumed this was because the lord chamberlain's Christian name was Henry. However, Southampton's Christian name was also Henry. I am absolutely sure no one was saying a word, least of all Aemilia, Will Shakespeare, or Henry Wriothesley (pronounced "Risley"), Earl of Southampton. Indeed, there may be nothing in it.

Shakespeare, as the sonnets imply, was back out on the road again. The plague continued. The theatre community was suffering. Shakespeare's archenemy Robert Greene died in penury, pleading with his wife, whom he had abandoned, to take care of his debts and look after the children (did she have any choice?). But this must have struck a note of alarm for Shakespeare. The Earl of Pembroke's Men were doing badly; they, too, were going broke, selling their costumes to raise capital, but it didn't work. Yet again Shakespeare changed companies. This time he joined Lord Strange's Men. Lord Strange was a descendant of Thomas Stanley, first Earl of Derby, depicted by Shakespeare in *Richard III*—on the good side. See how incestuous all this was? But Lord Strange's company of players wasn't working terribly well, either.

I love the suggestion made by Ian Wilson in *Shakespeare: The Evidence,* that Lord Strange (patron of Shakespeare's current troupe) gave money to Shakespeare to make sure he depicted Strange's great-grandfather in a favorable light in *Richard III;* and that Clifford played a dominant part in *Henry VI* because Margaret Clifford was Strange's mother. Also, Margaret Clifford brought up Aemilia Bassano after she left the Countess of Kent and before she got to court. The Strange/Derby/Clifford family were all Catholic, so Aemilia, like Shakespeare, got both sides of the argument.

In 1593, the year Aemilia gave birth, the playwright Thomas Kyd was arrested for atheism and immorality. He was tortured, and under torture implicated Christopher Marlowe. Kyd was released from prison but never recovered; he died a year later.

Meantime, the authorities were out to get Marlowe, perhaps for his writing, perhaps for atheism and immorality, perhaps because he had swung back and forth between Catholicism and Puritanism, but most probably because he was a spy who knew many important people in both Protestant and Catholic camps. (All spies were religious spies at this time.) He was spying for Walsingham, he was spying for France and Spain, and, if Charles Nicholl's book *The Reckoning: The Murder of Christopher Marlowe* is to be believed, was a counterspy. In any case, he was murdered in a pub in Deptford, stabbed through the eye with a knife, ostensibly over a row about a bar bill—but probably because of his spying activities.

Greene's death must have been salutary, Kyd's tragic, but Marlowe's must have been a great blow to Shakespeare. And a great blow for the theatre community as a whole—Kyd and Marlowe were the leading talents.

These events were deeply disturbing, and Shakespeare wrote a long poem, *The Rape of Lucrece,* which took on the violation of women with an understanding and empathy not witnessed before in his writing (or anyone's, for that matter, as far as I can tell). It's written in a complicated form of rhetoric called Rime Sparse. Shakespeare's mind was expanding as he forced himself into word patterns that were not familiar to him and over which he did not yet have mastery. Lucrece is the loyal, beautiful wife of Collatine; while he is away, Tarquin, King of the Romans, stays at their house. Tarquin knows rape is a horrible thing and he shouldn't violate Lucrece, but after a short internal struggle he does anyway. (This struggle about desire and suppression is a forerunner to Macbeth and his conscience over Duncan's murder.)

Lucrece gives voice to these unspeakable acts perpetrated upon her; she inspires her husband and Junius Brutus (ancestor of the Brutus in *Julius Caesar*) to revenge the wrong; all of Rome swears to get rid of Tarquin—thus bringing monarchy to an end in Rome. And then Lucrece kills herself. It is a pivotal poem, because it was the first time Shakespeare took on a woman's voice to articulate what it felt like to be at the mercy of a man who violently pushed aside a woman's self-hood and used her body for his own desires.

It was a breakthrough. Not a great poem—it has too much self-conscious strain in it—but it was a breakthrough for Shakespeare and literature. It takes us some sixty verses to set out the background that leads up to the rape. The rape itself takes around thirty verses, and then there is one very honest verse about the outcome.

> But she hath lost a dearer thing than life,
> And he hath won what he would lose again.
> This forcèd league doth force a further strife,
> This momentary joy breeds months of pain;
> This hot desire converts to cold disdain.
>   Pure chastity is rifled of her store,
>   And lust, the thief, far poorer than before.
>
>   THE RAPE OF LUCRECE (687–93)

Then we have around 120 verses about the effect the rape has on Lucrece, what her body feels like, how her mind divides, the effect this will have on her relationship with Collatine, rage, grief, shame, taking the shame into herself, knowing it will never come right, what the outside world will say, is there any way to right what has happened? It is, of course, what women have been asking themselves for centuries. Every day around 244 women are raped in the United States—and those are only the ones we know about. In places where war is happening, rape is an accepted part of the assault (finally declared a war crime in 2008 by the United Nations).

Women everywhere are coming to the aid of other women; in many parts of the world, every town has a rape crisis center; there have been some extraordinary cases, such as Eve Ensler's supporting the women in the Congo to build the City of Joy.

But for Shakespeare to write this picture of rape sometime around 1592–93, and then to give Lucrece's voice such emphasis, was unprecedented.

Of course, I say that Shakespeare learned this from Aemilia. He began to see how women were bought and sold for their bodies. Women could use their bodies as one way to advance themselves—but if they lost their reputation, they would be nothing. A tightrope. And if they were raped, could they ever speak of it? It could also be that for the first time he met a nonaristocratic woman who was educated, who spoke out, who was funny and talented, who interacted with whomever she pleased without asking permission from a man. Shakespeare was finally giving to women voices that belonged to women. The women of *Love's Labour's Lost* do speak out—but they discuss the nature of love, beauty, form—as the women and especially the Countess of Pembroke did in the academies. Not until *The Rape of Lucrece* did he speak of a woman's outrage about violation. The dedication to Southampton for this poem is far more intimate—much more a friend speaking to a friend. Shakespeare and Southampton's relationship had changed.

On the acting front, the troupe was in trouble again, because Lord Strange died—and in somewhat mysterious circumstances. It seemed as if he had been poisoned. So Shakespeare needed to find another troupe. He went back to the Burbage family. (Many of the actors in these troupes changed companies frequently, and Shakespeare often found himself working with the same people, even if they belong to different troupes.) If Shakespeare had been earning money during this time, it wasn't much, for the playhouses were still closed. He would do much better each year around Christmas at the court—the Queen knew and liked him. But that doth not a wife and three children keep, nor does it provide a steady income stream.

Then he spent these two or three years becoming friends with people in high places, moving in and out of the great houses in the country, and possibly the town houses by the Thames, sharing an emotional life with the people around him (even if the only accepted field for its expression was poetry), disappearing on tour and returning, probably worn out, to resume the discussion about the meaning of life—it all paid off for Shakespeare on a professional level.

The lord chamberlain himself became the patron of the players (did Aemilia have a word?). It was a great arrangement, because the lord chamberlain chose all the Queen's performances. And, together with the Lord Admiral's Men (Edward Alleyn's company), they became the leading acting troupe in the country.

But what of Shakespeare's heart? He was about to write the play that would become the most famous play about love ever: *Romeo and Juliet,* which lives on a different level from anything that came before.

London today is nearly eight million people; then it was around two hundred thousand, thus a town about the size of Boise, Idaho, in the United States, or Portsmouth in Britain. The chances of residents' knowing one another was much higher then. And although the society was obsessed with social rank, the different classes did know one another, often quite intimately, and were dependent upon one another.

Sir Philip Sidney, as we know, had been married to Frances Walsingham, daughter of Elizabeth's spymaster. But the romantic love of Sidney's life, according to his sonnet sequence, was Penelope Devereux, elder sister to the Earl of Essex, who had been married off early to Lord Rich. And Essex married Sidney's widow, Frances Walsingham.

Lord Strange, onetime patron of Shakespeare's players, was the son of Margaret Clifford, who had sheltered Aemilia Bassano for a time. Strange was married to Alice Spencer (yes, same family as Princess Di). Alice's sister Anne married Henry Carey, son of Henry Hunsdon, the lord chamberlain, patron of Shakespeare's players, lover of Aemilia Bassano.

Philip Sidney lost his life at the siege of Zutphen. A cousin of the Earl of Derby, father of Fernando, Lord Strange, also fought at Zutphen and was left in charge of the army and the town after it had been secured from the Spanish. Incredibly, nine days before Mary, Queen of Scots, was executed, he handed the town back to the Spanish—because, it was thought, the Derby/Strange family was Catholic. You can see that no one quite trusted the Derby family—and yet their lives were intertwined with those of the Queen and other aristocrats for generations. All this is to give a sense of how close these families were—and how the poets and musicians who served them were also affected by everything they did.

When you look at Shakespeare's plays and you look at Aemilia's life, you can see connections and resonances between the two stretching across the next twenty years. Whether this was because they knew each other for the next twenty years or because "one good heartbreak will furnish the poet with many songs," as Edith Wharton says, we do not know. Some of the parallels and coincidences . . .

Shakespeare wrote two plays about Venice. In one, *The Merchant of Venice* (written in 1596), in which the Jew Shylock dominates the play, his daughter marries a Christian, and the race relations and business practices are put under heavy scrutiny. The hero's name: Bassanio. He has no money, but he does have friends in high places. In the other, *Othello* (written in 1603–4), our hero comes from North Africa, and the plot hinges on a prized possession, a silk handkerchief embroidered with spotted strawberries. Desdemona's gentlewoman is called Emilia, and it is she who steals the handkerchief to give to her husband, Iago. Iago is angry because Othello is not advancing his career, and he tells the audience he suspects Othello has been sleeping with his wife. In 1597, Alphonso Lanyer left the Queen's service as a musician and went to try and make his fortune as a sailor/soldier on Southampton and Essex's expedition to the Azores. Although the first Azores expedition had been highly successful, this one wasn't, and Lanyer came back with neither knighthood nor money. He followed Southampton to Ireland and was equally unsuccessful in furthering his career. Aemilia told Forman that her husband dealt "hardily" with her, and spent all her money and jewels from the lord chamberlain. And, obviously, he did poorly as a soldier in the service of his wife's ex-lover.

In the three plays with lovers' names as the title–*Romeo and Juliet, Troilus and Cressida,* and *Antony and Cleopatra*–all three women have qualities in common. They are quick-witted, can change an argument in a nanosecond, and are sexually passionate, with no demure "I am a virgin, please help me" anywhere to be seen (though Cressida is very aware that her virginity is her *only* bargaining tool, for she has no family status or money to make a good match). They fight for their love as men do. Two succeed, and one fails–but nowhere do they pull back once they have made the commitment to love. The quick-witted, outspoken, sexually adventurous woman remained Shakespeare's ideal of womanhood. In the comedies, Rosalind in *As You Like It* and Beatrice in *Much Ado About Nothing* are bewitchingly adventurous.

Aemilia had two children, Henry and Odillya. She started writing poetry and was one of the first published women poets in England. Her verse is strong but not sublime. What is extraordinary about it is her feminine voice, speaking out on behalf of women. In her long poem *Salve Deus Rex Judaeorum* (*Hail to God, King of the Jews*—she said the title came to her in a dream), she defends Eve's picking of the apple:

> Our Mother Eve, who tasted of the Tree,
> Giving to Adam what she held most dear,
> Was simply good, and had no power to see,
> The after-coming harm did not appear . . .
>
> SALVE DEUS REX JUDAEORUM (763–66)

She pointed out that the wife of Pontius Pilate told him not to do it; she described in detail the agony of the women at the cross; she defended the great women of history, Cleopatra, Deborah, Esther. She demanded that women stop being punished for Eve's "sin":

> Then let us have our Liberty again,
> And challenge to your selves no Sov'raigntie;
> You came not in the world without our pain,
> Make that a bar against your cruelty. . . .
>
> SALVE DEUS REX JUDAEORUM (825–28)

It was one of the first feminist tracts.

Her husband died in 1613, and that year Shakespeare bought a house in London (though he had retired back to Stratford four or five years earlier). It was in Blackfriars, the converted monastery, where the new indoor theatre was situated, and where Aemilia's relatives the Johnsons owned a house. He set up a complicated ownership so that his wife, Anne, could not inherit her widow's third of it. And someone called William Johnson was one of the executors.

Aemilia wrote the first country-house poem (*before* Ben Jonson, who usually gets the attribution), "Description of Cookham," the home of the Countess of Cumberland, where she stayed in her youth, and she actively sought the patronage of women and only women, from Queen Anne downward. She wrote nine poems to women in high places whom she admired, and I have to say it would have been a revolutionary moment if she could have gathered those women into an academy and together they could have discussed women's position in the world, whether they agreed with Aemilia that it was not women's fault that there was sin in the world, however the church might have chosen to emphasize the idea. She was the first woman to publish her poetry in order to find a sponsor. *Salve Deus Rex Judaeorum* was printed in 1611—same year as the King James Bible and Chapman's translation of Homer's *Iliad*. It has taken four hundred years for her to begin to get acknowledgment.

Her husband had won a patent from James I to weigh hay and grain, but after his death she was in litigation with his relatives for the next twenty years to keep it. She started a school in 1617 (a year after Shakespeare's death), for the children of rich merchants, so her own education was extensive enough for her to do this. She ran into many problems with her landlord and only kept it going for two years.

Her daughter had died when she was ten months old, on September 6, 1599, so she had this grief in common with Shakespeare. Susanne Woods, who edited an excellent version of Lanyer's poems, suggested that the name Odillya was a created name, made out of "Aemilia" and "Ode." (Usually children took the names of their godparents.) If this is so, Aemilia was declaring that she enjoyed creating meaning through new words—something Shakespeare did all his life—that her daughter and creativity were synonymous. This, too, was a theme close to Shakespeare's heart, especially in his late plays. Aemilia's son became a court musician, and Nicholas Lanier, her cousin by marriage, was Charles I's chief of music when the Civil War broke out.

Aemilia died in 1645, in the midst of the Civil War—outliving Shakespeare by twenty-nine years, never becoming a silent or timid person. She lived life fully, in the end was probably far more daring than Shakespeare could cope with—but she was a flame that burned not just for him (if she did), but for women everywhere.

After leaving Stratford and learning his craft for a couple of years, Shakespeare encountered the roughest period of his professional life—the plague, touring, deaths of fellow playwrights, three successive deaths of aristocratic patrons of the companies he belonged to!

But he made friends in high places, joined an intellectual circle, and was exposed to ideas about poetry, playwriting, and music that inspired him to think of his calling as an honorable one—an artistic endeavor that could have an effect on the world as well as being entertaining and earning money. He could live an examined life, free to explore, to know his life was a journey, growing in strength to meet any challenge.

His relationship with the Earl of Southampton became one of friendship; Southampton not only gave him insights about the men's world of battle and leadership, but shared with him, for a short while, a common love, the Dark Lady of the sonnets. It has been suggested that Southampton might have given Shakespeare the money to buy a share in the company, thereby giving him power over his own financial life, although I am not sure he needed that kind of help when the opportunity arose in 1599.

From the Dark Lady, he finally got it about women. This understanding led him to a spiritual truth and connected him to a deep sexual passion, fomenting his creativity, releasing the Promethean fire needed to write the plays. Once he saw women as they truly are, he was able to understand the bind that an intelligent, creative, sexually desirous woman was in—and he started to write in her voice. So empathetic was he with his lover that he told of rape, repressive parents, and unprotected women; he saw that women's desires were as great as his own, he honored them—and he saw that two human beings passionately in love could move mountains. Love itself was the force that propelled his life in the theatre, his subject matter, the core of his creativity.

THE SEXUAL MERGES WITH THE
SPIRITUAL: NEW KNOWLEDGE

SCENE 1: *Romeo and Juliet*

What is passion, sexual/psychic passion? Is it a verb? A noun? An emotion? A state of being? Where does it live? In our bodies? Our minds? Can we see it? Smell it? Hear it? Touch it? Taste it?

We know that it's powerful, that it can cut across all social boundaries, that people who experience it find that ethnicity, gender, age, language, economic differences, all dissolve before its powers, calling lovers to be true to each other rather than family, friends, political parties, class distinctions. It has its own overwhelming volition—and thus is feared by people in power who want to reinforce the norms of society. Transgression is its journey—lovers are married to someone else, belong to different religions, live in countries that are at war.

But what is it exactly? We can see what it does. It changes everything. It turns a good writer into a great writer. A playwright who is technically adept, proficient at turning out a light comedy or an action saga, becomes a playwright who, through words and form, can conjure life itself, inspiring worlds to open for other souls to see and know themselves. But what is it exactly?

It's the mysterious electricity that generates between two people; it fills the body and triggers the imagination, paints the world in vivid color; the emotions break free, and the separate realities of two people become one symbiotic energy, able to cut through the accepted bounds of everyday life. It is the force that replenishes itself—as Troilus says of Cressida, she has "a mind / That doth renew swifter than blood decays"; it calls the lovers back to each other again and again; it has all the power of unbridled violence, yet exposes a vulnerability that can withstand almost any atrocity. It is a force for creativity. It could be called the soul.

Something happened to change Shakespeare's understanding of the world. There are hints of a different kind of knowledge in women-men relationships here and there in the early plays: in the Margaret/Suffolk farewell in *Henry VI Part 2*; in the Princess of France's knowledge of what she must do after her father's demise in *Love's Labour's Lost*. But it is in *Romeo and Juliet* that Shakespeare wrote about a sexual passion which was so consuming and so enlightening that it created an energy between the two lovers which in turn led them to understand the very source of spirituality itself.

I don't think Shakespeare could have found this visceral knowledge simply through his reading or studying. The desire to understand something means we may look for meaning in written texts, painting, music, chanting, psychoanalysis, philosophy. But, ultimately, we learn about life through living, through our relationships with other people. And the only way to understand the deepest sexual/spiritual love is through experiencing sexual/spiritual love. So I declare: Shakespeare knew it. He lived it. And the language to say it flowed from his pen because of it. And he didn't just experience it from the man's point of view. He experienced the woman's position just as deeply, felt her emotional journey as if it were his own. The masculine and the feminine, if you will, touched each other at the source, and merged into one power.

Why was Shakespeare able to see the woman's position, write entirely as if he were a woman, in a way that none of the other playwrights of the age were able to?

First and foremost, he was an actor; he'd been acting for about six years by this time, enough so that it was second nature to him: "embodying" a part, feeling it through the blood, muscles, bones, skin, was natural, whether playing man or woman. Whatever happened to him in life or onstage, he felt it with the whole of his being.

The second reason: for the first time he'd fallen in love "beyond reason"–with someone different from anything he knew before, someone over whom he had no control–and the love between them was volatile in its manifestation. The reading, studying, thinking he had been doing perhaps gave him a perspective about what he was now feeling; and perhaps that feeling opened the door to the esoteric knowledge, so much a part of the Elizabethan age, that he had been studying. And that, in turn, gave him a framework for writing more coherently about what was happening to him. But without the event itself, without the falling irrevocably in love, knowledge would be only brain-deep. It wouldn't manifest in the whole being—essential to the actor/playwright.

In *Richard II* (written in 1595, a year after *Romeo and Juliet*), Richard is alone in prison—except, of course, he isn't—he's an actor onstage with a couple thousand people watching him. And out of this dual reality, Shakespeare tried to explain how imagination creates reality.

> My brain I'll prove the female to my soul,
> My soul the father, and these two beget
> A generation of still-breeding thoughts;
> And these same thoughts people this little world
> In humours like the people of this world.
>
> RICHARD II (5.5, 6–10)

If you want to watch it, Mark Rylance has a beautiful interpretation on YouTube.

The brain, where all his thoughts seemingly are given birth, are sired by the deepest core of him, his soul. (Shakespeare has reversed the genders normally assigned to these entities.) The thoughts engender other thoughts. The world is actually made up of thought, and thought is what creates our idea of reality. And all you audience members are actually creating me as Richard, and I, accepting your definition of me as Richard, am able to create you as proof of my existence. To create this world, it takes a sexual act between brain and soul. This understanding belongs to Neoplatonic thinking—and has reflections today in modern physics. But, elegant as the above excerpt is, it doesn't hold a candle to the imaginative leaps that pour out of Shakespeare as he writes *Romeo and Juliet*.

In our story of *Women of Will*, following the development of Shakespeare's women, we are now at the first great quantum leap. The new territory we are inhabiting becomes the basis of everything that is to follow. Shakespeare's falling in love and actually experiencing a sexual/spiritual merging—it was not an abstract idea—ignited his imagination: he found the mind of his beloved exhilarating, the body mysterious, and the act of making love a conscious choice (not a rutting), consciously experienced: all attributes he wrote about in the plays that directly explored this theme, principally *Romeo and Juliet, Much Ado About Nothing, Troilus and Cressida,* and *Antony and Cleopatra.*

At the top of the play, Romeo says he is in love with a Rosaline, but his love is making him sick, solitary, even suicidal. Romeo identifies it as love, he's obsessed with it, but there is no parity in the relationship. In fact, there is no real relationship. Rosaline does not return his love. Romeo clings to it. Friar Laurence is right when he says Romeo was "doting, not loving" Rosaline. It doesn't matter what Romeo does; Rosaline has no response to his poems, his attention, his money, presents.

Juliet, on the other hand, has never been in love—but when her parents suggest she should think of marriage and loving Paris, a suitable match, she's willing to entertain the idea.

There's a big masked ball at the Capulet house, in order for Juliet and Paris to meet. Romeo finds out Rosaline is invited, so he and his mates Mercutio and Benvolio decide they'll crash it (which they can because they will all be masked). The Capulets and the Montagues, Romeo's family, are deadly enemies. In fact, there has been a fight between the two sides that very day. The Prince of Verona had to break it up and threaten death to anyone who would disobey his edict of no fighting. Death images abound in the opening act of *Romeo and Juliet*—the fight, Romeo's state of mind, the Prince's threats, even the nurse bringing in the death of her own daughter and husband—and then Mercutio goes into a diatribe worthy of a warrior with post-traumatic stress about battles, the pox, economic ruin. He's describing Mab, the fairies' midwife (again an imaginative symbol that brings forth teeming thoughts):

> Sometime she driveth o'er a soldier's neck,
> And then dreams he of cutting foreign throats,
> Of breaches, ambuscadoes, Spanish blades,
> Of healths five fathom deep; and then anon

> Drums in his ear, at which he starts and wakes,
> And being thus frighted, swears a prayer or two,
> And sleeps again. This is that very Mab
> That plaits the manes of horses in the night,
> And bakes the elf-locks in foul sluttish hairs,
> Which once untangled much misfortune bodes.
> This is the hag, when maids lie on their backs,
> That presses them and learns them first to bear,
> Making them women of good carriage.
> This is she—
>
> ROMEO AND JULIET (1.4, 84–97)

These are all consuming fantasies. (Shakespeare supposedly played Mercutio.) Whether it's Mercutio's state, or his own depression, Romeo is sure something cataclysmic is going to happen—which, of course, it does, but very differently from his own desperate fantasies.

Juliet, in the meantime, is having a good time at her first grown-up party. It is while she is dancing with Paris that Romeo notices her. He calls her "a rich jewel in an Ethiope's ear"—again the light and the dark. And then he touches her. Their masks come off. They see each other, they are revealed to each other, they are vulnerable, they are immediately and absolutely in love.

Shakespeare wrote the encounter in the form of a sonnet: Fourteen lines. Rhyming pattern. Listen to the spiritual language as it leads the way into their absolute aliveness to each other's bodies—sexual and spiritual images merging and emerging.

> ROMEO (to Juliet, touching her hand) If I profane with my
>   unworthiest hand
>   This holy shrine, the gentle sin is this:
>   My lips, two blushing pilgrims, ready stand
>   To smooth that rough touch with a tender kiss.
> JULIET Good pilgrim, you do wrong your hand too much,
>   Which mannerly devotion shows in this.
>   For saints have hands that pilgrims' hands do touch,
>   And palm to palm is holy palmers' kiss.
> ROMEO Have not saints lips, and holy palmers, too?
> JULIET Ay, pilgrim, lips that they must use in prayer.

ROMEO O then, dear saint, let lips do what hands do:
   They pray; grant thou, lest faith turn to despair.
JULIET Saints do not move, though grant for prayers' sake
ROMEO Then move not while my prayer's effect I take.
   He kisses her

ROMEO AND JULIET (1.4, 213–26)

They touch fingers, then palms, and then lips. They travel from profanity to unworthiness to holy sin, pilgrimage, prayer, sainthood. And this all before either knows the other's name; once they know, they also know their lives are changed forever.

   My only love sprung from my only hate!
   Too early seen unknown, and known too late!

ROMEO AND JULIET (1.4, 261–62)

Just to make sure we understand the kind of lower-self sexuality Romeo is now leaving behind, Shakespeare has him fleeing the company of "the boys" (Mercutio and Benvolio and their pages), who are fantasizing out loud about Rosaline and her lower parts, in an effort to force Romeo out of his hiding place.

   I conjure thee by Rosaline's bright eyes,
   By her high forehead and her scarlet lip,
   By her fine foot, straight leg, and quivering thigh,
   And by the demesnes that there adjacent lie,
   That in thy likeness thou appear to us.

ROMEO AND JULIET (2.1, 19–23)

In leaving them behind (symbolically, psychologically, practically), Romeo leaps over a wall into Juliet's orchard. (All monasteries were surrounded by walls in the Middle Ages—so, if you were going to lead a holy life, you leapt over the wall to begin your spiritual journey.) He sees the light from her balcony and calls it "the east"; even then the East was the mysterious place of ancient religions and understanding. And he declares that the light is caused by Juliet's being the sun; the sun, of course, is the alchemical symbol of purity, change, and growth. He invokes the sun to kill the moon, which, like

Romeo, was "sick and pale with grief." And at that moment, almost as if he has invoked her, Juliet appears:

> *[Enter Juliet aloft]*
> It is my lady, O, it is my love. O, that she knew she were!
> ROMEO AND JULIET (2.1, 55)

In the First Folio (the closest thing we have to the text Shakespeare gave to his actors), there are sixteen beats in that line instead of the usual ten; to say Romeo has an excess of feeling and emotion in that moment, as his fantasy turns to reality, would be an understatement (ten staccato notes, interspersed with an ecstatic "O"; followed by a great ecstatic "O" and then longer notes with vowel sounds of "knew" and "were").

Then Romeo goes into an imaginative journey about her eyes being stars, and how he'd like her eyes to twinkle in heaven and they would light up the world. It's a journey that allows Romeo's spirit to fly upward. We have lost our connection to the heavens; we rarely look upward or downward (although we do look downward more often), but to be out at night, in silence, with the stars, and to let the mind fly up to the heavens—it's possible to get an experience of why the Elizabethans believed that all that was outside there, in the universe (the macrocosm), was directly correlated with what was inside here, our organs, blood, and bones (the microcosm).

Juliet is far more practical. She thinks about his name, and that the name of a person or thing—a rose, say—is not the essence of it. The essence of Romeo is whom she loves. Get rid of the name, or she'll get rid of hers, so that their souls can be together. ("It is my soul that calls upon my name," says Romeo.) Once they find each other, and get through the fear that Romeo will be killed if he is found there, without hesitation they set about planning their life together. How can they be so sure? Juliet says it herself, about giving her love to Romeo:

> And yet I wish but for the thing I have.
> My bounty is as boundless as the sea,
> My love as deep. The more I give to thee
> The more I have, for both are infinite.
> ROMEO AND JULIET (2.1, 183–86)

I don't know if you can imagine what it is like saying that to some-one night after night and really tapping into absolute love, which exists. It actually feels as if you are swimming in the midst of some-thing infinite (I wonder if babies feel that in the womb) and you feel that there is no end to this love, it will never not be there. It leads to a state of infinite truth in the goodness of humanity, a relief, a relax-ation, a surrender that can take you anywhere.

And, of course, it does take them everywhere—marriage the next morning (Juliet's idea), followed by consummation that night. But the world intrudes. They are tested. After the marriage, before evening comes, Romeo is accosted by Juliet's vicious cousin, Tybalt, deter-mined to fight. Romeo offers love, gentleness, wisdom, and Tybalt rages. Mercutio, Romeo's unbalanced and renegade friend, can't bear what he thinks of as loss of honor in Romeo's responses. (This is the first time love and honor are put up against each other in the canon.) Mercutio fights Tybalt. Tybalt kills Mercutio, in part because Romeo tries to stop the fight—and here Romeo loses his balance. He drops into grief and rage, kills Tybalt, and is banished by the enraged Prince of Verona.

When Juliet hears what has happened, she, too, is poised between anger and hatred for the Romeo who killed her cousin, and love and compassion for the man who is her husband. And love wins. Juliet does not turn against Romeo; she joins with him in his predicament. And so the story, with the battle between the dark forces and light, can begin to come right.

Romeo and Juliet spend the night together. Their spiritual selves can experience their sexual selves. He leaves before dawn. The next day, Juliet (you can call her the epitome of the feminine spirit if you wish) is tested repeatedly. Her father is going to move her marriage day to Paris forward; first she opposes him, then finds a way, through their friend Friar Laurence, to pretend to consent, but instead take a poison that will make her seem dead. They will then prepare to bury her, and Romeo can come for her and they can escape to Mantua. She carries this plan through, despite all her fears. Unfortunately, Romeo hears that Juliet is dead—so he returns to Verona to die with her in the tomb. He kills yet again—this time Paris, who has come to strew flow-ers on Juliet's grave. Paris sees Romeo, thinks that, as a Montague, he has come to desecrate Juliet's grave, determines to kill him; they fight,

and Paris dies. Romeo lays Paris next to Juliet, Paris's dying wish—even
here Romeo's love expands out to others. Romeo then gathers the
dead Juliet in his arms and drinks poison so he can die kissing her.
Listen to the imagery of the words, the commitment of the act.

> Here, here will I remain
> With worms that are thy chambermaids. O, here
> Will I set up my everlasting rest,
> And shake the yoke of inauspicious stars
> From this world-wearied flesh. Eyes, look your last.
> Arms, take your last embrace, and lips, O you
> The doors of breath, seal with a righteous kiss
> A dateless bargain, to engrossing death.
>
> ROMEO AND JULIET (5.2, 112–19)

Death, orgasm, unity, merging, dateless bargain: Juliet wakes with
the dead Romeo beside her and knows she can only live where he is—
which means death. And so she kills herself, too. In this play we do
not get a sense of what happens to them in the afterworld, as we do
in *Antony and Cleopatra*. But we do see what happens in this world.

Their joint suicide so deeply affects their parents that the Montagues and Capulets resolve to love each other for the rest of their
days. Indeed, in their shared grief over the deaths of their children,
they are closer to each other than anyone else can be. Both sides were
responsible, both sides are in deep grief; good can come out of this.
The revenge story that drives the history plays and *Titus Andronicus* is
turned to love, responsibilities, painful understanding.

They resolve to erect statues of their children together, in gold
(again the alchemical symbol of purity and change), and to tell this
story.

So, out of this absolute passion and commitment to each other,
acting upon it in truth and goodness, Romeo and Juliet do change
the world. Whether Shakespeare thought of this as an ultimate good
that could change the layers of vengeful feelings, old arguments, pat-
terning in the mind and in society's rules, I'm not sure. It is a theme
he would turn to again and again, and we will follow it in the plays
that come immediately after. Shakespeare held up this story as one of
the great truths about human behavior, and about how we are able to

find our way through the morass of human interactions, which gird our lives about, to a deeper knowledge of the question he asked all his life: "What does it mean to be a human being?" And for Romeo and Juliet it means to commit themselves to love, come what may.

Out of that knowledge of love, Romeo and Juliet naturally ask, "How shall we act?" and "What must I do?" The answers they find go beyond their individual lives, taking them into a unity of such power that the world has been telling their story every since. This love story becomes the template for others. It spreads into the lives of their families in Verona. And, of course, it now fuels a tourist industry that keeps many people employed, and a film industry that retells the story in a million ways.

There is one other way in which this story of Romeo and Juliet is groundbreaking–both in world literature and in Shakespeare's canon. The woman enjoys absolute equality with the man. Shakespeare wrote about Juliet with as much insight, nuance, and detail as that with which he wrote about Romeo. Nowhere in Shakespeare's psyche is Juliet "less than" Romeo; nor is she "more than" Romeo. They are equal, in both the form and the content of the play; the actions of both are given equal attention. In many ways, Juliet's position is more difficult than Romeo's–because she's a woman and thus will have no independence in the social structure of her family or in society at large. Shakespeare reported that; the problems Juliet faces have to do with family expectations, her father's absolute dominion over her. What Shakespeare didn't do, in any way, is shortchange her in his creative imagination; this was a great breakthrough for Shakespeare, in his writing and his thinking. Men and women in their very essence–in their souls, if you wish–have natural parity. If one has dominance over the other, it means spiritual life is suffocated, for both! This was a relatively new idea at the time. It ran counter to the teaching in the Bible–Eve's being made out of Adam's rib to be his helpmate–which was the basis for the idea, held for so long, that women do not have souls of their own but are dependent on their fathers' and husbands'. So, before we move on to the plays immediately after *Romeo and Juliet*, we need another interlude, to examine the idea of the soul, what it meant in Shakespeare's day and what it means to us now.

We don't talk about the soul much; it's not a topic we deem essential to our collective, or even individual, thinking. We might invoke it every now and again, but it probably wouldn't turn up in a presidential speech, say, or these days even in a Church of England service. It's true that Thomas Moore and James Hillman have written popular books with *Soul* in the title, but these are books for seekers—we don't talk about "souls" in our everyday lives.

However, to Shakespeare and his contemporaries it was a burning issue—what is the soul, how do we know it, what is its function, is it part of the body or separate from the body, where does it go after the body's death?

Pamphlets, treatises, sermons, academic institutions, Shakespeare's works, all searched for its meaning and the role it plays in our lives. The question of whether women had souls was a divisive issue. The reactionary schools said, Definitely not; a woman's father or husband has a soul, and the woman derives her soul from him. The more enlightened schools—and that included Shakespeare—said, Yes, women have souls of their own; their salvation, their innermost selves, their essential essence is their own.

That the soul was usually depicted as feminine is illustrated by the popular myth of Psyche and Eros, an old tale told by Apuleius, a North African follower of Isis. Its other manifestation is of course the Holy Spirit in the Trinity, as in the Father, the Son, and the Holy Ghost (gender not identified, but it pretty much has to be feminine, or the father and the son were not going to get very far!). But neither the tale of Psyche nor the Holy Ghost tells us what it is, in a scientific way.

Searching for the soul and trying to understand the function of the soul has been a driving force for centuries. How Shakespeare talks about it, in both the plays and the poems, gives us a sense of his development as a human being, for his relationship to women and his evocation of the soul run on a parallel course, being intimately tied to love, both *éros* and *agápe*. That the soul is manifested in myth as Psyche clearly influenced Shakespeare; he quoted the story directly in so many of the plays, as painstakingly mapped by J. J. M. Tobin in *Shakespeare's Favorite Novel.* And out of this we see how women draw the power of the soul around them to strengthen who they are and then to manifest what is important to their lives. Psyche, in the story, is the one who has to go on the journey, do impossible tasks, know despair and hopelessness, give birth—while Eros just goes home to his mum and sulks, until, finally, he finds he misses Psyche and plays his part.

So what is the soul, why was it so important then, and why do we practically ignore it now?

Then the accepted answer was: "Plainly, the reasonable soul is a spiritual and immortal substance breathed into man by God, whereby he lives and moves and understandeth, and so distinguished from other creatures." That's the answer Sir Walter Raleigh got from his exasperated and out-of-his-league interrogator, when the interrogator was trying to find out if Raleigh was an atheist (a prosecutable offense) and Raleigh turned the tables on him and pressed him to define the soul.

The soul was an important idea for the Christian Church (they adopted it from the Greeks around the third century), because in its crudest form it keeps a tally of good deeds and bad: the soul that is beset with evil deeds will be cast down into hell; do good deeds and you'll go to heaven. Joan is willing to trade her soul to the devil, in *Henry VI Part 1,* if he will help her conquer the English in France. So in this respect you could say the soul keeps a tally of good deeds and bad, and also is a thing that can be traded if you want something badly enough and the devil can supply it. (That also means you have to believe in the devil, too.)

Shakespeare began to experiment with the idea of the soul being breath—and not just the breath of God (as we see in Michelangelo's painting in the Sistine Chapel of God symbolically breathing life into Adam's body) but the breath of the lover who pours his soul into the beloved.

Here could I breathe my soul into the air,
As mild and gentle as the cradle-babe
Dying with mother's dug between its lips.

HENRY VI PART 2 (3.2, 392–94)

Suffolk says this to his lover, Margaret, in the second part of
Henry VI, obviously lying with his head upon her breast. He goes on:

To have thee with thy lips to stop my mouth,
So shouldst thou either turn my flying soul
Or I should breathe it, so, into thy body—
And then it lived in sweet Elysium.

HENRY VI PART 2 (3.2, 397–400)

The idea that lovers can generate each other's souls, or that the
lover can be the soul of the other, came into being. The Greeks had
liked this idea, too, though for them (or at least the ruling class who
wrote about such things) the lovers were an older man and a younger
man. Breath as a life force is a potent idea, because, as most every
human being knows, the breath of the lover is deeply erotic, and it
does feel as if new life is being breathed into you.

"It is my soul that calls upon my name," Romeo tells the audience
in the balcony scene, speaking of Juliet, knowing she is calling him to
his truest self, his highest self.

As we already saw in the previous chapter, Shakespeare found his
way toward the act of creation's being the driving purpose of the soul
in *Richard II:*

My brain I'll prove the female to my soul,
My soul the father . . .

RICHARD II (5.5, 6–7)

The soul penetrates the brain, an erotic act (and here the soul
is male, the brain female). At this moment, there is no difference
between Richard and Shakespeare. Richard embodies the words of
Shakespeare the writer, Shakespeare the actor says them, the audience
hears them, and the audience members in turn create all these people

and plays in their imagination. The actor/playwright Richard is a formidable teacher; knowledge is spreading exponentially.

And we see how the imagination creates the realities it lives in; it forms images, harmonies, and disharmonies; it plays, it generates. And that is true in life as well as at the Globe. This idea of the soul as a creative act has a resonance throughout the rest of Shakespeare's writing.

There are still examples of people being called soulless brutes, usually an accusation being hurled at a "stranger"—Shylock, Aaron the Moor, Caliban, people who have been dehumanized but who also possess exquisite sensitivities, unrecognized by the person hurling the accusation. The accuser has always done something reprehensible himself—stolen an island, discriminated against someone because of his race—and is, in fact, in that moment, a soulless brute himself. Shakespeare's diagnostic skills of projection are alive and well, and we the audience realize that without love it is not possible to recognize the soul in the other.

Benedick asks Beatrice if "in your soul" she thinks Count Claudio has wronged Hero; Beatrice answers, "As sure as I have a thought or a soul"; and Benedick, because of his deep love for Beatrice, takes on her demand that he challenge Claudio: "Enough, I am engaged."

To support the soul and its truth, action is taken on behalf of the beloved person. The soul is manifested in action. And if I had to define what Shakespeare believed the soul to be, I would say: a verb, not a noun; that sweet state of emotional clarity that manifests itself in serving someone else, no matter how difficult.

In *Measure for Measure,* Shakespeare plunged back into the medieval, deeply Christian world of closely argued principles of what belongs to heaven, to earth, to hell. The soul is defined pretty much as Raleigh's interrogator defined it. The techniques of debate that Angelo and Isabella use in sparring belong to the art of logic: proving again what is already agreed upon. This form of scholasticism (as it was called) squeezes out the soul; deductive reasoning alone cannot see the soul. The two religious persons arguing these points, Angelo and Isabella, are almost totally lacking in self-knowledge; they'd need at least five years of twice-weekly therapy to work out their stuff. Although both are deeply concerned with their souls, their approach to the world is narrow-minded and destructive. Truth and justice prevail, just about, in the end, but little love has been generated. And their souls are not set free—yet they both belong to institutional Christianity.

In a clumsy ending, Shakespeare pointed out, but didn't particularly generate, the experience of the way in which the soul could reach God. The Duke, the supreme power in the land, like God, offers marriage to Isabella, the nun, the bride of Christ. She doesn't answer, so we don't know if she's going to open her heart as a human being and leave her nun vows. But at least we know Shakespeare was saying that man-made laws and religious structures may be necessary but they are not sufficient for human growth. That can only come by finding a deeper knowledge of oneself, and by love.

The merging of two souls is of course the central theme of the lovers in *Romeo and Juliet, Troilus and Cressida,* and *Antony and Cleopatra.* Their souls call on them to renew and re-create their love for each other again and again, against all the most atrocious odds, and the outcome of the play is dependent upon their success. This idea of the soul looking for its partner, a dominant idea in classical Greece, is taken much further by Shakespeare, in both sexual and spiritual terms.

The idea that the soul resides in the creative act and is generated out of love finds momentum in the great tragedies. Whereas Claudius (in *Hamlet*) still holds on to the old picture of the soul as a thing ("O limèd soul, . . . struggling to be free"—but it cannot, because he still possesses the things for which he committed the sin), Hamlet's soul is in full creative mode, driving him to ask questions about the Ghost, revenge, moral philosophy, what is man, the nature of being. This is such good stuff that it creates one of the most fascinating plays of all time. However, Hamlet turns away from love, the one state of being that could have held his restless soul. Ophelia, likewise, cannot rise to meet him in a commitment to their love. They cannot help each other, and so they both fall into a form of madness and despair.

Othello knows his love for Desdemona is his soul.

> Perdition catch my soul
> But I do love thee, and when I love thee not,
> Chaos is come again.
>
> OTHELLO (3.3, 100–02)

Again, he cannot hold to love, and perdition does catch his soul. Lear's soul finds freedom in prison when he's reunited with his daughter Cordelia.

> Come, let's away to prison.
> We two alone will sing like birds i' th' cage.
> When thou dost ask me blessing, I'll kneel down
> And ask of thee forgiveness; so we'll live, . . .
> And take upon's the mystery of things.
>
> KING LEAR (5.3, 9–12, 17)

The last exchange he has with her is as her breath or soul rises from her body and he follows her into death.

> Thou'lt come no more.
> Never, never, never, never, never . . .
> Do you see this? Look on her. Look, her lips,
> Look there, look there. *(He dies)*
>
> KING LEAR (5.3, 324–25, 327–28)

It is in the late plays that the soul finally becomes both the creative act *and* the courage to stay with the beloved through every vicissitude, in both the external world of events and the internal world of the psyche. What we call neurotic behaviors the Elizabethans thought of as an imbalance of the humors, or character flaws; they believed that chaos has to find form again, truth in beauty out of suffering. Out of that journey, what is dead is turned to life, what is stone becomes flesh, what is comatose awakes, and despair becomes joy. This is never the work of just one person, but a collective collaboration between a young woman—usually brought up in nature—her lover—who prizes love above all worldly gain—a witch or magical spirit, the artist, and the imaginative help of the gods.

Prospero, who has alchemical powers to be able to act as God, but no love, must release his creative abilities and start again. He must acknowledge the thing of darkness in his soul, stop putting his daughter to sleep when she says what he doesn't want to hear, and leave the island where he has had complete power for fifteen years.

But Leontes in *Winter's Tale,* who recognizes the havoc he has caused, can, through contemplation and prayers, with the humility to be guided by the witch Paulina, be given back his feminine half, his grace, his wife, Hermione.

So I think in the end where Shakespeare comes out is: The soul is a verb, not a noun. It is substantive but not material. It lives in every breath we take. Therefore, the potential to be open to life is there within our bodies in every moment. The soul is the ability to sustain love—real love, which renews itself in the creative act. It is the maiden phoenix, the bird of the spirit, which burns up itself (which is painful) and, out of the ashes, creates itself anew (which is often hard but ultimately joyful). It can join with another, or many. It fills the body, is deeply erotic, and generates new life.

Those of you who are Shakespeare buffs can probably expand this argument with some of the other 548 times Shakespeare uses "soul" in the canon; it is ever changing—as I said, a verb, not a noun.

So—why don't we talk about the soul today? For several reasons. There's little desire, because there is no space in our lives: we are being entertained to death with all the toys that are marketed to us, the stimuli with which we are bombarded. We separate our minds from our bodies. It happened long before Descartes: as we left nature and went to work in factories and in the mines, we closed down our bodies in sheer will to survive, unhooked the knowledge of the mind from the suffering of the body. Puritanism passed on the mores of sexual repression to the Victorian era—stifle the "bad" feelings. The Victorians were great empire builders, and when you live far from home it is much easier to run empires if you don't empathize with the colonized. And now the modern technology we have invented has us in its thrall—we hook up our brain waves and forget all about the body (unless it's porn we are watching—but even that is disassociated sex). So the separation between mind and body is spreading at unprecedented speed around the globe. Who knows if we can stop it? Probably not: these ideas have their own volition. But we can be conscious of it.

And, of course, with the rise of science and rationalism (only believing what can be proved), the soul could not be identified. The dissection of the brain proved there was no *there* there, no soul to be seen. People like Richard Dawkins and Christopher Hitchens write with great insight about the joys of science and the lunacy of religion; they, if I may say so, write with great soul!

Conversely, Carol Gilligan in her radical book *Birth of Pleasure* maps the parallels between the Psyche myth, modern marriage, the educational development of young girls and boys, and the way to a deeper knowing.

In Shakespeare's world, the desire to discover is ultimately where the source of the soul resides, and with each breath we have the opportunity to touch it; the desire to be at one with ourselves and others is love, and active love is how the questions are generated. It takes an enormous amount of courage, because you have to stay there, asking the question, even if you are in dire pain, or have done deeply reprehensible things, or have had deeply reprehensible things done to you.

In *Richard III,* the women are the only opposition to Richard as he climbs to power, killing everyone in his way. They oppose and expose him through their words and their insistence on naming all the people who have died. They will not be put down—as the mothers of the Plaza de Mayo in Argentina would not be put down, parading for a decade each Thursday with white scarves on their heads, holding pictures of their children and others, "the disappeared," who were brutally tortured, imprisoned, and murdered by the fascist regime during the Dirty War (1976–83). They eventually turned world opinion and became a symbol for vocal, nonviolent action. This is an act of creative bravery; this is love; this is the work of the soul, then and now.

We begin to see that soul does exist in our culture: it just may not be called that. Sometimes we do speak it. Its most common use is in "soul music," the music that was made out of the horrors of slavery, taking the ancient rhythms of Africa, using them to express the present pain of enslavement and death, lifting the spirit from the depths up to the heavens, creating joy where none existed before. This is the soul. In a small way, one of Shakespeare's most famous sonnets follows the same trajectory. "When in disgrace with Fortune and men's eyes," he begins, "I all alone beweep my outcast state," and then maps out his unending, mostly self-inflicted miseries. In the midst of this, he remembers the person he loves:

and then my state,
Like to the lark at the break of day arising
From sullen earth, sings hymns at heaven's gate. . . .

SONNET 29 (10–12)

The soul straddles life and death; it uses both; it is in both body and spirit; it is love and a call to action.

SCENE 2: *Troilus and Cressida*

Before we look at the women who come immediately after Juliet, I want to examine as a whole the plays Shakespeare wrote that have lovers' names as their title: *Romeo and Juliet, Troilus and Cressida,* and *Antony and Cleopatra.*

Of the three, I think we can safely say that *Romeo and Juliet* and *Antony and Cleopatra* have become indelibly marked on the human psyche as archetypal lovers. People who have never seen either play know that Romeo and Juliet are the epitome of young love, and Antony and Cleopatra are aging lovers more passionate about each other at their deaths than ever, after a long, tumultuous coupling. Few people know *Troilus and Cressida.* If they do, it would be to say "As true as Troilus, as false as Cressida."

Yet these three pairs were connected in Shakespeare's mind, and it was through them that he explored most deeply the sexual/spiritual merging. They are romantic stories about two people who love each other with ultimate commitment—and each of these three plays encompasses not only the love story, but the love story within a context, a social and political context of harsh realities. Before *Romeo and Juliet,* all love stories in Renaissance drama were happy love stories, arch comedies. Shakespeare was the first to tell a love story by framing it in *reality*—and thus it became a tragedy.

According to most scholars, he wrote *Romeo and Juliet* in 1594, *Troilus and Cressida* in 1601 (I would put it somewhat earlier, for reasons I'll explain later), and *Antony and Cleopatra* in 1607. A fourteen-year span. *Romeo and Juliet* and *Antony and Cleopatra* have never gone out of fashion. *Troilus and Cressida* was not performed in Shakespeare's lifetime (or if it was, once, privately or at the Inns of Court), and he certainly did nothing to promote its performance while he was alive.

These three plays have much in common. All are set against a backdrop of violence, so the love of the protagonists is in direct contrast to the violence of the setting. Two of the plays—*Troilus and Cressida* and *Antony and Cleopatra*—happen at seminal moments in Western civilization—the Greek-Trojan War, the subject of the *Iliad;* and the Battle of Actium, the moment when the Roman culture defeated the Hellenistic culture. And *Romeo and Juliet* was written shortly after a notorious family feud in England, in which teenage members of the Danvers family killed a member of the Long family. The Earl of Southampton, Shakespeare's friend and patron, was heavily involved in getting Charles and Henry Danvers out of England to escape the law.

So, in one play, Shakespeare had some personal relationship to the violence, and in the others, it was alive in his imagination through his reading, and probably the work of his fellow playwrights.

Why is the violence so important to the story of sexual/spiritual merging? Because in these stories the lovers are forced to make life-and-death choices; they are tested in a way few of us are. Antony and Cleopatra and Romeo and Juliet ultimately choose death to stay true to love. (Can you imagine choosing death to stay true to love?) Troilus and Cressida do not. They do not pit themselves against the forces of power that dictate their separation, and they cannot hold their union. Putting two stories against the backdrop of founding stories allows us to see turning points in our history and what the cost has been to individuals and to the people who surrounded them. And what got passed on to the culture. Shakespeare gave us three levels in each of these stories: personal, societal, epic! We identify with the lovers on the personal level. But the plays are heart-stopping as we scratch below the surface finding the perspective they reveal about our political situation *now*, how we have inherited the world Shakespeare was writing about. We see how the political circumstances and cultural mores define the context for love.

Shakespeare also did something else in these three plays—he put the rage and connection felt in battle right up against the force of love, as if to test these two ultimate states of knowledge and merging, to see how they related and if one would prevail over the other.

Beatrice and Benedick in *Much Ado About Nothing*–a fourth couple, who have a wonderful coming together–are not tested in this ultimate way. The wars Benedick has been fighting are tin-pot wars, skirmishes that came to nothing; there is no military machine with its own demands (although there is a brotherhood between officers which Benedick must break)–Benedick only has to issue a challenge for a duel to unite with Beatrice. His willingness to do it–and it could mean death–is the turning point of the love between Beatrice and Benedick. The play can end in a gentler, very personal way–and therefore *Much Ado About Nothing* is a comedy (and one with a marriage that will truly endure), not a tragedy of epic proportions, as the others are!

How important was it to Shakespeare that he set *Troilus and Cressida* within the *Iliad,* and *Antony and Cleopatra* at the time when the Hellenistic civilization was overthrown? That he told a different version from the one accepted in Elizabethan times? It was, it is important. He did it deliberately. He changed the vision of the story, showing that traditional stories, always accepted as "right" and "heroic," are not necessarily so–in fact, may have outcomes that do not serve a world attempting to live with compassion.

We understand the Trojan War and Actium more clearly as a result of Shakespeare's illuminating work. Thanks to historians and social commentators, we can track the huge effects these wars have had on our institutions and on our personal lives. And I think Shakespeare knew exactly what he was doing. The *Iliad,* the founding story of Western civilization, is the story that Greek writers, historians, and philosophers went back to again and again in order to define themselves, create new events, plays, models of behavior that influenced the search for both Greek and Roman identity. We can now see, four hundred years after Shakespeare, how that identity in turn became both European and American identity, and lives in our lives today.

The debacle which was the Greek-Trojan War was understood by most people in Shakespeare's times and before in heroic, morally simplistic, vibrantly present-moment storytelling. Yet to Shakespeare it was a duplicitous, hypocritical, stupid mess–and he wrote his version as such, which he may or may not have shown to anyone. Then he imported a love story from Chaucer to illustrate that war's callousness and consequences for love.

Similarly, the Battle of Actium was pinpointed by Octavius Caesar, once he had become the emperor, as the most important battle of his ascendency. He identified it as the moment when the Roman Empire became the Roman Empire, so to speak, and Egypt as an independent state ceased to exist. It was written down by his historians in terms of Cleopatra's cowardice, Antony's besotted love, and Rome's superiority. Octavius Caesar believed this moment was so important that he called himself Emperor Augustus. Shakespeare took Octavius Caesar's reading (via Plutarch) and turned the Battle of Actium into the first testing of Antony and Cleopatra's maturing love, and out of that the story became, not the stupidity of Antony or the cowardice of Cleopatra, but the beginning of a journey of constantly tested and regenerating love. The tragedy eventually was the destruction of Egypt and all that it stood for—and that was a tragedy. We are very conscious of the world we have inherited through Rome, and many of us mourn what we have lost by the annihilation of Egypt.

Shakespeare, as we have said, wrote on three levels. First there is the personal level, what is happening to the leading individuals in the story; then there is the context of their lives, who's dead, who's alive in the family structure, who is married to whom, their background, status, the laws that govern their lives. Finally, there is always a larger knowledge, an acknowledgment of the world from time immemorial, our humanity, the events that got us here, from the Bible and before, through all the great stories, many gods, and the historical ramifications of where we have come from and where we are going. Each person has the possibility of becoming a huge presence in this expansive canvas, yet the smaller personal details are also recorded.

It is because Shakespeare wrote on these three levels simultaneously that his stories speak to many cultures, can be performed anywhere in the world, are as much about the colonized as the colonizers, the repressed as the repressors, the workingman as the aristocrat, the woman as the man, and the potential in all of us.

And so, as I break open *Troilus and Cressida*, perhaps we will see why this pair of lovers couldn't in the end stay true to love, universal love as well as individual, and yet Antony and Cleopatra could and did.

There are three women besides Cressida in *Troilus and Cressida*.

Each has a distinctive role, and each reflects a facet of a woman's predicament.

Andromache is the great warrior Hector's wife, and when she pleads with her husband not to go to the wars one day, because every instinct within her tells her Hector is going to get killed, she is pushed aside and told she is shaming him. Hector has given his word to Achilles that he will fight that day—and this promise takes precedence over Andromache and their children (who will, we know, be sold into slavery when Troy falls). But it may also be that Hector's *desire* to fight Achilles has a far greater pull on him than wife and children ever can—that his love of war, and his deep attraction to the end-game he is playing with Achilles, is where his passion truly lies. Andromache, on the other hand, has only one role in Hector's eyes: wife. The honorable wife is submissive and supportive of her husband.

Cassandra, sister to Hector, Paris, and Troilus, is a prophetess—but her predictions about the downfall of Troy, although correct, are an embarrassment to her brothers. She can predict, but they will not listen.

The ravishing and ravished Helen is, of course, the queen stolen from the Greek Menelaus by Paris, the official reason for the war. Paris stole her at the behest of the princes of the House of Priam because the Greeks had stolen an old aunt of theirs. It's a sexual act which is a political act, which everyone approved of! The war has now been going on for seven years, with many thousands dead. Helen herself offers no opinion on the matter. In fact, the way Shakespeare has portrayed her, she is as vacuous and unthinking as any Valley Girl. (Valley Girls are from Los Angeles. They live in the valley where the shops are. Maybe we should call her a bit of a bimbo.)

The Greeks suggest to the Trojans that if they just give Helen back the war will be over: the Greeks will make no further demands. Neither side really wants to fight anymore, yet the Trojans, led by Hector, turn the offer down because of their "honor."

Enter Cressida—the beautiful daughter of the spy Calchas, who has gone over to the Greek side. She is a woman of indeterminate birth, so has absolutely no status, has no protector in Troy, but she has wit, clarity, and courage. She has an uncle Pandarus, who, as his name suggests, scrapes a living by doing people favors and "pandering" to them.

Troilus, the youngest son of Priam, doesn't want to fight the war anymore, because he can only think of his love for Cressida. There is a war within him. The first thing he says is:

> Why should I war without the walls of Troy
> That find such cruel battle here within?
> Each Trojan is master of his heart,
> Let him to field—Troilus, alas, hath none.
> TROILUS AND CRESSIDA (1.1, 2–5)

He is trying to get Pandarus to effect a meeting between himself and Cressida.

Cressida is equally smitten, but, as she tells the audience, she is not going to let Pandarus set up a meeting, because she must protect her virginity. That is the only thing of value she possesses—and without it she can never make a marriage, and marriage is the only way she can live a life with status and dignity. Yet she is also passionate. She knows "joy's soul lies in the doing." So she, too, is at war with herself, because she knows it is men's sexual desire that makes women "angels" before they have been able to possess them; once possessed, women are "things."

> Yet hold I off. Women are angels, wooing;
> Things won are done. Joy's soul lies in the doing.
> That she beloved knows naught that knows not this:
> Men prize the thing ungained more than it is. . . .
> Then though my heart's contents firm love doth bear,
> Nothing of that shall from mine eyes appear.
> TROILUS AND CRESSIDA (1.2, 225–28, 233–34)

Finally, in Act 3, they meet. They are in love. Troilus realizes that Cressida, with the astuteness of her mind as well as the beauty of her body, is his life partner.

> O that I thought it could be in a woman—
> As, if it can, I will presume in you—
> To feed for aye her lamp and flames of love,

To keep her constancy in plight and youth,
Outliving beauty's outward, with a mind
That doth renew swifter than blood decays!

TROILUS AND CRESSIDA (3.2, 129–34)

Again and again Cressida begins to give herself to Troilus, only to stop herself when she realizes if she does and he is not true to her, she will have lost everything.

This is where Shakespeare is so brilliant. These lovers are as passionate as Romeo and Juliet. Yet their status is completely unequal. She has no status; or any way of earning a living; or any family. Troilus is a prince; a warrior; has a voice in his father's council. Troilus has power, she has none. But because he's young, never been in love before, and seems to be ignorant about the position of women, he doesn't truly understand the cost to Cressida of becoming lovers.

In any case, she tells him her fears—and he swears he will always and forever be true to her. Once she believes that, she swears the same. They in effect make their own marriage ceremony, and they go to bed. One is forced to ask: why not a proper marriage ceremony? Why doesn't Troilus ask her to marry him? In any case, if someone you were passionate about swore this to you, would you not believe it?

True swains in love shall in the world to come
Approve their truths by Troilus. . . .
As true as steel, as plantage to the moon,
As sun to day, as turtle to her mate,
As iron to adamant, as earth to th' centre . . .
"As true as Troilus" shall crown up the verse
And sanctify the numbers.

TROILUS AND CRESSIDA (3.2, 145–46, 149–51, 154–55)

And if you invoked time, place, and the spirit of eternity in your answer (as Cressida does), would you not say this is the deepest vow language can make?

If I be false, or swerve a hair from truth,
When time is old and hath forgot itself,

When water drops have worn the stones of Troy
And blind oblivion swallowed cities up,
And mighty states characterless are grated
To dusty nothing, yet let memory
From false to false among false maids in love
Upbraid my falsehood.

TROILUS AND CRESSIDA (3.2, 157–64)

No sooner does consummation take place than Cressida is traded for the warrior Antenor—she is going to be handed over to the Greeks to get a warrior back. She is given no choice; she certainly doesn't want to go. Troilus does not challenge the order; he accepts it as inevitable, because it's what the Trojan council has decreed. Yet, a few scenes earlier, in the council, he has argued that, if he were married and no longer loved his wife, he would still be honor bound to fight for her. This gap between the ideals men espouse and their actual actions is the hallmark of *Troilus and Cressida*. So, even though the war is being fought because Paris is in love with Helen and it's a matter of "honor," Troilus never says, "Cressida is my love and she's not going." He fails the first test; no matter that he swore there was no imposition too great that his mistress could impose on him.

As soon as Cressida gets to the Greek camp, she's handed around the room to be kissed by all the Greek generals. It's an unpleasant scene, symbolically a rape scene (no "honor" toward women here—"she's asking for it" is the general attitude—starkly contrasting with the way Hector is welcomed into the Greek camp when he visits). She's rescued by Diomedes, who takes her to her father. Her father then proceeds to offer her to Diomedes. In the scene where she and Diomedes are together, she calls him "guardian" repeatedly, naming the role he must perform for her. She flirts, she comes back to her true self, she gives him the come-on, she rejects him—games women play when they are desperate. She ricochets round the room, at one time promising she will give herself to him, at another remaining true to Troilus. And Troilus is watching this scene from afar. You would think he would step in and intervene on her behalf—but he doesn't. He believes she's unfaithful, never recognizing the perilous position she's been put in, and he leaves vowing to kill Diomedes in battle the next day. At the end of the scene, Cressida, full of self-loathing, seems to find Diomedes attractive—and therefore acquiesces to the idea that he can be her protector and her lover. But her character is falling to pieces before our eyes. The intelligent, courageous Cressida, who told the audience so clearly why she should not give up her virginity, is gone; instead, her mind is splintering. She has lost all her spirit, and her sexuality is up for grabs. Cressida, who is equal in mind and body to any of the men, is abandoned by Troilus and by Shakespeare. And so Shakespeare leaves it. (In some stories by other authors, she ends up as a whore in a leper colony.)

Troilus, abandoning love, becomes a great warrior, taking over the leadership of the Trojan forces after Hector is killed. Shakespeare begins his portrait of Troilus with love, and ends it with revenge. When we last see him, he is killing everyone he can, admitting no mercy.

> I do not speak of flight, of fear, of death,
> But dare all imminence that gods and men
> Address their dangers in. Hector is gone. . . .
> Strike a free march to Troy! With comfort go:
> Hope of revenge shall hide our inward woe.
>
> TROILUS AND CRESSIDA (5.II, 13–15, 31–32)

Why do these two fail all the tests to their love? Indeed, why does the failure turn them into damaged human beings? It's the war, the nature of the war, the position of women, the love of honor, and the blind assumption of power and the warriors' ways of doing things.

Shakespeare imported this story of Troilus and Cressida from a story Chaucer had written two hundred years earlier—it doesn't exist in the *Iliad* itself. So what was Shakespeare doing when he imported a medieval story of courtly love and put it in the midst of the founding story? I think it's clear. Love, the passion experienced by Troilus and Cressida, has the potential to stop—for a moment, at any rate—the inevitability of the daily slaughter. Troilus doesn't want to fight. Paris often doesn't fight, because he'd rather stay with Helen—though he wants everyone else to fight, because he wants to keep her. Hector knows Helen's not worth it.

> Let Helen go. . . .
> If we have lost so many tenths of ours
> To guard a thing not ours—nor worth to us,
> Had it our name, the value of one ten—
> What merit's in that reason which denies
> The yielding of her up?
>
> TROILUS AND CRESSIDA (2.2, 17, 21–25)

Yet he reverses his argument once he realizes his honor is being impugned.

The women never unite in their fight to stop the war (although Andromache and Cassandra try), and we never see Hecuba, the mother to all these sons. Everyone is splintered.

Shakespeare piles on his anger about the stupidity of the war. He has Diomedes tell Paris what he really thinks about Helen:

> She's bitter to her country. Hear me, Paris.
> For every false drop in her bawdy veins
> A Grecian's life hath sunk; for every scruple
> Of her contaminated carrion weight,
> A Trojan hath been slain. Since she could speak
> She hath not given so many good words breath
> As, for her, Greeks and Trojans suffered death.
>
> TROILUS AND CRESSIDA (4.1, 73–79)

But the greatest vitriol is expressed by Thersites, a kind of fool/servant attached to Ajax, who defects to Achilles. At every turn Thersites tells the audience what he thinks of what is going on, how hypocritical, stupid, unnecessary all this violence is; he gets beaten for it, but he persists. I have to ask, is this Shakespeare's direct voice?

> Lechery, lechery, still wars and lechery! Nothing else holds fashion.
>
> TROILUS AND CRESSIDA (5.2, 213)

And the great Greek hero Achilles, with his sidekick Patroclus, is arrogant, lazy, full of a false sense of himself; he uses his sexuality to manipulate men and women and is a thoroughly despicable character. He doesn't even kill Hector honorably: he gets his Myrmidons to surround Hector and stab him to death, then ties the body to his horse's heels and drags it around the battlefield in triumph.

The story of the battle between Hector and Achilles gets as much stage time as do Troilus and Cressida—and again Shakespeare seems to be paralleling these two "love" stories. Men's love of honor is as strong as the love between men and women—maybe more so—but in the end there is no "honor," only the desire to win.

Troilus can't stay true to love, because he neither sees the power he possesses nor has the insight to change the way things are done. War, honor, the military machine, bravery in battle are the way men identify who they are. To break that accepted assumption is to be "untrue." The only time Troilus finds he can't fight is in that moment when he's so impassioned about Cressida at the beginning of the play. Once he's slept with Cressida, he reverts entirely to conventional male thinking. The reason Cressida can't stay true is that her position—indeed, like that of all the women in the play—is untenable. The women lack the ability to break out from their assigned roles. They can't create an alternative world. Their circumstances are so inculcated into their psyches *and* the social system that there's no breaking out.

Ulysses has a famous speech about degree and harmony:

> The heavens themselves, the planets, and this centre
> Observe degree, priority, and place,
> Insisture, course, proportion, season, form,
> Office and custom, in all line of order. . . .
>   But when the planets
> In evil mixture to disorder wander,
> What plagues and what portents, what mutiny?
> What raging of the sea, shaking of earth?
> Commotion in the winds, frights, changes, horrors
> Divert and crack, rend and deracinate
> The unity and married calm of states
> Quite from their fixture. O, when degree is shaked,
> Which is the ladder to all high designs,

The enterprise is sick. . . .
Take but degree away, untune that string,
And hark, what discord follows.
            TROILUS AND CRESSIDA (1.3, 86–89, 95–104, 110–11)

He claims that the reason the Greeks are not winning is that they have lost the proper respect for hierarchy—and this chaos and failure to follow Agamemnon means they cannot fight and overcome the Trojans.

This is lip service. The only people who observe the proper hierarchical pattern are the women—and then three of them end up destroyed. The men who pay lip service to a degree but then do what they want are happy to fight another day—which they do. This war has another four years to go, though at the final moment at the end of Shakespeare's play each side claims honor and victory. The *Iliad* doesn't tell the story to the end of the war. Its most important point is that when Troy eventually falls it gives birth to a new myth—a myth that becomes the founding story of Rome. And here we see how thought patterns, assumptions, and ways of doing things are passed down through the generations, so "the way it is" becomes reality itself. We internalize it—and no one needs to police us to let it be "the way it is."

Troy falls (as Cassandra and Cressida predict), but the warrior Aeneas escapes and eventually will go on to found Rome. He first travels to Carthage, in North Africa, and falls in love with the great, sensitive, art-loving Queen Dido—absolutely, intensely, spiritually, sexually—but he will abandon her to found Rome. He has a greater calling: Rome. Dido goes mad and kills herself. They meet again in the underworld, and that's where Shakespeare invokes them.

When Antony is dying, he invokes Dido and Aeneas as lovers whom he and Cleopatra echo—though, of course, Antony does not abandon Cleopatra—but Alexandria does fall to Rome, as Carthage did. Rome not only destroyed Carthage, they razed it to the ground, killing every person in it, and ground the stones into dust. Cressida uses this image in her betrothal speech to Troilus. She says if she prove false—when "mighty states characterless are grated / To dusty nothing"—then all false lovers should be known "'As false as Cressid.'" And so they are.

But perhaps if Rome didn't insist on absolute hegemony and raze states to dusty nothing, the feminine spirit might be able to flourish, take its place, and help create a world in which true love, coexistence, variety, and true sexuality, instead of war and honor, would be the name of the game.

That is the context for the greatest sexual/spiritual merging that Shakespeare examines in *Antony and Cleopatra.*

The reason I think *Troilus and Cressida* was written before 1601 is that it shows signs of coming together in fits and starts. I think Shakespeare wrote it over a period of time, starting somewhere after 1592, when the two fateful plague years changed the course of his life. His fellow playwright George Chapman (probably the playwright referred to in the sonnets who also has Southampton's patronage) was translating the *Iliad* in these years and for many years thereafter. Southampton and Essex were finding wars to fight—the Huguenot cause first, but then they mounted several expeditions against Spain, mostly at sea, at Cadiz, the Azores, really anywhere they could find Spanish ships (especially those laden with gold from the New World) to destroy and plunder. Eventually, of course, there was Essex's ill-fated expedition to Ireland, the failure of which led to his personal rebellion against the Queen. How much Essex's and Southampton's characters were affected by these wars I do not know. In any case, London was full of foot soldiers who had joined or been conscripted into the armies and come home without limbs, their minds frayed, unable to earn a living or support their families. Shakespeare really didn't like war or what it stands for.

But he also saw how deeply attracted some men are to war: that their lives do not seem relevant to them if they don't have a war to fight.

Essex, who caused trouble wherever he went, was one such man. His behavior and his writing from the Tower in the hours before his execution are exemplary—brave, calm, thoughtful to others, humble, even poetic. It seems to me that the passion to prove you can look death in the face, straight on, is the hallmark of masculinity for some men: it offers them a challenge they cannot find elsewhere. Certainly not in love, if the Earl of Essex, Alexander the Great, and General Patton are the examples we look at!

Shakespeare, however, was interested in studying a man who not only was, reportedly, the greatest soldier in the world, but who also loved a woman even more than he loved battle. This woman was as mercurial, emotional, and powerful as any battle, with intelligence second to none. She was Cressida grown up and elevated to power. She was, of course, Cleopatra.

The sexual/spiritual merging of Antony and Cleopatra is legendary; they changed all our lives, and we live with the effects of who they were.

SCENE 3: *Antony and Cleopatra*

We have inherited the Roman world which triumphs at the end of *Antony and Cleopatra*. There is a direct link between the world we live in today and the forces that triumphed at Actium. Two ways of being in the world met in that sea battle. The world Octavius Caesar inhabited dominated that day; Octavius then sought to obliterate the world Antony and Cleopatra lived in. What may have been possible before the Battle of Actium was no longer possible after it. I say all this very aware that Actium was not much of a battle in reality, but the *idea* of Actium became the turning point in the thinking of all the people who wrote about it: Plutarch, Caesar, and Shakespeare included.

The founding of America came out of two strands of European development—the one based on its argument with Britain, a sense of injustice that had its origins in the rights established by English common law, such as no taxation without representation (with which some people in the English Parliament, led by Edmund Burke, deeply sympathized); and then a second, idealistic and idealized strand, ideas strongly shared by the Founding Fathers—the idea of the Roman Republic. And just as the Roman Republic turned into the Roman Empire, and then, for better and for worse, collapsed, leaving the Christian Church intact, stretching across Europe, so America has turned the American Republic into the American Empire—and the American Empire will collapse except for our church—the American Corporation. The corporation will continue to dominate the world, much as the Roman Church once dominated lands formerly controlled by the Roman Empire. But in this new world order, the

American people may be crushed under their survival-of-the-fittest mechanism, as were the people of the Roman Empire. As the majority of people under the Roman Empire had no idea why their world came to an end, so, I think, most ordinary Americans do not understand the forces that are at work today. But I get ahead of myself.

Antony and Cleopatra is set against the backdrop of the known world. The Roman Empire, born out of the Roman Republic, with its ideas of democracy among a certain group of wealthy men (no vote for men without land—as with our Founding Fathers—and certainly no vote for women and slaves. Why are democracies built on top of one form of slavery or another?). Three men dominate the Roman world—Octavius Caesar, who rules Europe and lives in Rome; Mark Antony, who rules the East and North Africa and lives officially in Athens; and Lepidus, who has Spain. There is some lip service paid to the power of the Roman Senate—those aristocrats who are supposed to make wise decisions on behalf of the whole populace—but by and large we encounter them as yes-men around Octavius Caesar. They also have an admiration and romantic attachments to Mark Antony. No one cares much for Lepidus. Into this Roman world comes a powerful woman, Cleopatra.

At the beginning of the play, Shakespeare gives us two totally different pictures of the relationship between Antony and Cleopatra. The first comes from the Roman soldiers, the second from Antony himself!

Antony is not living in Athens but in Alexandria, with Cleopatra. Alexandria is the center of learning in the known world—a multiracial city with a great library, the center of astrology and medicine—as well as being a great trading city and the capital of Egypt. Egypt is a client state of Rome. Rome protects it with its armies and asks Egypt to pay tribute to Rome, but technically Egypt is independent, not part of the Roman Empire—just its bread basket and a source of revenue. Cleopatra and Egypt are well aware, however, that if Rome chose to crush Egypt it could. Has before and will again.

Cleopatra, for her part, has developed her influence in Rome through her personal relationships. Julius Caesar, her first lover (no Roman can marry Cleopatra: she's a foreigner, and Romans are only allowed to marry Romans), helped her get rid of her kid brother so she could become sole ruler of Egypt. There is a hint that perhaps General Pompey was her lover, too, when he arrived to seek support in his wars against Julius Caesar; he was executed instead. Her second lover is Mark Antony.

Cleopatra is the incarnation of Isis. The worship of Isis gives women just as much power, if not more, than men. There is no shame in Egypt about Cleopatra's being Caesar's or Antony's lover. She can have whatever lovers she pleases. She has great beauty and intelligence. She speaks five languages, is the first Ptolemy who has bothered to learn Egyptian, travels to Middle and Lower Egypt, and is very dear to her people. She doesn't know this, but she is the last of the Ptolemies. The original Ptolemy, some three centuries earlier, was Alexander the Great's general. So this family is in fact Greek, but they have adopted most of the customs of the Egyptians—especially the worship of Isis. They continue the learning, building, equal rights of women, support of the arts, and trading, activities that the Egyptians have practiced for centuries. Alexandria is the most exciting place to be in the world. In comparison, Rome is a backwater.

And Mark Antony, of course, is far more attuned to Athens and the Greeks than he is to the Romans (he wears Greek clothes, loves Greek art, chose Greece as his part of the empire, and so on).

In any case, at the beginning of the play we get the Roman soldiers' take on what's happening to Mark Antony in Alexandria.

> Nay, but this dotage of our general's
> O'erflows the measure. Those his goodly eyes,
> That o'er the files and musters of the war
> Have glowed like plated Mars, now bend, now turn
> The office and devotion of their view
> Upon a tawny front. His captain's heart,
> Which in the scuffles of great fights hath burst
> The buckles on his breast, reneges all temper,
> And is become the bellows and the fan
> To cool a gipsy's lust.
>
> ANTONY AND CLEOPATRA (I.I, I–IO)

And then Antony and Cleopatra arrive and we get his take:

Let Rome in Tiber melt, and the wide arch
Of the ranged empire fall. Here is my space.
Kingdoms are clay. Our dungy earth alike
Feeds beast as man. The nobleness of life
Is to do thus; *(kissing her)* when such a mutual pair
And such a twain can do't—in which I bind
On pain of punishment the world to weet—
We stand up peerless.

ANTONY AND CLEOPATRA (1.1, 35–42)

Which is the truth? That, of course, is the question that dominates the play: is Antony's sense of his union with Cleopatra the higher truth, or is his calling as a Roman soldier?

It will be no surprise that I think (and I think that Shakespeare thinks) the relationship between Antony and Cleopatra is the higher truth—and that, if it had survived the Roman onslaught, Egypt would have proved a different and healthier model for the Western world! But for most of the centuries since the play was written, and indeed since Mark Antony died, the idea of Cleopatra being a whore who has seduced the noble Antony away from his honorable self has been the picture presented, by academics and theatre directors alike. In the last ten or twenty years, the perspective has been changing. But I would like to make an unequivocal stand, both as a director and as someone who has played Cleopatra, that the sexual and spiritual merging of these two takes us on an extraordinary journey of learning, unparalleled anywhere onstage or in literature. And it is the story we are following in *Women of Will.* It's Shakespeare's most committed attempt to see what the possibility for the world could be if we had real equality between men and women, if both had power in the social and political world, and if their highest spiritual calling was their sexual passion for each other.

Antony and Cleopatra was written in 1607. It was the last play Shakespeare wrote before plunging into the despair of *Coriolanus* and *Timon of Athens.* He'd already started the journey into darkness with *Macbeth* and *King Lear.* In *Antony and Cleopatra,* the setting stretches across most of the known world, though it focuses on Alexandria and Rome. The two capitals are very different. Shakespeare was aware of the history and the immediate past of the two protagonists, and predicted the future for us all; he gave Antony and Cleopatra equal attention; he idealized neither, nor did he demonize either, but allowed them to have a complexity, both individually and together, which shifts, changes, backtracks, develops. He constructed a pace that signals the swift cutting of modern movies; he took known historical events and mixed them with small moments from unknown fictitious (but very real) people and allowed the "spin" on events to be told by many different people. It is an achievement difficult for us lesser mortals to live up to—which may be why theatrical productions are often flawed in some way.

Indeed, the two frames he offered at the beginning of the play—that of the Roman soldiers and that of Antony himself—force the question: how do we look at this? At the end of the play, Shakespeare again gave us two pictures—Cleopatra joining Antony in the afterlife in joyful merging; or Octavius Caesar taking over the world, and his pity and lament for the folly of their actions.

It was twelve years since he had written *Romeo and Juliet*, about two lovers who have very little history, are together only for a few days, are mourned by everyone, and manage to bring about change with their deaths. It was nine years since he had written *Much Ado About Nothing*, in which Benedick chooses to commit himself to Beatrice's world rather than stay locked into military custom—and it ends happily. It was more than six years since *Troilus and Cressida*, in which the lovers get mashed up in the war that supposedly founded Western civilization. Through all the plays from 1596 onward, he had been examining the masculine world of honor, "pride, pomp, and circumstance of glorious war," its exclusion of women, its cost to ordinary human beings; he never sidestepped the thrill and pull of men who bond by facing death together. Nor did he shortchange women's friendship and their enormous practicality in organizing the daily lives of themselves and others, the friendship and camaraderie that come out of that. Now he put all these strands together in one enormous play, which has at its center the most intimate relationship between one man and one woman.

So which is the picture that we, the audience, think is the correct one?

Nay, but this dotage of our general's
O'erflows the measure. . . . His captain's heart
. . . is become the bellows and the fan
To cool a gipsy's lust.
ANTONY AND CLEOPATRA (I.I, I–2, 6, 9–IO)

Or

Let Rome in Tiber melt, and the wide arch
Of the ranged empire fall. Here is my space.
Kingdoms are clay. . . . The nobleness of life
Is to do thus; *(kissing her)* . . .
ANTONY AND CLEOPATRA (I.I, 35–38)

These are the alternative frames Shakespeare gave us to measure the message of the play—and nobody needs me to say that for the last two thousand years men's valor and honor in war and "doing the right thing" has always taken precedence over love between a man and a woman. Men who don't come up to that, or fall away, are not real men, and society does not honor them in any way.

In any case, immediately after those opening statements are made, news arrives from Rome, and Antony refuses to hear it. Cleopatra is very aware that the message may be from either of the two people who legally can call on Antony's loyalty—his wife, Fulvia, or his fellow triumvirate Octavius Caesar. Antony and Cleopatra go off together, but when we see them again, it's clear not only that Antony has heard the news from Rome, but that he heard it while Cleopatra was not there—he separated himself from her to deal with it, and now she's looking for him and intuitively knows something momentous is happening.

When he comes to tell her he's leaving—obviously, his statements about Rome in Tiber melting didn't stand up under pressure—Cleopatra plays every emotional trick she can to get him to stay, or at least to make him understand how painful it is for her to have him leave. He hopes the news of Fulvia's death will reassure her, but it seems to make matters worse, because now Cleopatra can see how unfaithful a husband Antony is (as if she didn't know before), but

Antony has to go—and we applaud him for going. His wife created wars in the Italian Peninsula, in large part to try and get him back to Rome; and now Pompey's son is creating all kinds of trouble, using pirates to besiege ships and ports alike (a bit like the coast of Somalia today). Antony is responsible for the millions of people living all round the Mediterranean; he has to go, because his authority, power, and influence are such that people will agree with him, go to war if he says so, negotiate peace if he says so, follow him and his reputation into difficult places in order to keep the peace. Just as decisively as he said, "This is my space," he now says, "I'll leave you, lady." Cleopatra stops her emotional acting out and tries to define what is going on with her, so they can part with some kind of depth of understanding:

> Sir, you and I must part; but that's not it;
> Sir, you and I have loved; but there's not it;
> That you know well. Something it is I would—
> O, my oblivion is a very Antony,
> And I am all forgotten.
>> ANTONY AND CLEOPATRA (1.3, 104–08)

When Cleopatra realizes he's going no matter what she says and does, she swiftly changes her behavior and becomes the good Roman wife, acquiescing to her husband's wishes, blessing his endeavors. Once in Rome, Antony finds a greater crisis than Fulvia's wars—and one that has to be dealt with before the Roman military strategy can be brought to bear on Pompey—namely, that Octavius Caesar thinks Antony supported Fulvia's insurrections and Antony is finding a way to get rid of Octavius Caesar. Lepidus is ineffectual in trying to bring them together; Agrippa (Octavius Caesar's wily general) is the one who comes up with an idea to heal this wound permanently: Let Antony marry Octavius's sister Octavia. Thus Antony and Octavius will then be family. Antony thereby shows he is not bound to Cleopatra (and Rome is always fearful of Alexandria, because it is richer, cleverer, more cosmopolitan), he's not going to use Egypt's millions to defeat Rome, he is sorry his wife challenged Octavius, and he'll prove he's a good Roman again.

Without too much deep thinking, Mark Antony agrees, and very efficiently marries Octavia. He meets with Pompey on his boat, does a deal with him, calms Octavius Caesar, and goes back to Athens with Octavia. He's returned to being a good Roman soldier, at least on the surface. When the pirate Menas says that Antony must now leave Cleopatra completely, Enobarbus, Antony's best friend and second in command, who has lived in Egypt as long as Antony, replies, "Never! He will not." He talks of Antony's heart being "tied up" from the moment he met Cleopatra. However, the audience never knows what Antony really thinks and feels about this, other than his opening sentences at the beginning of the play.

Cleopatra, meantime, is waiting for Antony to return—and in these scenes with her court—and particularly her women, Iras and Charmian—we realize that this relationship with Antony has been in existence for many years.

> Think on me,
> That am with Phoebus' amorous pinches black,
> And wrinkled deep in time.
> ANTONY AND CLEOPATRA (1.5, 32–34)

(As an aside, Cleopatra had four children: one with Julius Caesar, and then twins and another son with Antony. Just like Isis, she is a mother as well as a lover.)

Their relationship has no puritanical restraints on it in any way; its intensity has always been guided by the sexuality between them. The political alliance (which also has disadvantages) has been secondary to their sexual passion. However, when Cleopatra hears of Antony's marriage to Octavia, she goes berserk—beats the messenger, herself, and anyone she can find. She summons all of her courage to let him go forever—but then cannot. He is still the most beautiful person in the world to her. So their love holds, despite this obstacle. Antony made a marriage to keep the Roman world together, but his deep personal attachment to Cleopatra is unchanged. Can these two positions live side by side?

After some unstated amount of time, Antony returns to Cleopatra. And Shakespeare doesn't say why. When I asked Nigel why he thought Antony did it, his answer was: "Simple. He misses her. His real life doesn't work without her. He can't be who he is without her."

Abandoning Octavia and returning to Cleopatra brings down the wrath of Octavius Caesar upon Antony and Cleopatra—and Antony seems to know that will be the consequence. Lepidus bites the dust shortly after Pompey was dealt with (Octavius got rid of him), so now there are only two men in charge of the world.

In what seems to be a pre-emptive move, Antony and Cleopatra stage a huge spectacle, getting married as Isis and Dionysus with all their Egyptian children around them. This link with the gods is difficult for us to hold in our conscious understanding, but it's worth trying, because Shakespeare used it in several ways in the second half of the play. The first half of the play is very much about establishing Antony and Cleopatra as ordinary human beings with a passion for each other, and as leaders who have responsibilities. The second half links their humanness to their godlike status. Their journey toward archetypes, if you will. Not that they are archetypes—they can only ever be human beings—but the effect they have on others is archetypal; the fantasy of who they are in other people's eyes has repercussions for them personally and for the world at large. We do this to our leaders—whether they be presidents, gurus, or movie stars. Antony and Cleopatra play into deification; they use it for their own ends, to prove that they are larger than life and therefore will prevail, as the gods prevail. Elizabeth I played this game as the Virgin Queen, or Astraea, or Gloriana (depending upon the occasion), so her knights would serve her in war, her clergy would serve her in religion, her lawyers would serve her in wisdom, and everyone would pay their taxes on time. England does best under female monarchs, who perhaps give us more room to maneuver. Whereas America wants its presidents to appear to be both puritans and warriors—an almost impossible combination! Washington, Lincoln, and Roosevelt were really the only ones who ever succeeded. This desire to have a god or goddess in charge, with supposedly superhuman powers, is a need in the human psyche: the desire to serve the god's will or know the god is on your side. Perhaps large states must have that kind of leadership. The fact that the "god" is also a human in life is one of the great tensions for that god/human. In the case of Antony and Cleopatra, we have two humans, two gods, and one war: the battle for the Roman Empire.

What's the difference between the two sides, and who is going to win? By crowning themselves as gods, Antony and Cleopatra declare themselves not only equal in sharing power, equal in the world's eyes, but also as mystical, worthy of worship, with a direct line to the power that created the world.

Most people in the audience will know that Octavius Caesar is not Augustus yet, that Christ was born in Augustus's reign, and that we've thirty more years until B.C. becomes A.D. These earlier gods, Isis, Dionysus, Hercules (Antony's other incarnation), and Augustus himself–for he, too, declares himself a god after his defeat of Egypt–are powerful, and they have much more complexity than the universal power of the Almighty God. A world without God doesn't compute. The question is: what kind of gods are Antony and Cleopatra manifesting, and if he wins, what kind of god will Octavius Caesar be?

As for actors, how the hell does one play a god? Well, get the clothes right first. Then, of course, do as they do in the movies–have everyone bow and crouch around you. But these are crutches. There is no way of playing a god–and you do so at your peril. So in some ways we already know that Antony and Cleopatra are on dodgy ground. Isis, Cleopatra's goddess, is not about empire and war, but about love, sexual desire, procreation, decimation, putting the pieces back together again, nurturing life, the lover and the son being one. Isis is not really a god to invoke in order to beat the Roman armies in battle. (In everyday life, her cult became very strong–not surprisingly, among women–and it spread all over the empire, including in Rome itself.) Dionysus, Antony's principal god, is great at crossdressing, something Antony and Cleopatra both like to do; Dionysus is terrific for creating the celebration that can bring Pompey, Lepidus, Octavius, Antony, and the pirates all together to sing about jolly Bacchus (the Roman version of Dionysus). But when violence is in the offing, the god Dionysus goes underground, having learned fear when he was tiny, when the Titans killed his nurse. He isn't a warrior god, though he does know that if he is suppressed indiscriminate violence will break out. This is the god Antony loves to be! However, Antony does have another god–a warrior god–a Roman god. It's Hercules, he who can do impossible tasks. In Shakespeare's play, Hercules deserts Antony just before his second battle with Octavius–

though Antony still wins, even as a mortal human being. But I think Shakespeare included it because he wanted us to know that warrior strength was leaving Antony. (Anyway, it's in Plutarch, the source material.)

The question is: is it possible for anyone, man or woman, to inspire/control/align massive groups of people without aspiring to be a god? Gods have to epitomize certain qualities humans have, or would like to have. They must have charisma, which means people are sexually attracted to them; they have to exude unutterable confidence, so people know they are safe with them; and it's a good idea for them not to be too complex—otherwise, the message gets muddled.

In their quest to be gods, Antony and Cleopatra are unsuccessful—mostly because they are riotously complex, too intelligent, and into each other, rather than presenting themselves as objects of worship for others. They live with power, because they've always had it and that's the game they learned to play at an early age. But it is no longer a dominant desire in either of them. Their love for each other is!

The Battle of Actium is the first test. By fighting at sea, Antony deserts his saner self, because he knows he can beat Caesar on land. But Cleopatra wants to be in the battle; she can do so by sailing with her well-equipped navy. Antony lets her have her way. It's either god-like hubris or stupidity—and he loses the confidence of his soldiers before he even begins.

When she gets scared in the middle of the battle and runs away, he follows her. Not only do they lose, but he also loses his honor, his reputation, all the things that made him great in Roman eyes. He is plunged into the greatest despair.

> O, whither hast thou led me, Egypt? See
> How I convey my shame out of thine eyes
> By looking back what I have left behind
> 'Stroyed in dishonour.
>
> ANTONY AND CLEOPATRA (3.11, 53–56)

Cleopatra goes to him, pleading for forgiveness, which he gives her—and again reiterates that she is the most important thing to him.

CLEOPATRA O, my lord, my lord,
  Forgive my fearful sails! I little thought
  You would have followed.
ANTONY Egypt, thou knew'st too well
  My heart was to thy rudder tied by th'strings,
  And thou shouldst tow me after. O'er my spirit
  Thy full supremacy thou knew'st, and that
  Thy beck might from the bidding of the gods
  Command me.
CLEOPATRA O, my pardon!
ANTONY Now I must
  To the young man send humble treaties, dodge
  And palter in the shifts of lowness, who
  With half the bulk o'th'world played as I pleased,
  Making and marring fortunes. You did know
  How much you were my conqueror, and that
  My sword, made weak by my affection, would
  Obey it on all cause.
CLEOPATRA Pardon, pardon!
ANTONY Fall not a tear, I say. One of them rates
  All that is won and lost. Give me a kiss.
  He kisses her

ANTONY AND CLEOPATRA (3.II, 57–77)

One of the most appealing aspects of both Cleopatra and Antony is how they are loved by people of their own sexes. Antony's relationship with his soldiers is one of the bedrocks of the play (which is why it is so disturbing when he loses it). Octavius Caesar reports on his tenacious endurance when he was leading his men on a forced retreat, famine at their heels; they ate the barks of trees, "strange flesh / which some did die to look on," and drank horse piss to stay alive. Mark Antony is a man among men; he eats with them, drinks with them, extols their virtues; when he's planning to kill himself, he wants them to be with him. They refuse to run him through, so he does it himself. He gives them all his worldly goods. He *is* the greatest soldier in the world—not the greatest strategist, but the greatest leader of the people, by being one of the people.

This makes it all the more heartbreaking when Enobarbus leaves him. But once he leaves, Enobarbus doesn't want to live, either, and dies of a broken heart.

Hercules, the warrior god, also leaves Antony. Late that night, as they prepare to go into battle again, the soldiers hear Hercules leaving him. Yet, the next day, Antony wins the battle and returns to Cleopatra.

> O thou day o'th'world,
> Chain mine armed neck; leap thou, attire and all,
> Through proof of harness to my heart, and there
> Ride on the pants triumphing.
>
> ANTONY AND CLEOPATRA (4.8, 13–16)

They lose the third battle, and Octavius now begins his diplomatic initiative to divide Cleopatra from Antony.

Antony's shame in defeat doesn't immediately make him take the way of the honorable Roman soldier: suicide. Instead, he turns on Cleopatra. She entertains Octavius's messenger when Antony isn't there. Antony comes across them (it's a scene comparable to the husband's coming home in the middle of the day and finding the wife in bed with the mailman) and immediately assumes Cleopatra is negotiating with Octavius behind his back. He's so enraged he's going to kill her. So she devises one of her childish tricks: she goes to her monument and sends him word she's dead, so he'll be sorry.

And, of course, he is. So sorry that he decides to kill himself. She, too, has now shamed him, by committing suicide first, doing the noble act. So Antony prepares to kill himself, asking his soldiers to help him (they refuse—they love him too much) but finally persuading his personal servant Eros.

Shakespeare calls Antony's servant "Eros" deliberately. It is Eros that takes off Antony's armor, Eros that's by his side as he philosophizes about life and how it will be when he meets Cleopatra in the afterworld.

> I will o'ertake thee, Cleopatra, and
> Weep for my pardon. So it must be, for now

All length is torture. Since the torch is out,
Lie down and stray no farther. . . .
Eros!–I come, my queen.–Eros!–Stay for me.
Where souls do couch on flowers we'll hand in hand,
And with our sprightly port make the ghosts gaze.
Dido and her Aeneas shall want troops,
And all the haunt be ours. Come, Eros, Eros!

ANTONY AND CLEOPATRA (4.14, 52–55, 58–62)

You notice he chooses the founder of Rome, Aeneas, to be in this heaven. But Aeneas is there with his great love, Dido, whom he deserted to go and found Rome. Dido couldn't believe he would leave their great love, and she killed herself. Aeneas loved Dido, the North African queen who also created a great center of learning and the arts, Carthage. Shakespeare seems to be saying that Aeneas the lover is more powerful than the Aeneas who founded Rome!

Shakespeare merged the ideas of Antony, Aeneas, sublime poetry, Eros, Dido, Cleopatra, Carthage, Alexandria, love, and the world of our unconscious minds, coalescing them all to inspire Antony to kill himself and be reunited with Cleopatra in a better world. It is one of the greatest creative acts ever drawn by an artist. It lives on so many levels–symbolically, atavistically, poetically, and, if the actors and director do it right, visually, musically, and emotionally.

Then what happens? Antony botches the job. Shakespeare has transported us to another realm. We have intuitively picked up all of these layers of understanding–and then Shakespeare blows it apart. "Oops, sorry, the greatest soldier in the world doesn't know how to kill himself." Now Antony discovers that Cleopatra is not dead–this is fast turning into a farce–and he's got a sword stuck through his middle. But he isn't angry, and he *is* dying: all he wants to do is get to Cleopatra to help her think through whom to trust in Octavius's entourage, and then to die by her side.

He gets to her monument; Cleopatra is high up, far above him. She is locked in, supposedly safe from Octavius's soldiers, so the only way for him to get to her is to be pulled up the outside of the building.

And yet, once again, Shakespeare started up on a great journey of symbolic, atavistic, and poetic imagery of drawing the god, the humans, human emotions, the afterworld, into a sexual/spiritual merging.

> O sun,
> Burn the great sphere thou mov'st in; darkling stand
> The varying shore o'th'world! O, Antony,
> Antony, Antony! Help, Charmian, help, Iras, help,
> Help, friends below! Let's draw him hither.
>
> ANTONY AND CLEOPATRA (4.15, 11–15)

As Antony gets hauled up the side of the phallic monument, in verse with building rhythm:

> O come, come, come!
> And welcome, welcome! Die when thou hast lived,
> Quicken with kissing. Had my lips that power,
> Thus would I wear them out.
>
> ANTONY AND CLEOPATRA (4.15, 42–45)

And so, after telling Cleopatra to trust no one about Caesar but Proculeius (he's wrong even in that—but it is mortal knowledge he's dispensing, not the wisdom of the gods, so it's the desire that's important, not the information), Antony dies, where he has lived, in Cleopatra's lap. And here we get the goddess Isis, with her son and lover Horus/Osiris. For the man to love completely, he must be able to love the mother, the wife, the virgin maiden—and all in one—not just love one and reject the others. And he has to love them bodily, spiritually, generously, with heart and aesthetic understanding. Otherwise, he will not love her wrinkled deep in time; only someone who knows and accepts all of his own imperfections can attain the sacredness of loving someone in her entirety. (The Christian Church dealt Christianity a wound that then perverted everything, made Mary a literal virgin, the clergy celibate, Christ a sexless saint and pious victim—but, then, you'll do that if you are bent on controlling people, not freeing them.) Antony is the person who can embrace all feminine power as he dies. He may have lost the empire, but he has won his love—the greater victory. And now Cleopatra has the fifth act in which to follow him.

For a moment, we see her considering whether to negotiate with Octavius or at least to save her children. When I directed the play, I'd had the children playing in the court, and at this point, while Cleopatra was distracting Octavius with her negotiations, I had the children escaping and leaving with their schoolteacher—which they did in life. Caesarion was killed shortly thereafter (in life), but the younger children were brought up in Athens by the generous and loving Octavia and so reached adulthood. (Octavia was an extraordinary woman; she is worthy of her own play.)

Finally, Cleopatra starts her journey toward the other world and Antony. She, as always, has her women around her. As Antony is loved by his men, so Cleopatra's strength is derived from her women, plus the odd eunuch and schoolteacher. They are friends who know and love one another—and if die is what they must do, they will do it. Cleopatra's going to die through the services of the snake (knowledge; healing; shedding of the skin and rebirth) brought by a clown, an ordinary person. When I played Cleopatra, the clown and I exchanged our first two or three lines in Egyptian—the language of the people—because we both knew what this was about and where it would end up. Shakespeare wrote one of his best funny scenes just before Cleopatra's death, drawing the audience, through laughter, into the open frame of mind needed to understand Cleopatra's ascent to the next world. Just as Eros went before Antony, so Iras goes before Cleopatra, leaving Charmian behind to tidy up the loose ends before joining her mistress. Cleopatra begins with the desire for death—"immortal longings"—hearing Antony calling her, leaving the frustrated Octavius behind in this world, feeling human jealousy that Iras might reach Antony before she does. She takes first one asp to her breast, her body filled with that orgasmic bliss which is often created in a mother's body as she suckles her child, hearing Antony calling her again. "Husband, I come. / Now to that name my courage prove my title!"

Applying the second asp, she says, "As sweet as balm, as soft as air, as gentle. O Antony!" and so dies, with a merging of mother, lover, and child, to join with Antony. You could say that she always was, and is, joined with Antony, because it's not possible to know the mother, lover, and child *without* an Antony.

We are left with Octavius Caesar and the Roman occupation.

Octavius Caesar is not unkind, but he is clear and absolute; he rules a hierarchical structure that is controllable. His people are trained to give orders and take orders, to speak with one voice, and to know their place in the order of things. There is security in this—it is the structure of organizations. But love is not possible here.

I think Shakespeare found himself asking: why is the war story often given so much more emphasis than the love story? Both stories demand great courage, sacrifice, and commitment—but in the end, one heals and the other decimates. And Shakespeare himself chose the love story, for it unites men and women, gives them equal status, and opens doors toward a new life.

What Romeo and Juliet knew about themselves and each other, which for them happened instantaneously and took place in one Italian town, then remained focused and true for the few days during which they loved each other, and for which they both died; this was also true on an expanded level for Antony and Cleopatra. They are many decades older, in a relationship that lasted twelve years, while both were rulers of the vast known world!

The difference is in the journey, not in the message. Antony and Cleopatra had countries at their command; millions of people were affected by what they did. They had years together, were unfaithful to each other (at least, Antony was in practice; Cleopatra probably only contemplated it, which, of course, is strange if you think of Cleopatra's reputation as a promiscuous temptress, and Antony's as a good soldier—but 'tis ever thus). They had children together and with others. They were excessive, played politics, hurt and loved those around them. But in the end, their journey is the same as Romeo and Juliet's. It is with each other they know themselves the best, whether through the deep sexuality they experience with each other, or the sense of each other's being the godhead whom they will merge with after death—and so the only way to find fulfillment is to join the other in death, wherever and whatever that might be!

Both pairs of lovers captured the imagination of the world, and everyone knows (whether or not they've seen the plays, and most people haven't) what they stand for: an ultimate commitment to full-bodied love that unites the lovers forever.

And I think, just as the younger Shakespeare could feel the passion in his veins as he wrote *Romeo and Juliet,* so as an older man he felt the weariness and lack of innocence that made up the layered connection, though even greater commitment, as he wrote *Antony and Cleopatra.*

He also would have been aware of the difference between the Hellenistic culture Antony and Cleopatra stood for, and the Roman culture Octavius Caesar stood for. Politically, Hellenism believed in alliances, treaties between equal states, not colonization; Octavius believed in colonization, which needed universal law and armies to keep everyone aligned to Rome's dominance. Hellenism believed in the arts, dancing, singing, storytelling. The Romans were suspicious of the arts, at least at the beginning of their history, preferring oratory, a simple hardworking life without too much frivolous distraction. Eventually, they learned to harness the power of the arts, but not until much later. Alexandria became the center of learning, experiment, and fun, but it didn't have the armies to protect itself. Rome extended its empire far and wide, encouraging trade, competition, field sports, and blood sports as it marched across the earth. It collapsed only when it stretched itself too far from the center, and those in the inner circle were psychologically bankrupt from too little examination, too much greed, too little curiosity, too little support for the artistic life.

If Antony and Cleopatra had defeated Octavius at Actium and taken over the leadership of Europe, North Africa, and what is now called the Middle East, would our lives be different? Could there be a society in which love, the arts, learning, and experiment are central? Or do these things always fall before armies, the law, and economic expansion? The latter live in this world; the former are always reaching toward the spiritual world beyond this material. Love is the path to that spiritual world; masculine qualities and feminine qualities (whichever gender possesses them) are in a perpetual dance to invigorate and balance and harmonize those states of being, which allow us to know more, feel more, hear more, see more—and so become ourselves, spiritually and sexually. In order to function efficiently, armies and the law demand a certain lack of questioning. Antony was the greatest soldier in the world, but he shed that skin to be with Cleopatra. She took the protection of the Roman world and its armies, until the price was giving up Antony. They each had to choose: individual supremacy in this world as it is, or being with the other in the next world, whatever that is, and accepting the possibility that it may not exist. Ultimately, they found that the higher calling was to be with each other.

We all have to choose. We have to choose how we spend our lives: Is our commitment only to ourselves, or is there a commitment larger than our individual selves? How do we serve a larger commitment and not lose sight of who we are? If only women commit themselves to the family unit, is that healthy? How do we feel alive in ourselves, know that we are increasing our sensitivity to others, to the state of the world, while knowing ourselves ever more deeply—and, with our increasing power, not being blind to the effect we have on others?

The only guide in this journey is love. And love has its own power. It takes us to unknown places, places where we may never have had the courage to go. The Greeks divided love into two kinds, *agápe* and *éros*. *Agápe* was the love of mankind, the love of family and other human beings; *éros* was the erotic love between two people. What Shakespeare saw was not only that the power of erotic love could turn into spiritual love, but that the erotic spirit evokes the very foundation of life, in all its complexity. So the power of the erotic spirit, if freed, spreads out into play, artistic endeavor, generosity toward others, a power to excel in whatever one is doing; it naturally flows into *agápe,* interacting with others on multiple levels (as when Romeo puts the dying Paris next to Juliet, for example). It only turns into jealousy, or the desire to win at the expense of others, if it forgets its origin, because then it believes love is limited and limiting. It is not: as Juliet says, "The more I give to thee, the more I have, for both are infinite."

The key is the commitment of the lovers to each other. The result is a spirituality which flows into the whole world, perhaps even after the lovers are dead.

Shakespeare created Romeo and Juliet, and Antony and Cleopatra, out of his own experience of erotic love. They have become icons in our minds, but if we go to the plays themselves and take on these characters, putting our minds and bodies into their minds and bodies, then we become aware, viscerally, of the enormous power of the erotic and how it can lead to stumbling, bumbling human enlightenment.

SCENE 4: The Women Who Follow Juliet

Immediately after finishing *Romeo and Juliet* in 1594, Shakespeare wrote *Midsummer Night's Dream, Merchant of Venice,* and *Richard II.* These are followed by *Henry IV Parts 1* and *2, King John, The Merry Wives of Windsor,* and, in 1598, *Much Ado About Nothing.*

The plays were coming in a poetic frenzy, we might say—and he needed to earn money. *Midsummer Night's Dream* is a play full of extremes, but nobody dies at the end. It's almost as if Shakespeare wrote the plot of falling in love five times over in *Midsummer,* but, with the help of magic, fairies, and the good intentions of stalwart artisans, it could all come right.

First couple up: Theseus and Hippolyta, belonging to classical Greece, myth, and storytelling. Theseus, the much-appreciated Athenian lawmaker and warrior, has conquered in battle Hippolyta and her Amazons. With his military victory absolute, Theseus is keen that Hippolyta love and marry him—a very clear symbolic picture of the masculine and the feminine, if we can reduce it to such. Hippolyta doesn't say much. Certainly she gives no indication that she cares for Theseus in any way: she's captive, she has few choices. Not an equal relationship by a long shot. Their "courtship" and marriage form the frame for the play.

Next two couples up: Hermia and Lysander, Helena and Demetrius, ordinary middle-class teenagers from Athens. In Shakespeare's writing, the girls are far more developed—in character and action—whereas it's hard to know the difference between Demetrius and Lysander (to this day I can never remember which is which, even though I've directed the play five times) other than that one—Demetrius, yes?—has Hermia's father's blessing to marry her, and Lysander doesn't. Hermia, of course, wants to marry Lysander. Her best friend, Helena, wants to marry Demetrius. They decide to run away to the woods (the wild, untamed place outside Athens, where anything can happen). Lysander suggests it to Hermia, so they can escape an Athenian law that gives Hermia's father the right to kill his daughter if she goes against him. And Helena suggests it to Demetrius because she knows he'll chase Hermia and Lysander, and then she'll chase Demetrius—

and for some reason she has confidence that, outside the walls and laws of Athens, she can somehow persuade Demetrius to love and marry her. Her belief in the wild place of nature to bring about change turns out to be accurate.

Once in the woods, we meet the fourth couple—Titania and Oberon, queen and king of the fairies, whose relationship has fallen apart because they've both been having to do with incompatible mythological creatures—principally, Hippolyta was Oberon's mistress, Titania was Theseus's (he had many others)—and then there's this human child Titania will not give to Oberon to be his page because "his mother was a votaress of my order." The fairies are what we would call in this day and age our unconscious minds. Shakespeare would think of them as ancient country knowledge, the links between the energies of nature and our abilities to be in touch with them.

This delicious mess of psychological relationships bewitched Shakespeare's imagination. Titania, Oberon, and especially Oberon's sidekick, Puck or Robin Goodfellow, belong to the world of Shakespeare's childhood and the Celtic influence so prevalent in Stratford. There are numerous Welsh names, both in the town and in the plays. Shakespeare's grandmother may have been Welsh. The fairies' sexual couplings with mythological characters, Theseus and Hippolyta, belong to Shakespeare's teenage years in school. The harsh laws of Athens, which give Hermia's father, Egeus, the right to kill his daughter if she disobeys him, gives credence to Shakespeare's clerking either at the Guild Hall in Stratford or at the Inns of Court in London. How women should be treated if they don't obey the males in the family was a topic alive and well in the treatises and pamphlets of Elizabethan England. The debate still goes on today; in some parts of the world, women pay the ultimate price for transgressing male laws.

Of all the couples in *Midsummer Night's Dream,* the only ones who are equal in their power over their lives and sexuality are the fairies Oberon and Titania, at least until Oberon uses magic to force Titania to fall in love with a "foul thing"—namely, an ass. But Oberon and Titania belong to the woods, to nature. All the others have to maneuver within the constraints laid on them by conquest or by law.

And so we come to the final pairing, another classic couple, Pyramus and Thisbe. These are roles to be enacted by the workingmen of Athens when they present a play for the wedding of Theseus and Hippolyta.

It is Shakespeare's genius that he gives us in Pyramus and Thisbe a rerun of the *Romeo and Juliet* story, two lovers who die mistakenly because they each think the other is dead. In this version, the presence of the actors playing the roles is far more dominant than the actual parts. The actors can arise from the dead and explain to their audience—the real lovers—how to interpret the play. The play within the play, with its double suicide, inventing a million methods of killing yourself, brings such laughter to all parties, and then to the actual theatre audience itself, that a great celebration of unity and community flows.

At midnight, the lovers can go to bed—all threat of death now removed from their lives—and be blessed by the fairies in their sexual/spiritual unions. In *Romeo and Juliet,* Shakespeare told it for real; in *A Midsummer Night's Dream,* he told it for joy.

The key to the difference in outcomes—real death in *Romeo and Juliet;* pretend death, sexual consummation, and new life in *A Midsummer Night's Dream*—rests on the ability to change the laws and institutional structures that sanction killing women who disobey. Plus a bit of magic.

When I look at women who are stoned to death under Sharia law, or burned to death under encrusted Hindu custom, or killed by their fathers or brothers because they have "shamed their honor," I can see how universal and ingrained the desire to control women's sexuality is! In the West we are being exploited in a different way. We are bombarded with images to manipulate women into conforming to an idea of female sexuality almost impossible to obtain—and that in turn leads to various psychological disorders!

Shakespeare was writing about love fast and furious, and not only in the plays: he was probably writing the last section of the sonnets, too. Love, far more than war, was occupying his mind and talents.

The next play Shakespeare wrote is *The Merchant of Venice,* a comedy that reveals more uncomfortable aspects of human nature. It's the second play Shakespeare wrote in which the women disguise themselves as men to get something done. Ostensibly, it's a comedy, but its racism and sexism leave an odd taste in the mouth. Still, it can be very powerful, as several recent productions have shown.

Merchant is a play I stayed away from for years, until I felt I really understood it. And then directing it was one of the most satisfying experiences of my life.

Money, the worth of metals, and the power of the father constrain the women in *Merchant of Venice*. It's a play whose symbolism and structure follow various esoteric forms and numbers—a pattern then obliterated by the power of Shylock's character, the outsider, the Jew. The play is ostensibly named after Antonio, the wealthy homosexual patron of Bassanio. But commodity comes into everyone's lives—and in the end it is hard to tell "which is the merchant here, and which the Jew?"

Among the women, Portia is the daughter of an extremely rich, dead man, who controls his daughter and her inherited fortune from the grave. She cannot marry unless one of her suitors answers the riddle of the three caskets made of gold, silver, and lead. If a suitor chooses correctly, she must marry. If he loses, he can never marry, and Portia awaits the next contender.

Nerissa, Portia's lady-in-waiting, is dependent upon her mistress for her livelihood—so, when Portia marries, Nerissa swiftly marries the best friend of Portia's husband, thereby staying in the same economic sphere.

Jessica, Shylock's daughter, is locked up each night by her father. She steals his money, and elopes with a Christian.

Portia's intelligence and courage are palpable. We don't know how long her father has been dead, but he must have known his daughter had a keen brain, capable not only of making her own decisions but also of constructing authoritative statements in a court of law. If he did know, he didn't care—he still "protects" her from unsuitable suitors. The contrast between the Portia who has to sit around at home (Belmont—the Beautiful Mountain—a Shangri-la where she lives in the imagination of men), waiting for a next suitor to come from some far part of the world, and the Portia who disguises herself as a lawyer and strides into the Venetian courtroom could not be more extreme. At home she talks wittily about nothing. In the law court she picks her way through a complicated lawsuit and finds the loophole to rescue her new husband's patron. She discovers things about herself, her husband, her marriage vows, the laws of Venice, the fate of Jews, and the process of being Christianized when she is disguised as a man. When she's dressed in her frock, she learns little. True, she gives herself to Bassanio, her husband-to-be, in a very genuine speech, handing over her worldly goods to him, but if the crisis about Antonio's loss of fortune and imminent death had not intruded, she would be living a dull, predictable life in her Beautiful Mountain.

Nerissa dresses as a man, too, law clerk to Portia's lawyer. In court she discovers what a racist loudmouth her husband is. In my production, I made Nerissa a Marrano (a Jew disguised as a Christian) to emphasize the predicament Jews found themselves in—which made this marriage even more complex, even more in need of forgiveness. Finally, Jessica disguises herself as a man to run away from her father. She not only steals his money, but spends it thoughtlessly, giving her father's turquoise ring from his wife (presumably Jessica's mother) for a monkey.

She converts to Christianity, again thoughtlessly. She and Lorenzo discuss lovers who have stayed true and lovers who have betrayed each other (including Troilus and Cressida and Pyramus and Thisbe) as they listen to music and seek to hear the harmony of the spheres.

The women do not know themselves. They are at the beginning of the journey of their lives. The men break their vows (they give away rings the women give them, having sworn never to take them off their fingers unless their love fails—which clearly it does at some level). Ostensibly, the play ends happily—except not really. We cannot forget Shylock's forced conversion at the end of Act 4; or Antonio's sadness at not dying for the man he loves; or the suspicion between Christians and Jews, centered on the crucifixion of Christ, but now exploited in monetary exchanges, pogroms, and the execution of individuals like Dr. López, Elizabeth's physician, accused of poisoning her, a year before *Merchant of Venice* was written. It is a disturbing play. But because it is set in Venice, where many people of many faiths found ways to write laws, trade, worship, create buildings of unbelievable beauty, there is an undercurrent of hope—this multicultural, vibrant, artistic city is never still, and it might, as its people rub up against one another, find a way to toleration and growth.

Even for the women, if they can leave the mountain and get into the streets.

SCENE 5: Benedick's Choice—Beatrice

And so we come to *Much Ado About Nothing*. It's a good title. Nothing; no thing; a "thing" in Elizabethan English is a penis, so "no thing" is a vagina. Much Ado About a Vagina—presumably Hero's, as the plot hinges around her virginity. "Nothing" also means "noting" (as in, noting what other people do), and a lot of noting goes on in this play—Claudio and Don Pedro spying on someone they think is Hero *in flagrante delicto*. On the comic side, the men expound on Beatrice's passion for Benedick, making sure he is overhearing them; likewise, the women talk about Benedick's love for Beatrice when Beatrice is "noting" them.

At the beginning of *Much Ado,* a visiting army—led by a Spaniard, Don Pedro—is coming to stay in Messina. They have been fighting nearby (not quite clear for whom—but Italy was full of mercenary armies, and skirmishes between city-states were common). There is much rejoicing, especially among the young women, because it means there will be a lot of men in the town. Leonato's household seems to be composed almost entirely of young and not-so-young unmarried women. Leonato, the governor of Messina, invites the officers to stay with him. Hero, Leonato's daughter and sole child, a virgin and inheritor of his fortune, is attracted to Claudio, a young officer. Claudio is likewise interested.

With Claudio and Hero, Shakespeare gives us a portrait of a well-arranged courtship and betrothal of two young people. They are attracted to each other. Claudio makes sure that she's rich and that Leonato is not planning to leave his money to anyone else. Don Pedro negotiates on Claudio's behalf, as suggested by the rules of courtly love, being a stand-in wooer for Claudio at the masked ball—thereby testing the girl's virtue and suitability.

In the meantime, Shakespeare is drawing another picture of an attraction between two lovers. They are older; they have been around the block a few times. They are Benedick (the good dick) and Beatrice (as in Dante's Beatrice—but a woman who is in flesh and blood, not so young—*not* an eight-year-old who remains an abstract inspiration for a lifetime). Their names also mean "benediction" and "the blessed." Beatrice and Benedick seem to have been lovers in the past, but now challenge each other only with words. Indeed, Benedick swears he'll never marry—though clearly he's a womanizer—and Beatrice seems to be of the same mind, though she keenly supports her young cousin Hero's marriage.

In any case, the first exchange between Beatrice and Benedick, witty though it is, allows the audience to know how powerful is the attraction between them, and leaves each lightly wounded.

The play follows the progression of our two more conventional lovers, the negotiations between the parties, and the preparations for the masked ball. At this ball, through the good services of Don Pedro, the young couple are betrothed (with a little hiccup here and there); Beatrice and Benedick manage to dance with each other, masked, and in this disguise she tells him what an idiot Benedick is and how no one respects him.

The play begins to darken and lighten. On the light side, the men persuade Benedick that Beatrice is in love with him, and to save her life, he decides to open his heart and allow himself to love her. Similarly, the women let it be known to Beatrice that Benedick is madly in love with her—and she finally admits to herself she's overwhelmingly in love with him. On the dark side, Don John, bastard half-brother to Don Pedro, determines to undermine the proposed marriage between Hero and Claudio—for no other reason than that he'll enjoy manipulating everyone into pain and loathing, rather than joy and celebration. So he arranges for Claudio to watch in the orchard two people making love on the balcony. (Shakespeare liked repeating his plots in different ways—though the repetitions may have had more to do with the fixed nature of the playhouse and what was possible to enact. If you had seen *Romeo and Juliet* recently, then, as an audience member, you would be bound to compare the absolutely sexual/spiritual ecstasy of that scene with the ludicrous "humpings" of a pretend Hero making love with a pretend unknown lover.) The charade works! It's enough for Claudio. His wounded pride and cuckolded spirit lead him to plan a public and irretrievable condemnation of

Hero. The marriage goes forward, and when the priest asks first Hero and then Claudio if there is any reason why this marriage should not take place, he exposes her "infidelity" in front of the congregation, Leonato, Don Pedro, and everyone in the town. "There, Leonato, take her back again. / Give not this rotten orange to your friend." Then he leaves, taking Don Pedro with him.

Benedick does not go with them—which is unusual, because one of his fellow officers has been humiliated, and the honorable action would be to join him. Leonato, for his part, believes the officers, and not his daughter. He wants her dead.

> BENEDICK How doth the lady?
> BEATRICE Dead, I think. Help, uncle.
>   Hero, why Hero! Uncle, Signor Benedick, Friar—
> LEONATO O fate, take not away thy heavy hand.
>   Death is the fairest cover for her shame
>   That may be wished for.
>   MUCH ADO ABOUT NOTHING (4.1, 111–16)

(The fathers who want their daughters dead in Shakespeare's plays are thick on the ground: Capulet, Egeus, Leonato, Lear, Cymbeline, Leontes, to name a few.)

Through the intervention of Friar Francis and Benedick, Leonato is calmed down and forced to think about Hero's predicament. She may be telling the truth. They will say that she is dead. She will retire to a nunnery, where she will spend the rest of her days if they do not find the reason for Claudio's accusations. Everyone leaves the church except Beatrice. She weeps at the altar in shame, rage, and helplessness about being a woman.

Benedick returns. This is the key scene of the play, and really shows Shakespeare's sensitivity to the predicament of women. As a man of real honor, Benedick will use his superior place in society to rectify this injustice; and if he truly loves, he will love the whole of her, with no caveats.

Benedick approaches the weeping Beatrice—"Lady Beatrice, have you wept all this while?"

"Yea, and I will weep a while longer."

"I will not desire that."

"You have no reason. I do it freely."

"I do love nothing in the world so well as you: is not that strange?"

So, at the time of Beatrice's greatest vulnerability, Benedick declares his love for her. And, as Nigel likes to point out, he goes first. He says he loves her *before* he knows for sure how she feels about him.

It leads her to declare her love for him—and at that moment of mutual love, he says, "Come, bid me do anything for thee."

"Kill Claudio" is the answer.

"Ha, not for the wide world."

So, at the very joining of the love between them, Benedick pulls back. Even though he thinks Claudio is mistaken, he will not violate the officer honor by fighting his best friend.

Beatrice's reply is "You kill me to deny it." And she tries to leave. Benedick stops her. So angry is she at Claudio, she screams that she "would eat his heart in the market-place."

Then they have an exchange about the true nature of honor—and this is key. In the world they live in, Hero has no way of redeeming her name or proving she's telling the truth. She cannot challenge Claudio, nor can Beatrice. What Claudio publicly proclaims about Hero will stand, unless a man takes on the voice of the women.

Benedick asks Beatrice, "Think you in your soul the Count Claudio hath wronged Hero?"

Beatrice's reply is "Yea, as sure as I have a thought or a soul."

And Benedick says, "Enough, I am engaged."

The reason this text is so important is, first, he knows that Beatrice has a soul (a truth still not universally accepted, as we discussed before) and, second, he takes Beatrice's thought as the thought that should guide him. He violates the honor between officers, choosing instead to follow his love. Love is the higher calling.

Of course, because it is a comedy, it all gets sorted out in the end, and no one has to die. When Hero's innocence is revealed, Claudio must go through public penance and a cleansing ritual. The young lovers are restored to each other. Whether the trials of their courtship will lead to a stronger marriage, Shakespeare leaves unsaid.

With *Much Ado About Nothing,* Shakespeare lines up Benedick's loyalty to the army, the men he fights alongside, and their male world, and, on the other side, his love for Beatrice and the world she is forced to live in as a woman. And he shows they are not compatible. Benedick has to choose.

Toward the end of the play, Benedick swears to Beatrice, "I will live in thy heart, die in thy lap, and be buried in thy eyes"—the heart being the place of love, dying being orgasm, eyes being the passage to the soul. So I think we can say that this marriage will last: both Beatrice and Benedick understand the ways of the world, and they put their love for each other into the enduring terrain of an ever-regenerative sexual/spiritual merging.

AN INTERLUDE: Dealing with Loss—
Lamentation Versus Honor

I have been subtitling the play version of *Women of Will* "Following the Feminine in Shakespeare's Plays." And if I categorize "the feminine" and "the masculine," the next few plays provide the clearest examples of the differences. Shakespeare reporting on "the masculine" stands in direct contrast to his exploration of "the feminine" in *Richard III, Henry IV Parts 1* and *2, King John,* and *Henry V.*

For two thousand years the definitions of feminine and masculine have been:

The feminine: Those qualities in a human being which have to do with feeling, valuing feeling more than the logical sense. The feminine is associated with the body, holding relationship to be of primary importance, willing to trust intuition and make decisions on intuition alone. Soft, tender, a gentle voice. Tends toward associative thinking.

The masculine: Goal-oriented, looking for abstract or logical reasons to go into action, challenging the body to obey the dictates of the mind, being careless of collateral damage when going for the top prize. Tough, independent, loving idea of justice. Tends toward linear thinking.

I would say these qualities are propelled by cultural rather than biological impulses—though they may have had their origins in biology.

It is considered honorable, "right," for a woman to have feminine qualities, a man to have masculine. Men and women who practice actions usually associated with the other sex are not respected; they may be silenced, vilified, called "unnatural." Margaret, when she captures, taunts, and beheads York on the battlefield, is unnatural because she is a woman; had she been a man, her behavior would be considered "valiant." Lady Macbeth has to unsex herself to do violent deeds. Henry VI is considered "womanish" because he won't fight. Albany is a "milk-livered man" because he won't take up arms against the invading French who have come to rescue Lear. And so on.

Let us briefly look at these five plays mentioned above, the words and actions Shakespeare gives to the two genders, the effectiveness of those words and actions, and then the actual events that happened in Shakespeare's life and what, if anything, the correlation might be.

In 1596, Shakespeare's son, Hamnet, died. Shakespeare wrote *King John* that year, a play immersed in the politics of power, in the midst of which a young son dies: Arthur, aged around eleven, the same age as Hamnet.

The grief expressed by Constance, Arthur's mother, is extreme: she tears her hair, lacerates her skin, hallucinates his presence, sees him in heaven, and excoriates the Cardinal for lack of understanding. Eventually, she disappears; her death is reported almost casually some two scenes later. She died "in a frenzy," but, says the messenger, it might be just a rumor. Having dominated the play for three and a half acts, she dribbles away, an inconsequential death.

Shakespeare's concentration on the manner of Constance's grief, making it one of the two most powerful scenes in the play (the other being the young Arthur persuading Hubert *not* to burn out his eyes), the articulation of her loss, the depth of her pain, must be a reflection of Shakespeare's own state. Perhaps he could say through Constance what would be "unmanly" for him to say in life. To lose a child is unimaginable; the helplessness of that grief must be articulated:

> Give sorrow words. The grief that does not speak
> Whispers the o'erfraught heart and bids it break . . .
>
> MACBETH (4.3, 240–41)

says Malcolm to Macduff on the loss of his son in *Macbeth,* written nearly a decade later.

The method Constance uses to express her grief belongs to the thousands-of-years-old rites of lamentation. Although banned at various times by various leaders, it remains the ritual of the people living in the countryside, folk who follow the old ways. Shakespeare would know it from two places: Greek plays and his Celtic neighbors.

So, slotted between the early plays on sexual/spiritual love and the slightly later *Much Ado* and *As You Like It,* come these four plays containing both lamentation (the expression of women's grief) and the expression of love between warriors, as well as the eulogy—"the noble death." They are in direct contrast to each other.

Death and birth were once the two life events in which women experienced power. Birth as an event still does belong to women, although with the advent of primogeniture the necessity of having a son (as Henry VIII's wives found out) took precedence over all other facets of birth—labor, health, joy, status—as the new soul came into the world. Death, when the soul leaves this world and goes to the next, no longer belongs to women—except in the rites of lamentation.

Lamentation evolved out of the stories about the dead and the place we believed souls went after death. When someone died, in most parts of the world—but certainly in Greece and the European civilizations that came after—the poets, usually women, sang long lamentation poems, remembering all the good deeds of the dead person, all the bad, and those in between. They also expressed the feelings of those that had been left behind, including cursing those who killed the person, if that was the way death occurred.

Nothing was left out, because the whole point was to say everything; otherwise, catharsis would not take place. And catharsis was the point. These stories would go on for days, with a great deal of wailing, hair tearing, thymus thumping, nails scratching the skin. The notes in the voice tapped into the place where grief was held (as great composers do), shaking loose the feeling held there. The dead body would be taken on a journey and set down at a crossroads or in a public place, so other people could join in the anguish of the death and the celebration of the life. The sound of the poets' voices had a function: it was carrying the soul from this world into the next. The living were helping the dead in their journey. The mourners knew the soul had completed its journey and reached the other world because they could feel in their bodies that it was done: there was nothing left to say, no more weeping; every story had been told, every possible hurt had been expressed, every joy had been re-created; the body and mind had been drained of all emotion. Catharsis had taken place.

This is what Anne is trying to do with Henry VI's body at the beginning of *Richard III*—she's lamenting his death in a public place.

She's putting the body down so others can join with her to mark his passing and tell their stories of his life. However, there's a problem: it's an act of insurrection against the new king Edward, on behalf of the deposed king Henry. Richard uses the frenzy of her emotion to manipulate her responses to him. When she is completely exhausted, he moves in on her. She has no will to resist.

Elizabeth, on hearing of Edward's death, enters "with her hair about her ears" and begins her lamentation for her husband's death. She's joined by the Duchess of York and Clarence's children—and they add Clarence's death to the lamentation. Elizabeth's son Dorset stops her by saying God is much displeased that she receives His doings with so little gratitude. Rivers, her brother, says she must act, and get the young heir crowned. And in that exchange you see the difference between the expression of grief as a rite, and the will of God as a belief. In *King John*, Constance turns on the Cardinal when he calls her lamentation "madness, and not sorrow":

> Thou art not holy to belie me so.
> I am not mad: this hair I tear is mine; . . .
>
> KING JOHN (3.3, 45–46)

One action is deeply "feminine," felt in the body, an expression of relationship. The other is "masculine": ignore the body and the emotion, and go to the goal—crowning, the next political move!

The rite of lamentation was banned at various times over the two thousand years during which it was practiced (and is still practiced in some parts of the world). In Shakespeare's time, Elizabeth I banned it because she thought the rite was too "Catholic." The Greeks banned it around 400 B.C. because it was antithetical to raising an army to fight for "Athens." (This happened as people were gathering into towns, a hundred families becoming "Athens" or "Thebes.") Greek military leaders needed to tell a story that *didn't* tell the whole truth but could instead weave together stories about the slain men as heroes. It needed to be a story about giving up your life to a greater good. When "Athens" became an idea, as well as a city-state, they needed all male citizens of a certain age to fight on its behalf. As Athens organized itself into a coherent community—regulating the women's role to run the household and bring up the children—the men were creating the legal system, the religious institutions, the academy, the gymnasium, and the army. Sexuality between men was idealized, because their sexuality (the pleasurable kind, versus the procreation kind with women) could be used to encourage certain kinds of behavior—fight to the death for your beloved, for instance. The battles needed to be heroic; the men often fought in pairs with their younger lovers, or their lovers would hear of the daring exploits and rate their "virtue." You didn't want some poet to say, "Well, he got terrified, turned around, and ran away, then got stabbed in the back and lay there for the next four hours screaming for his mother." Truth about how human beings behaved in battle might not coincide with how you wanted men to behave in battle. Therefore, the story must be told to inspire the troops, not create catharsis. I have told this story in a simplified form. There were many facets to banning lamentation—the distribution of property away from the tribe and toward the family and primogeniture, the deliberate encouragement of the hero story, the suppression of women's voices generally. Gail Holst-Warhaft, among many others, tells the story powerfully in *Dangerous Voices*.

In the fifth and fourth centuries B.C., the idea of "spin" was born. Heroes do not run away. Heroes face death. Heroes are prepared to sacrifice life itself, to uphold the idea of the state. Whether it be Athens, or Germany, or America, the name of our country embodies all the things we believe to be good. And women bravely offer up their sons and husbands in duty to the country.

"Your son, my lord, has paid a soldier's debt. He only lived but till he was a man . . ." Ross tells Old Siward in *Macbeth*. "Had he his hurts before?" Siward asks. "Ay, on the front" replies Ross. Siward responds:

> Why then, God's soldier be he.
> Had I as many sons as I have hairs
> I would not wish them to a fairer death;
> And so his knell is knolled.
>
> MACBETH (5.7, 89–92)

The funeral of Philip Sidney was glorious because he gave up his life willingly, in the cause of his country. Shakespeare must have been studying the Earl of Essex and the Earl of Southampton, who had positioned themselves as the heroic warriors of the Elizabethan age. But he also saw a very different picture of death through the women's eyes.

The idea of honor in battle has been passed down for generations. It went from Greece, to Rome, to the medieval world and the Crusades. It was beloved of Sir Philip Sidney, Essex and Southampton, Richard Coeur de Lion and Philip the Bastard, Hotspur, Henry V, Coriolanus. In many ways, the British Empire was founded on it—and it certainly inspires the Navy SEALs and the Green Berets. The idea came to a halt in the First World War, when the slaughter was so great, carnage so mundane, and no one knew why they were fighting. The poets, led by Wilfred Owen and Siegfried Sassoon, told the truth about what was really happening. Wilfred Owen's poem says it all:

DULCE ET DECORUM EST

Bent double, like old beggars under sacks,
Knock-kneed, coughing like hags, we cursed through sludge,
Till on the haunting flares we turned our backs,
And towards our distant rest began to trudge.
Men marched asleep. Many had lost their boots,
But limped on, blood-shod. All went lame; all blind;
Drunk with fatigue; deaf even to the hoots
Of gas-shells, dropping softly behind.

Gas! GAS! Quick boys!—An ecstasy of fumbling
Fitting the clumsy helmets just in time,
But someone still was yelling out and stumbling
And flound'ring like a man in fire or lime—
Dim, through the misty panes and thick green light,
As under a green sea, I saw him drowning.

In all my dreams, before my helpless sight,
He plunges at me, guttering, choking, drowning.

If in some smothering dreams, you too could pace
Behind the wagon that we flung him in,

And watch the white eyes writhing in his face,
His hanging face, like a devil's sick of sin;
If you could hear, at every jolt, the blood
Come gargling from the froth-corrupted lungs
Obscene as cancer, bitten as the cud
Of vile, incurable sores on innocent tongues—
My friend, you would not tell with such high zest
To children, ardent for some desperate glory,
The old Lie: *Dulce et decorum est*
Pro patria mori.

The First World War poets, like Shakespeare, wanted to tell the truth about battle—yet also wanted to understand why men so loved it and women encouraged them to go!

What happens when the grab for power happens *within* the country? A Pinochet, or the Russian Communist Party, or Richard of Gloucester as he knocks off contender after contender—the young princes, his brother Clarence, Hastings, Vaughan, Grey, his former ally Buckingham; his wife, Anne. The result is usually civil war of one kind or another. But England in the *Richard III* play is sick of civil war. It hasn't solved anything. Some men flee to the Earl of Richmond in Brittany and prepare to be part of an invasion. But at home the only people who oppose Richard overtly are the women. And they do it through lamentation: first Anne taking the body of Henry VI through the streets of London; then Richard's mother, the Duchess of York, the Queen Mother, Elizabeth, and Lady Anne going to visit the two princes in the Tower. Though the Duchess of York and Elizabeth are deeply opposed to Richard, they wish Anne no harm to herself as she goes to be crowned. Finally, the two Yorkist women, and the surviving Lancastrian women, come together to lament and recite the violence of the past. Margaret (yes, Margaret of Anjou, wife to Henry VI, living like a bag lady in the portals of the castle), the Duchess of York, and Queen Elizabeth go through the litany of who killed whom, going back over the deaths, trying to find the release of catharsis. By this time, it is clear that it is not just Richard who is to blame, though he is the final horrendous manifestation; it's the whole system and everyone involved, action after action driving the two sides to kill each other and decimate the kingdom. All under the rubric of honor and primogeniture.

> MARGARET If ancient sorrow be most reverend,
>   Give mine the benefit of seniory. . . .
>   If sorrow can admit society,
>   I had an Edward, till a Richard killed him;
>   I had a husband, till a Richard killed him.
>   Thou hadst an Edward, till a Richard killed him;
>   Thou hadst a Richard, till a Richard killed him.
> DUCHESS OF YORK I had a Richard too, and thou didst kill
>   him;
>   I had a Rutland too, thou holpst to kill him. . . .
> MARGARET From forth the kennel of thy womb hath crept
>   A hell-hound that doth hunt us all to death. . . .
>   RICHARD III (4.4, 35–36, 38–44, 46–47)

We find it so difficult to listen to those women in *Richard III*—the scenes are often cut to shreds. "Too much emotion," we say. "They keep on going on about what happened. We *know* what happened. Let's get on with the action." In one production I did, I decided I was going to go for the full lamentation: hair tearing, chest beating, cries going up to heaven. It was powerful and unbearable. It certainly showed that the women were an opposition to Richard—their efforts were not to be dismissed (as they usually are)—but it was excruciating to listen to. We have no emotional stamina anymore, so it's hard for us to hear deep grief and not try to stop it. But the women in *Richard III* are precursors of more modern women who have banded together to stop war. I have mentioned the Mothers of the Plaza de Mayo in Argentina; but there are also the Russian mothers of soldiers in Afghanistan a decade before America invaded that country; the women of Greenham Common who camped out at the nuclear-weapons base in Berkshire, England, in 1981, protesting cruise missles; even the actions of Lysistrata and her women in the play of that name. In the last production I did of *Richard III*, Nigel played Richard. He crawled into his mother's lap like a three-year-old, desperate for love before he went into battle. Anne Sandoe, who was playing the Duchess of York, cradled him as if he were her baby again, as she told him she hoped the other side would win, and "Bloody thou art, bloody will be thy end: Shame serves thy life and doth thy death attend." It was profoundly moving—she loves him and he must die!

I think the reason we cannot bear lamentation now (or any excessive emotion) is that we survive by cutting ourselves off from ourselves. We do not experience what we are saying when we are saying it (as Elizabethans did). We are fed news round the clock, nearly all of it violent. We don't watch children playing, we watch men killing—to feel it too would drive us mad. Yet feeling it is what the women do in *Richard III* and *King John;* and what both men and women do in lamentation rites. Babies feel and express exactly what they are feeling. But after that we train ourselves *not* to feel, and if the body cannot feel and let go of deep grief, what does it become? Without catharsis, does suppressed emotion change into neurosis, which works its poison in our psyches? In *Richard III* there is much lamentation and very little honor.

But *Henry IV Part 1* is a play with much "honor." Honor is its central theme. So let's examine *Henry IV Part 1* for a moment, to understand the ingredients of "honor."

"What is honor?" "How do you get it?" and "What good does it do?"

You will notice there are not many women in these plays—and when they appear, they are usually whores or faithful wives. Honor is not a woman's story.

At the top of the play, there are two young men—Hal, the King's son, and Hotspur, the son of the Earl of Northumberland. Hotspur cares only about honor, winning honor in battle.

> Send danger from the east unto the west,
> So honour cross it from the north to south. . . .
> By heaven, methinks it were an easy leap
> To pluck bright honour from the pale-faced moon, . . .
> HENRY IV PART I (1.3, 198–99, 204–05)

Hal, on the other hand, is a very troubled young man—he drinks, whores, and steals, and his father is both desperately worried about him and ashamed of him. Hal has a best friend, Falstaff, a man fat from eating and drinking, but very funny; he loves his friends, having a good time–(very "feminine" you could say) and he doesn't have much time for honor. Because he's a knight he's supposed to gather soldiers to fight on behalf of the king. This is what he says directly to the audience, when he knows he must fight in the wars.

> Well, 'tis no matter; honour pricks me on. Yea, but how if honour prick me off when I come on? How then? Can honour set-to a leg? No. Or an arm? No. Or take away the grief of a wound? No. Honour hath no skill in surgery, then? No. What is honour? A word. What is in that word "honour"? What is that "honour"? Air. A trim reckoning! Who hath it? He that died o'Wednesday. Doth he feel it? No. Doth he hear it? No. 'Tis insensible, then? Yea, to the dead. But will it not live with the living? No. Why? Detraction will not suffer it. Therefore I'll none of it. Honour is a mere scutcheon. And so ends my catechism.
>
> HENRY IV PART I (5.1, 129–36)

Now, if Falstaff is talking directly to the working people standing in the pit at the Globe and they answer his questions as if in a catechism (which Jonny Epstein did brilliantly when he played Falstaff), you can see that, *finally*, they have a voice speaking on their behalf. Because, if the ordinary people come home with a limb lost or a face blown up, there isn't any VA hospital or hero's pension for them–they are likely to starve on the streets.

Eventually, Hal's father, Henry IV, is able to shame his son into fighting Hotspur–basically, by telling him he wishes Hotspur was his son.

> Now, by my sceptre, and my soul to boot,
> He *[Hotspur]* hath more worthy interest to the state
> Than thou, the shadow of succession;
> For, of no right, nor colour like to right,
> He doth fill fields with harness *[armor]* in the realm,
> Turns head against the lion's armèd jaws,
> And, being no more in debt to years than thou,

> Leads ancient lords and reverend bishops on
> To bloody battles, and to bruising arms.
> What never-dying honour hath he got. . . .
>
> HENRY IV PART I (3.2, 98–107)

Self-interest, desire for his father's approval, and desire to be a manly man finally shift Hal into being a soldier instead of a layabout.

Hal fights Hotspur and kills him. He learns the ecstatic state of battle. The scene is almost a love scene—because, by killing Hotspur, Hal is able to redeem himself in his father's eyes and inherit all those honors Hotspur (Percy) has accrued.

HOTSPUR
> O Harry, thou hast robbed me of my youth.
> I better brook the loss of brittle life
> Than those proud titles thou has won of me.
>
> HENRY IV PART I (5.3, 78–80)

Thus, death is preferable to handing over his honors.

HOTSPUR They wound my thoughts worse than thy sword
> my flesh.
> But thought's the slave of life, and life, time's fool;
> And time, that takes survey of all the world,
> Must have a stop. O, I could prophesy,
> But that the earthy and cold hand of death
> Lies on my tongue. No, Percy, thou art dust,
> And food for—
PRINCE HARRY For worms, brave Percy. Fare thee well, great
> heart.
> Ill-weaved ambition, how much art thou shrunk!
> When that this body did contain a spirit,
> A kingdom for it was too small a bound,
> But now two paces of the vilest earth
> Is room enough. This earth that bears thee dead
> Bears not alive so stout a gentleman . . .
> Adieu, and take thy praise with thee to heaven.

Thy ignominy sleep with thee in the grave,
But not remembered in thy epitaph.

HENRY IV PART I (5.3, 81–94, 100–02)

The eulogy has replaced lamentation.

And that's where *Henry IV Part 1* ends. We go into *Part 2*. Shakespeare is studying government and what is right for a king to do. (Can he promise his enemies terms sufficient so that they will lay down their arms; then, once they've done that, can he go against his word and execute them? Not much "honor" there—but by this time Machiavelli's *The Prince* is as widely read as Castiglione's *The Courtier*.) However, Hotspur's wife takes up the theme of her dead spouse's honor. She says his honor

. . . stuck upon him as the sun
In the grey vault of heaven, and by his light
Did all the chivalry of England move
To do brave acts. He was indeed the glass
Wherein the noble youth did dress themselves. . . .
He was the mark and glass, copy and book,
That fashioned others. And him—O wondrous him!
O miracle of men!

HENRY IV PART 2 (2.3, 18–22, 31–33)

But she is invoking his honor to prevent her father-in-law from going to war again. He deserted his son in battle before Hotspur got killed; he should not go into battle now. "For God's sake, go not to these wars."

At the end of *Henry IV Part 2,* there is a big scene between blood father and son. Hal thinks his father is dead; he takes the crown and puts it on his head. His father wakes up, and they have a horrible scene of recrimination. Again Hal is shamed, and the only way he can get his father's love and respect back is by swearing to put down all enemies and unite the land (there are mini–civil wars everywhere), and by finding an outside enemy (in this case, yet once again, France) and returning to England triumphant, the universal idea of greatness through conquest!

Of course, there is one person who cannot be allowed to distract, and that is Falstaff. Falstaff's iconoclasm and truthful vision about honor and hierarchy and money cannot live alongside this spiritual but cynical idea of honor.

Falstaff is rejected publicly (very important, that—so all can see Hal is "not the man he was").

> I know thee not, old man. . . .
> Presume not that I am the thing I was,
> For God doth know, so shall the world perceive,
> That I have turned away my former self.
>
> HENRY IV PART 2 (5.5, 41, 50–52)

And as we go into *Henry V,* the first thing we learn about is Falstaff's death. A little later, Henry V puts a few more of his old mates to death. He threatens Harfleur into submission.

> I will not leave the half-achieved Harfleur
> Till in her ashes she lie burièd.
> The gates of mercy shall be all shut up,
> And the fleshed soldier, rough and hard of heart,
> In liberty of bloody hand shall range
> With conscience wide as hell, mowing like grass
> Your fresh fair virgins and your flow'ring infants. . . .
>   . . . Therefore, you men of Harfleur,
> Take pity of your town and of your people
> Whiles yet my soldiers are in my command,
> Whiles yet the cool and temperate wind of grace
> O'erblows the filthy and contagious clouds
> Of heady murder, spoil, and villainy.
> If not, why, in a moment look to see
> The blind and bloody soldier with foul hand
> Defile the locks of your shrill-shrieking daughters;
> Your fathers taken by the silver beards,
> And their most reverend heads dashed to the walls;
> Your naked infants spitted upon pikes,
> Whiles the mad mothers with their howls confused

Do break the clouds. . . .
What say you? Will you yield, and this avoid?
Or, guilty in defence, be thus destroyed.

HENRY V (3.3, 8–14, 27–40, 42–43)

Of course, they yield. You'd think after that Henry would declare victory, call it a day, and go home. But he doesn't. He marches inland. Then comes the Battle of Agincourt:

We few, we happy few, we band of brothers.
For he today that sheds his blood with me
Shall be my brother. . . .

HENRY V (4.3, 62–64)

These words are profoundly moving. They have been the clarion call for England in every war that has followed since. And once England has won against all odds (though the ordinary English soldier who dies is part of "five hundred of no name"), the King marries the French princess, in order to make nice, and all things seem triumphant. So, to put it crudely, we got a whore at the beginning of the play describing Falstaff's death, and a trophy wife at the end. Oh yes, and French Queen Isabel joins the negotiations. "Haply a woman's voice may do some good."

Shakespeare does add a little epilogue pointing out that Henry V died shortly thereafter, France was lost—and, of course, England plunged into civil wars, those of the *Henry VI* plays that we have already dealt with. And there is very little honor anywhere to be seen in the *Henry VI* plays, after the death of John Talbot!

There are several things we can see in all this. The first is that war is a man's game, it is intolerable, and the only way you can get people to do it is to make the alternative seem a hundred times worse—that, if you are a captive in war, you will have no "self" left. Therefore, valor must be glorified, if not deified. It must look as if you are doing it to protect loved ones (and you may well be, because by and large the opposite side will be telling the same story to their armies, and your infants, reverend fathers, and daughters are likely to be slaughtered if you lose). But in order to kill, men must be trained to kill. As Lieutenant Colonel David Grossman points out in *On Killing*, the majority of men will not kill, not even in war. They have to be taught. They have to turn from empathetic creatures to berserkers—people who go toward danger, not away from it. Stephan Wolfert carefully maps this out in his one-man play *Cry Havoc*, his own story of a veteran who found insight and a form of peace through Shakespeare's warriors.

In *King John*, Shakespeare puts the idea of honor and the expression of lamentation right alongside each other. I find *King John* a riveting play. I don't understand why it's not done more often—it's true, Act 5 drops off a bit, but before then it's electrifying. The long lamentations of grief are expressed by Constance for Arthur, her son, same age as Hamnet, Shakespeare's son, when he died. This seems far more personal to Shakespeare's own life than Hotspur's desire for honor. Shakespeare must be writing about himself through Constance's stages of grief, her lack of belief in an afterworld where they'll meet again, and her rage at the Cardinal who tells her she is too fond of grief.

> Thou art not holy to belie me so.
> I am not mad: this hair I tear is mine;
> My name is Constance; I was Geoffrey's wife;
> Young Arthur is my son; and he is lost.
>
> KING JOHN (3.3, 45–48)

Shakespeare didn't have a battle he could fight in and be "valiant" (and so subvert his grief). He had a playhouse, and in *King John* none of the English nobles are valiant. Lewis, the French Dauphin, plays at valor, but it's of little avail, and he gets washed up on the sands. The bastard who at the beginning of the play cynically extols the virtues of "Commodity" is the *only* person holding the kingdom together by the end. He is truly honorable. And where does he get his sense of honor from? Well, it turns out he's the bastard son of Richard the Lionheart, so he beats the Duke of Austria (who was responsible for his father's death), takes back his father's lion skin, wears it, and becomes the embodiment of bravery in battle and fearless courage.

He inherits the idea of honor and courage through the story of his father—and with it the tales of his valor. The fact that in life Richard was an appalling king, only set foot in England once or never, and plunged Europe into all kinds of skirmishes with "the infidel," bankrupting the country, is neither here nor there—it is the story of bravery that wins the day, inspires the Bastard, and goes down in history so today we still learn the valiant myth of Richard Coeur de Lion, hero of Hollywood movies.

So there's the reality and then there's the spin. And Shakespeare, at the earliest age, started to understand that it was the spin that endured. The spin can be created out of many strands—it can be a mix of actual heroism and later storytelling (revision after the fact); it covers shame and lack of love; it's the human mind wanting the story to be other than it is.

King John, the man who is meant to be a fearless leader, is dominated by his mother, Elinor. The Pope is a scheming villain, the French King changes sides when self-interest calls, and the Magna Carta is nowhere to be seen. John orders the killing of a child, and is ignominiously poisoned by a bunch of monks at the end of the play.

The most moving scene is between the boy Arthur and his jailer, Hubert. For some reason, John has ordered Arthur's eyes to be put out, though it makes no sense—why blind the boy before he's killed? However, it makes sense on an emotional and symbolic level. Arthur, through loving Hubert, awakens compassion in him, and Hubert then risks his own life in order not to blind or kill the child. This scene stands in sharp contrast to one earlier, when John, professing love for Hubert, gets him to agree to the murder. Arthur does die, but not by Hubert; it's an accident, when he escapes and falls from a high wall.

The women's actions in both *Richard III* and *King John* may have no direct effect on the course of the war, but they do change the way we look at death, what an honest response may be, and how they, like Wilfred Owen three hundred and twenty years later, attempt to tell it like it is. Looking at death the way it is, rather than inspiring men with the idea of honor, changes the story. The ethos of killing is automatically accepted in the *Henry VI* plays. Then the women ask: Is killing the only way to solve this? In *Richard III* Elizabeth finds an alternative. And, eventually, other women in other plays will find a way. So it is my hunch that, even at this relatively early stage in his writing, Shakespeare wanted to look at the heroic war story in a different way, and study the elements that get human beings to break out of the habitual, accepted ways of honor and violence. The women prove better at it than the men.

And none of the skills you need to acquire in order to live with other people—especially people who are not like you—have, at this time, a place in the culture. Or did not.

Here is where Elizabeth I's age differs from those that came before. Although she used the imagery, metaphors, and stories of honor as well as the next man (much of it borrowed from her father, Henry VIII), she used it to unite her country. But she didn't act upon it. Elizabeth, and especially her chief minister, Burleigh, were not particularly keen on war as a way to solve problems. Better to have diplomacy. Better to have potential marriages. Better to build a country that had an education system, which taught people how to use language to debate, persuade, and influence. Learn the universal language (Latin), but also learn five or six other languages, so you understood how other people thought. Encourage playhouses where the *big* issues could be debated. Discourage extremism of any kind—but especially extremism of religion, because once people are sure that God is on their side, there's no stopping them, especially if they don't have to do the actual fighting themselves. Mainland Europe learned this over and over again, to its great pain.

If you take away the people's drive to act on the idea of "I am right, I live in the best country in the world, God's blessing is upon us, and He doesn't like anybody else," what do you put there instead? Shakespeare was really clear about this: *love*. And for it to be real, palpable, so that you can feel it all through your body, groin, heart, and head, women have to take their equal place with men. Then perhaps the world will fill with celebration, poetry, emotional turmoil, and eventually children and new life. It is a new world order.

LIVING UNDERGROUND
OR DYING TO TELL THE TRUTH

AN INTERLUDE: Switching Genders

In Elizabethan times, only boys played women; men would play the older female roles. No women ever played women. I also want to record some of the conversations, as actors, Nige and I had about gender switching as we rehearsed and performed *Women of Will*.

Putting real women on the professional stage seemed to be unthinkable in the sixteenth century in England (which makes Shakespeare's relationship to women all the more remarkable), though it happened in France and Italy.

In medieval times, women throughout the British Isles had taken part in country revels and religious festivals. But no longer. And certainly not in the professional playhouses. Just as the grammar schools were only for boys—and the plays enacted there were with boys only—so the new playwrights wrote female parts knowing boys and men would perform them.

Boys dressed in girls' clothes bothered certain sections of society in London and drew criticism about the "encouragement of vice." However, the general public who went to the playhouses seemed to find it normal, and occasionally salacious fun.

Every actor in Shakespeare's company influenced him. It goes without saying that most of the clowns, especially William Kempe, danced to their own drummer, no matter what Shakespeare had written for them. But of the "straight" actors, let's take the most obvious example of Richard Burbage. (I think we can safely say that Burbage,

John Heminges, and Henry Condell were the players closest to Shake-speare—he left money in his will for memorial rings to be made for them, a common practice among special friends at the time.) Bur-bage played Hamlet, Othello, Richard III, Macbeth, and Lear; when Shakespeare was writing those parts, there is no way that Burbage, and everything he knew about Burbage, was not informing his creative process. They were born a few years apart, both in Stratford-on-Avon. Did they know each other as children? If the original Burbage home was in Stratford, they probably did: there were only fifteen hundred people living in Stratford, so everyone knew almost everyone. If James Burbage, Richard's father, was out on the road with the Earl of Leices-ter's Men, and his wife and children stayed in Stratford, that would increase the chances of Shakespeare's talents being recognized by the Burbages, and vice versa. Maybe both Burbage and Shakespeare were boy actors at some point. Every conversation, every book they read, every major event in their lives, they knew about each other. Bur-bage died just three years after Shakespeare, and at every performance Burbage gave, Shakespeare was right alongside him, either onstage with him or listening to him from the tiring-house. Besides being an actor, Burbage was a painter, built theatres with his father, and had probably been onstage since he was a teenager. He had an emotional range and depth second to none; his voice, strong and nuanced, was exercised for many hours each day; he could fight and dance and probably had a grammar-school education, like Shakespeare. When Burbage died, the funeral procession went on for miles, because the general populace and the aristocracy associated Hamlet with Burbage, Othello with Burbage, Lear with Burbage, far more than they associ-ated Shakespeare with those roles.

When a playwright knows the actor who will play the part in the piece he is working on, he knows the depths he can go to; he knows how the actor's voice will shake the theatre in the storm scene, knows he's capable of dying of a broken heart and then making a joke; there are two people present in the creation of the roles—the actor and the playwright. Shakespeare and Burbage knew each other for at least thirty years—and maybe the whole of their lives, fifty-two years in Shakespeare's case.

Put this up against the boy actors who played the women's parts.

The boys seem to range from thirteen to twenty. It probably depended on when each boy's voice broke and how soon his beard stubble came in. There were two kinds of boy actors.

Some of them belonged to the children's companies, either Saint Paul's or Merchant Taylors', and they acted only with other boys. The boy companies were a bit faddish—they came and they went—and the public seemed to like the idea of them, especially when they played rather sexy scenes, a bit of a turn-on. Playwrights often used these boy companies to perform plays that pushed the envelope, testing out some of their more outrageous statements, both politically and sexually. However, these companies didn't have the staying power of the adult companies, maybe because the boys grew up too fast—or their parents intervened. They were much cheaper than adult companies; a boy earned three shillings a week, whereas grown-up actors in London received up to five shillings a performance. This cost saving alone would threaten the Lord Chamberlain's Men, especially if they saw their audiences dwindling because of these kids (which is what happened to the troupe of players in *Hamlet*—they were on the road because some boy company had stolen their business). As far as we know, Shakespeare never wrote for these boy companies, as, say, Ben Jonson did.

The other kind of boy actor was one attached to a professional company. Some of the actors from the all-boy companies did end up in the grown-up companies, but most went on to live regular, more stable lives outside the theatre. Nathan Field was probably the best-known example of someone who started in a boy company, then switched and played women for several years in Shakespeare's company, later becoming a well-known adult actor performing in male parts.

Usually, the boy actors showed an early talent and were sent by their parents to join a company as apprentices. This is where it gets interesting. In order to train for a trade, it was necessary to be apprenticed to a master in that trade for around nine years. Richard Field, Shakespeare's friend from Stratford, was apprenticed as a printer to Thomas Vautrollier for nine years. At the end of that time, he was welcomed into the "brotherhood" of printers and could set up his own shop. (Field's master conveniently died, so Field married his widow and took over Vautrollier's press—a not uncommon practice.)

But there was no such thing as an acting guild. So what happened, according to John Astington in *Actors and Acting in Shakespeare's Time,* was that a boy would become apprenticed to an actor who was a member of some guild. Shakespeare's friend John Heminges, for example, who had himself been apprenticed at the age of eleven, became a member of the Grocers' Company at twenty-one, and at one point had ten apprentices all training to be actors with him—but officially they signed up as would-be grocers. Ben Jonson belonged to the Bricklayers' Guild, Robert Armin to the Goldsmiths' Guild, and the Burbages were joiners. To be a citizen of London, you had to be a member of a guild. Shakespeare lived at least twenty years in London but was never a citizen. Most apprentices at the playhouse did double duty—learned the trade of a guild and acted. It must have been a hard working life.

Add to all this that you had perhaps three days to rehearse a play, but more likely one day, and you were performing the next afternoon— and doing this several times a week, because the play changed each day. The workload and memorization load were overwhelming—to us, impossible. We like to have six weeks' rehearsal for one Shakespeare play; if we only get four, we feel hard done by! And we like to have long discussions about motivation and backstories, and it takes us forever to get a fight right.

So a young boy, working under this pressure, was going to be nimble of mind, a quick study, be naturally coordinated in mind and body, say his lines clearly, and not have a lot of life experience to draw upon. That doesn't mean he was going to be bad—it's just that the meaning of the lines he spoke would be best heard through their clarity and simplicity, allowing the text to speak for itself.

I do think it is worth thinking about Shakespeare himself as a boy actor. Some scholars think he left school early because of the decline in his father's financial position. But it could be because he was such a talented actor that he was apprenticed to a touring group at an early age. Then, when he was seventeen or eighteen, his voice broke, his beard came in, and he returned home. And then he got Anne pregnant! (There were several examples of mini-apprenticeships in the theatre: three years was probably the longest any actor could play women onstage. If Shakespeare did play women's parts, it would add to his deepening empathy for women as he got older.)

At Shakespeare & Company we run many, many school programs—and we do productions with the kids themselves performing. We gender-bend all the time—mostly, but not always, girls playing boys' parts. We work at the high-school level, in middle schools, and elementary schools. We also work with children in the justice system. And we have undergraduates who come to us. But, whatever their age, the young people who are the most successful are those who can say the lines clearly, to allow the text to take them where it wants to go. A young actor who thinks he's got to act up a storm can be painful to behold and often makes the text indecipherable. Likewise, a child who doesn't have the ability to think into her words, or doesn't really know what the words mean, loses both audience and her fellow actors. Conversely, hearing a child say "Here is my hand," and another answer "And mine, with my heart in it," clearly, strongly, and simply, is a joy to behold!

There is evidence that many of the boy actors in Shakespeare's company were strong and imaginative. But it is unlikely that any of them would have had the kind of influence on Shakespeare that Burbage had; they would be vessels for the words, rather than forces of nature who lived in Shakespeare's consciousness as he wrote the plays.

In many ways, I think this allowed Shakespeare to be freer when he was writing the women. He might not have known which boy would play the part—the boys didn't stay in the company as long as other talented members did. And even that would release Shakespeare from constraints. With luck, he would get a boy in touch with his feminine side, un-self-conscious, open to the poetry, and able to say the text clearly enough that the audience's imaginations would soar with the possibilities of meaning that resided in the words.

So, when Shakespeare was writing Cleopatra, he was thinking only of the Cleopatra in his imagination; he was allowing Lady Macbeth to unsex herself without worrying too much that she was already unsexed or had no breasts to give suck; Isabella's spiritual desire and sexual repression could be complicated and dense without wondering if the young boy playing her would understand even a hint of what she was going through. Perhaps the gender bending of Rosalind, Imogen, and Viola was fun because of the theatrical circumstances: here was a boy pretending to be a girl who then dressed up as a boy (and, in the case of Rosalind, then pretended to be a girl so Orlando would woo her). The audience—and of course there were men, women, and children in the audience, from most strata of society—found this cross-dressing exciting, but the contribution the boys offered when playing the women's parts was necessarily limited. So Shakespeare was free to have the women do exactly what he wanted them to do, or to follow them to wherever they guided him in his imagination as he wrote. And the power the women wielded in his inner landscape took him to places no playwright had been before him—places where women have been able to find themselves ever since, as many great actresses have attested.

We should also register the effect boy actors playing girls had on some members of the population. The Puritans would get into rages because of the kissing that went on among men onstage in the playhouses—not to mention the actors' dressing up in clothes that legally they weren't supposed to wear. It made many people uneasy that actors were able to swap their clothes and embody—truthfully—a king or a queen or a cardinal. Dressing as aristocracy and monarchs, when they were butchers' sons—what was the world coming to! Could rank really be just a matter of clothes?

Theatre knows about stereotyping: we dress up, swap genders, explore sexuality, adopt different personas, allowing the outside appearance to dictate one aspect of a character while finding the truth within. In *Women of Will*, I play only one man's role—Caius Martius, later named Coriolanus—but Nige plays three women—Adriana from *Comedy of Errors,* Olivia from *Twelfth Night,* and Volumnia in *Coriolanus.* Playing Olivia allows him to know things about himself he's not normally in touch with.

> I particularly like playing Olivia in *Twelfth Night*—in fact, she's probably one of my favorite roles in the canon, male or female. I love the way my body softens as I play her; an inner calm and confidence come over me; I feel I am in control. "Grounded," "feline," "legato"—these are the words I associate with her. She's heavy with grief about the deaths of her brother and father, but then she falls in love, so unexpected, and the heaviness evapo-

rates. She's been in a dormant state—and suddenly she's alive again, with a freedom she never had before. She speaks her passion so honestly. As an actor, I just love the moment I feel the feminine dropping into my body, I am miserable on those days I don't get it—then I start being self-conscious about my biceps and neck. I love the labile quality of being a woman. I like the way the cloth of my dress moves with my body. But I don't feel there's much difference between falling in love as a woman or a man—it's all harder as a man, because you're supposed to be more aggressive, and as a woman I feel as if I am opening, inviting.

As a man, I love chasing balls, kicking, dribbling, hitting, controlling, being one with the ball—but it's a physical sensation, I'm not thinking about it when I'm doing it; the pleasure is in the doing. But it's not an "inner" life. With a woman, I feel the same kind of "at one" emotion, but it's on the inside. I can feel the flow of the relationship, my attention to the other person, the moment-to-moment exchange between us, whether it is spoken or not.

Adriana, in *Comedy of Errors*, is angry because her husband isn't there a lot of the time; he's out on the street, where she can't go. She's always sitting around, waiting for him, and sitting around is so boring. Her little sister is boring, too—she knows nothing about life. Adriana is just fed up with the role of being a woman, so, once she gets a chance to go after her husband in the street, she flings herself at him—and of course that's where a lot of the comedy lies. But as Adriana, all I can feel is the tedium of being left at home, waiting, waiting, waiting. And Adriana is middle-class, whereas both Olivia and Volumnia are aristocrats—they have status.

And Volumnia has a strong sense of her own "rightness." She knows the contribution she's made to the state, and she doesn't mind whether she's at home sewing or in the street greeting people—her status is assured. And she also knows she would fight physically if she ever had to. Wounds, to her, whether psychic or physical, are to be treasured; so, whether it's the wounds her son has received, or the wings being pulled off butterflies by her grandson, or death by burning of the whole town, she can endure all that, mostly because she identifies with "Rome." It is her religion, her faith, her God—and to sacrifice for it is an honor.

When I was playing Volumnia in an all-male production, my desire to be with Caius Martius at the end of the play was overwhelming. I wanted to touch him, to smell him. It was a powerful need. There was something about his being "mine": I gave birth to him, he and I grew together, his father was never there, it was just the two of us. But even that connection I would sacrifice for "Rome" if necessary.

I, as Nigel, would hate to bring a baby to term, having watched my wife go through it twice; it's not something I want to do. But as Volumnia, I know it's what makes Caius Martius and myself one. I know the energy between us is so deeply connected he'll do what I want him to do in the end. I (Nigel) could feel my own mother doing that to me, and I hated her for it. I ran away. And whenever I gave in to her, I was full of self-loathing.

This is what I, Tina, learned about playing a man, or at least this one man—whether what I say is applicable to other men, I do not know. When I first started to take on Caius Martius, everything revolved around my mother: was she pleased with me or not, could I win status for us as a family unit, could she say she was proud to be a Roman and I was the embodiment of that? Then, of course, there was the fear that perhaps I couldn't be all the things she said I was. But as I fought the wars she sent me to, I began to find my own identity. Among men's bodies I not only felt fear, danger, anger, euphoria, but I *liked* feeling those emotions, I inhabited them, and I could feel reciprocal feeling from both fellow and enemy officers (something I never got from my mother—only approval or disapproval from her). We respected one another because we knew one another and we had the same rules. In this world, my mother was far away; here I could grow, I could excel, because I was good at it and killing the enemy was an honorable thing to do—for them and for me.

I chose a wife who said little, but would be a buffer between me and my mother. I had a son whom I left to the women to bring up—I was absent from his life, as my father had been absent from mine. My mother neither told me who my father was, nor mentioned what had happened to him. He was absent because he was not worthy of us.

When I took the town of Corioli by myself and was granted the honorific Coriolanus—thereafter being known by the name that would mark my courage, skill, and superiority—I knew I was my mother's equal, and if I remained a warrior she could never diminish me again. But both she and Rome expected me to become a consul. And that meant asking for support from others, pleasing others, especially the working people, whom I despised. It meant putting on the "gown of humility," showing the working people the wounds I had received fighting for Rome. It meant playing politics, a role I knew I didn't want to play; it meant compromise, not saying what I meant. It took away the identity I had forged ("Would you have me / False to my nature? Rather say I play the man I am"). And my mother could insert her way into my political life in a way she could never do on the battlefield.

The greatest love of my life was my greatest enemy, because twelve times we had fought body to body, in a world the two of us created, a world where the death of one or both was the end-game. It was an ultimate intimacy. We were locked in perfect symmetry; neither could overcome the other, nor would we submit to the other. So, when I left my mother and Rome, there was no question about where I was going—I was going to Aufidius and the Volsci.

Living in the complexity of Coriolanus's skin, I, Tina, learned things about men only dimly registered before: that my (Coriolanus's) passion was for my archenemy, that he was the only person in the world who knew what I knew, that we held knowledge for each other and we would never tell. Dressing up as a warrior, feeling my extraordinary strength, was my protection from the little boy who wanted protection, who felt he could get it if he could wear his mother's clothes. That is why the gown of humility that I had to put on to ask for the support of the workingmen made me feel far too vulnerable, too close to that little boy; my warrior self couldn't cover that vulnerability. I can't bear remembering those days—it's why I don't protect my son. So not only do I tear off the gown in the marketplace, but I verbally abuse the commoners, and swear I will never fight for them again. They banish me, and I banish them! But I know my physical strength will never fail me. Not only did it separate me from my mother; I was able to find my identity there, and it kept me apart from the common men, people who have to plead for food, for a voice, who spend their days scrabbling for a living. Every choice in my life can be only an extreme—because I (as Coriolanus) cannot entertain complexity. It weakens me, and if I am weak, the terrible potential of merging with my mother lurks in the background. She is absolute, and I would not exist. It even allows me to make sense of why I want to return to Rome and kill everyone in it, including my mother, my wife, and my son. Tina understood these things, and it allowed me to play Coriolanus. Coriolanus understands them only dimly. He is driven by unconscious forces far too strong—and he gives his reason for doing what he is doing under the rubric of one word, "honor."

Shakespeare not only switched genders, he played many ages, inhabited spirits and witches, killed, loved, sacrificed, knew God and the devil. No wonder he kept a relatively low profile in the world—no killing a man in a duel for him (as Ben Jonson did), or dying as a pauper (as Greene and Kyd did), or being stabbed through the eye for being a spy (as Marlowe was).

As an aside, I think (this is Tina talking now) we should listen carefully to what transgender people have to say about how the world works. They may be able to break open some of the stereotyping that has dominated our world for so long; we may be able to learn something from them about how the development of gender differences over the millennia perhaps feeds into violence and separation—how much is nature and how much is nurture? It takes courage to parade your difference to the world. And why does difference make us so uneasy?

Why are uniforms so important? We put trust in the uniform, the status, the outside. We all wear uniforms of one sort or another to advertise something to the world, trying to strengthen our perceptions of ourselves. Actors, of course, change their uniforms all the time, catching glimpses into worlds of other classes, races, sexes, dispositions, sightings of what it means to be a human being who does not look like them. "Serious" actors tend to dress down in life, looking slightly scruffy (especially the Brits), neutral, waiting to don the clothes to become the man or the woman. And as men played women's parts through the first two thousand years of theatre's history, they both perpetuated some ignorance and accumulated some knowledge about what it meant to be a woman. Shakespeare inherited that knowledge. He inherited the right to write about women—and, fortunately for us, he took it on so deeply, it would be difficult to know it was a man writing the women's roles. You would think—once he had transitioned away from projecting onto women, and become the artist embodying the women—that it was a woman writing about what it meant to be a woman, so sensitive are his insights.

SCENE 1: Overview of the Progression of the Cross-Dressers

Women dressing as men appear in other Elizabethan plays besides those of Shakespeare. And, as already discussed, men dressing as women were just part of the playhouse ethos, so the actors of Shakespeare's world were used to gender bending. And they were good actors and good storytellers—which meant that they sought to understand everyone they were presenting, take on their mantle, understand their thinking, and stand in their desires and fears.

It's fair to ask, doesn't *As You Like It* come under the heading of "The Sexual Merges with the Spiritual: New Knowledge"? (Or even the plays with Viola or Imogen?) And, of course, the answer is yes, it does, but these later works differ in several ways. The major way is that the heroine/hero has to go on a solo journey first (both physical and psychological) to get to know herself before she makes a commitment to anyone else. That journey is not just a sexual one or a spiritual one; it is also a journey of independence. Once the spirit is free, then a commitment to sexual bonding can take place, and usually the marriage comes at the end of the play.

If one looks at the progression of the women who dressed as men in Shakespeare's canon, one can see the deepening of his understanding of women's predicament. Start with Julia in *The Two Gentlemen of Verona.* She cannot travel unless she's disguised; she cannot serve Proteus, and understand who he really is, unless she's disguised. What she finds out as his servant is very different from what she saw as his lover. However, she doesn't use her disguise to start taking over the action of the play—which is what the women do who come after Julia.

Portia, Nerissa, and Jessica all disguise themselves as men in *The Merchant of Venice*—and Portia reveals herself as more learned, more skillful, and ultimately more forgiving than any of the men do. Nerissa and Jessica both dress as men, but their journeys have little to do with anything but convenience, and they both end up with dodgy marriages.

Then comes Rosalind—the greatest of the cross-dressers, with Viola/ Cesario in *Twelfth Night* and Imogen/Fidele in *Cymbeline* coming in close seconds. Rosalind's character undergoes a profound change— a change she must undergo by herself. If she revealed her love to her lover at the beginning of the play, there would be no journey—or play, for that matter. Viola/Cesario finds her strength through her disguised sexuality. Imogen/Fidele goes through the extremes of emotional turmoil, lives as a poor person rather than a princess, and faces battle.

All of these women find new selves in their disguise, facets of themselves they then use to forward the story and their relationships.

And to play these women cannot but affect the actors who play them. The act of speaking out—and, in the past and even the recent past, women were trained *not* to speak out—demands courage. In many parts of the world, it still demands great courage for a woman to say publicly and privately what she thinks. But women from India, Pakistan, Egypt, Syria, Nigeria are stepping forward, often paying a high price for doing so. In the theatre, Vanessa Redgrave played both Rosalind and Imogen. While performing those roles, she was arranging rallies and meetings, using her voice to focus public attention on pressing issues.

SCENE 2: Rosalind and 1599

Shakespeare's personal life bears on what he was writing. He'd finished *Much Ado About Nothing*—a play that illuminates the real power of man/woman relationships, for Beatrice and Benedick are so much more themselves when with each other; their power infuses each the other, and it's a joy to behold.

Southampton and Essex were separated, Southampton having been made a part of Robert Cecil's delegation to Paris to help negotiate peace between France and Spain. But he had got Elizabeth Vernon, one of the Queen's ladies-in-waiting, pregnant. Elizabeth Vernon was not a good political or economic match for Southampton, so perhaps there was real affection between the two. When Southampton found out, he sneaked back to England and married her. Seeing his patron, now his friend, go through the same predicament that he, Shakespeare, had been through fifteen years earlier must have given him pause, as well as amusement that Southampton had finally married without the aid of any sonnets! The year 1598 also saw Ben Jonson, the playwright Shakespeare had probably supported and brought into the company, kill a fellow player, Gabriel Spenser, his friend and probably a really good actor, in a duel—and be put in prison for it, only escaping the death penalty by pleading benefit of clergy. (Because he was able to read and write so fluently, Jonson claimed he had the protection of the church—the benefit of clergy—and therefore could not be tried by the state.)

Then, toward the end of 1598, in the cold of winter, the Theatre in North London was dismantled and taken across the river to be reassembled on Bankside, a few hundred feet from the Rose. The story goes that the Burbages did it in the middle of the night—but Peter McCurdy, the timber framer who built the current Globe, says this is not possible. It would take at least a week to take down, and maybe longer to reassemble. However, whatever the time frame, whatever the cost, the Burbages were willing to offer a share to all their long-standing colleagues—John Heminges, Augustine Phillips, Thomas Pope, William Kempe, and Shakespeare. So, by May of 1599, Shakespeare became a shareholder in his company.

The story has it that Southampton gave him the money—but I think he may have earned enough himself to buy his own share. He'd bought New Place in Stratford in 1597, and Richard Quiney had asked him for a loan, and the Stratford town fathers inquired whether he was interested in investing in tithes.

Being a shareholder is very different from being a hired hand. In effect, you are part owner of the theatre. That means you are responsible for all the assets of the company, the plays it buys, the box-office income, how many actors you employ, your appearances at court; you are a practicing shareholder in a business.

The new playhouse is called the Globe, and I do wonder if that was Shakespeare's choice. Shakespeare wrote up a storm in 1599–doubtless inspired to make his mark in the Globe.

The first play he wrote in 1599 was the great hero play *Henry V*–and, yes, Essex and Southampton were back together again (Southampton having been chucked in jail for a short time for getting Elizabeth Vernon pregnant, not getting the Queen's permission to marry her, and so on). Essex and Southampton went off to Ireland to subdue Hugh O'Neill, Earl of Tyrone (who had been brought to England by Philip Sidney's father and lived at Penshurst, home of the Sidneys, from age eleven to sixteen–so he knew personally all the leading figures in the English court). O'Neill was now challenging the English supremacy in Ireland. At the beginning of *Henry V,* Shakespeare included several lines about his friends' returning gloriously to London. How much did Shakespeare believe it?

In any case, as we've already seen, the women in *Henry V* are of little importance, as would be women in the Irish campaign. There is no place for women in the hero story.

Next Shakespeare wrote *Julius Caesar.* The women fare a little better. Calpurnia, Caesar's wife, tells him *not* to go to the capitol that day; her intuition tells her it's a terrible idea, because she's had a dream of a statue spouting blood. So Caesar says he won't go. But when his friends come to take him to the capitol and he tells them he's not going because Calpurnia doesn't want him to, they say, You're not going to listen to a woman, are you? And Caesar says:

> How foolish do your fears seem now, Calpurnia!
> I am ashamèd I did yield to them.
>
> JULIUS CAESAR (2.2, 109–10)

He goes to the capitol with his friendly conspirators. And we all know how that turned out!

We never know what happens to Calpurnia, but we do to Portia, Brutus's wife.

Portia knows what Brutus is up to, but she wants him to *tell* her what he's up to. At this point in Roman history, men and women, within the bond of marriage, were meant to be equal in status, and she makes a most compelling argument why he should tell her his secret. Eventually, he says he will—after she has shown him the wound she's made in her thigh to prove her loyalty and discretion. But then a potential conspirator arrives, and he promises he will come up to bed after he's left, and tell all.

Of course, he leaves *with* the conspirator to go and kill Caesar—and he never tells her. She sends a messenger to him to say she knows what he's up to and she supports him, but that's the best she can do. Civil war breaks out immediately, and the final time we hear about Portia is before the big battle, Brutus and Cassius versus Mark Antony and Octavius Caesar.

She has killed herself by swallowing fire: My voice was useless; I will burn it out. When Cassius expresses his sympathy and grief to Brutus, Brutus says, "Speak no more of her." Later, when her death is reported again, Brutus pretends he didn't know, and again receives the news with ideal stoicism.

Somewhere in here, in life, Essex and Southampton returned ignominiously from Ireland, not having accomplished their task but instead signing a humiliating (from the English point of view) treaty with O'Neill, giving him more or less everything he wanted. Essex had also knighted a lot of his friends for their nonexistent "bravery" and made Southampton General of the Horse—all on Elizabeth's behalf but without her permission or blessing. It was a mess, and Essex and Southampton were locked up in the Tower.

Shakespeare, meanwhile, wrote *As You Like It,* producing his best heroine yet, Rosalind.

At the beginning of the play, Rosalind says little, but once she is banished, disguises herself as a man, goes on her journey to the Forest of Arden, interacts freely with everyone around her, and you cannot shut her up.

Great freedom came to Shakespeare, just as it did for Rosalind, in this year 1599: it *was* as he liked it!

He became a co-owner of his company. He could play a leading part in their success (indeed, his name appeared near the top of the list of representatives from the Globe in official documents hereafter), and he had every intention of exerting his business acumen as well as his acting and writing skills.

The people who were his mentors, at least in aristocratic terms, turned out not to be too wise, and honor in battle made no more adored appearances in his plays after 1599—in fact, Shakespeare seemed to be released to speak as he really felt in *Hamlet, Troilus and Cressida,* and *Coriolanus.* The lid came off: no more restraints. He was his own man. And his own woman.

And so Shakespeare journeyed from falling in love several years earlier (and not just sexual passion, but that overwhelming love for another which, no matter how unsuitable, no matter what the practical difficulties, no matter that both are married with children, have responsibilities, must earn a living, still continues to grow) to owning a theatre and writing freely for his own company, bringing together his artistic, personal, and economic interests.

He now plunged into a series of plays that focus on man/woman relationships—but they differ somewhat from the sexual/spiritual merging of a *Romeo and Juliet.* These plays could not have been written without Shakespeare's understanding of how deeply people can love, and that parity of status is a natural state of being.

Because the promise in the power of that kind of union is so overwhelming, the mind (that voice in your head) will do everything it can to mess it up, debunk it, make it not true. Not loving is more comfortable than meeting the challenge of loving—even though we all yearn for the loving state, we usually settle for a more comfortable arrangement.

If you don't have the burning, swift fire that catapults you into immediate actions, like Romeo and Juliet, but you do feel love at that kind of depth, how do you deal with it? What are the building blocks that allow you to know the other, try to strengthen your frightened self, and really see if you can live in this consuming passion?

The answer is revealed through Rosalind in *As You Like It,* the last play that Shakespeare wrote in 1599. She disguises herself as a boy, drops all the covering inhibitions of femininity, and really searches for her true self, including her electrifying attraction for Orlando. She lives underground. Her disguise gives her the ability to find out about herself, what she really thinks and feels. It also allows her to teach Orlando what Rosalind thinks and feels, and to guide him from his romantic version of love into an honest, tough love that will endure. And she can do all this freely, without having anyone in power tell her how women should or should not behave.

At the beginning of the play Orlando, the son of honorable Sir Rowland de Bois, is constrained by his jealous brother Oliver to fulfill the role of lackey. He's given no education, nor is he allowed to behave in any way that would allow him to become a gentleman, though he is an intelligent, caring, cultured man.

> My father charged you in his will to give me good education.
> You have trained me like a peasant, obscuring and hiding me
> from all gentleman-like qualities. The spirit of my father grows
> strong in me, and I will no longer endure it. . . .
>
> AS YOU LIKE IT (1.1, 45–48)

Similarly, Rosalind and Celia live at the court of the bad Duke Frederick, Celia's father. Many years earlier, Frederick stole the kingdom from his older brother, known in the play as Duke Senior. Duke Senior is living in exile in the Forest of Arden, but his daughter Rosalind was kept behind to be brought up and become best friends with her cousin Celia. And they are best friends. This friendship sustains them through many vicissitudes, and their friendship is a real "women's" friendship—Shakespeare observed the strength women get from one another and observed that their perpetual "talking everything through" is more than idle chatter.

Orlando is so fed up with his state that he determines to fight Frederick's professional wrestler, Charles. There's a reward if you can beat him, and Orlando is determined to win the money.

At the fight, the two women first try to persuade Orlando not to fight (because he is seemingly so outmatched and Charles is a known killer), but Orlando is in such despair that he won't be dissuaded. And he wins.

After the match, the girls congratulate Orlando, and at that moment Orlando and Rosalind fall deeply and violently in love—so much so that they are struck dumb. Neither can say a word to the other, though Rosalind does manage to hang a jewel around Orlando's neck.

At first Frederick is attracted to Orlando, but when he discovers his father was Sir Rowland de Bois (a legendary figure who stood for goodness and honor) he tells him to go away. When Orlando returns home, jewel around his neck, his jealous brother Oliver is seeking to kill him. So, warned by the faithful old servant Adam, Orlando flees to the Forest of Arden.

Frederick is now in a very bad temper and turns his anger upon Rosalind—banishing her from the kingdom. When he's stormed out, the women turn to each other, and Celia commits herself to going with Rosalind. In fact, in this first third of the play, Celia has been a more dominant figure than Rosalind. She talks more, stands up to her father, and suggests they both run away to seek Duke Senior in the Forest of Arden.

Celia's determination to share Rosalind's exile is the first practical triumph of love over hate. Then she suggests that they take the clown, Touchstone, and some jewels with them. This is good practical advice if the shit is hitting the fan: remember friendship and laughter, and scrape together a bit of money if you can.

They decide to disguise themselves.

> Were it not better,
> Because that I am more than common tall,
> That I did suit me all points like a man?
> AS YOU LIKE IT (1.3, 110–12)

Celia dresses as a country maid, and so off they go, as Ganymede and Aliena, on the journey from court to country, traveling to the Forest of Arden.

The idea of the journey is classic (not only in Shakespeare, although he used it repeatedly)—leaving behind the old life and trying to find your way into the new. To go somewhere that you don't recognize, where the tastes, smells, and language are different, so stimulates the senses that your perception of yourself begins to change. The people you meet don't know you, so the picture of whoever your regular friends and family think you are disappears—it's possible to see yourself differently, to reinvent yourself.

And that is exactly what Rosalind/Ganymede does. When she gets to Arden, she doesn't visit her father; she meets him by chance, but he doesn't recognize her/him, and she passes on her way. Instead, she has adventures. A woman falls in love with her. She helps a local shepherd in his courting of the aforesaid woman. She debates with the resident philosopher. With the money they've brought along, she and Celia buy a little cottage and some sheep—and she/he thinks about the world, undefined by any expectations of others.

And then there's Orlando. He spends his time writing poems to the woman he saw for all of two minutes at the wrestling match. She has sparked his creative muse, but his poetry is hopeless. He doesn't know who the real Rosalind is!

This is where playing Rosalind and Orlando actually gives the key to experiencing what is going on: it's not possible to understand it just by reading the words on the page. And it only has a little to do with "boy plays girl, plays boy, plays girl" (i.e., Shakespeare's boy actor is playing Rosalind, Rosalind is pretending she's a boy, and this pretend boy offers to play Rosalind for Orlando, so he can practice wooing her!).

What happens to the actor playing Rosalind is that she first learns the art of turning a bad situation (banishment in this case) into an adventure (off to the Forest of Arden in disguise). When she meets the man she loves, Rosalind is struck dumb, but Ganymede adopts the persona of a "saucy lackey" and baits and jeers at Orlando as one man to another. Orlando likes the saucy lackey, and when the saucy lackey offers to pretend to be Rosalind, Orlando agrees. Disguise allows the layers of the real self to be experienced, each disguise stripping away social constraints.

And so can begin the examination of courtship. Orlando can be honest with Ganymede because he knows he's not really Rosalind, so that what Ganymede thinks is not threatening to Orlando. He can put himself into the states of love "as if" the person opposite him were Rosalind, and he can "rehearse" what he'd do with Rosalind.

Rosalind, for her part, is not constrained by her persona as a good and proper young woman, but can let loose in whatever way she wishes as Ganymede. I found having an accent (my own regional Nottingham accent—justified by the text "indeed an old religious uncle of mine taught me to speak, who was in his youth an inland man"—Nottingham is in the Midlands) gave me enormous freedom. I was *not* a Duke's daughter, or in the marriage market, or anything I didn't want to be—I was a lackey, speaking in a voice that had nothing to do with my court self (although quite a lot to do with my Tina self), and in this character I was able to read Orlando the riot act when he was late, tell him not to be so daft when he said he would die for love, and allow myself the freedom to feel the sexual passion I had for him without running away or being struck dumb. As this Ganymede played Rosalind—"Why, how now, Orlando, where have you been all this while? You a lover? An you serve me such another trick, never come in my sight more!"—I began to see that she was not the Rosalind I thought I was, the Rosalind everyone else had developed. The real Rosalind was much nearer to Ganymede, actively wooing Orlando, getting him to marry her, voicing her fears that he would abandon her as soon as they'd slept together ("Men are April when they woo, December when they wed") though he swore he would love her "forever and a day"—or, worse still, that she would change toward him when they were married ("Maids are May when they are maids, but the sky changes when they are wives").

Somewhere in the midst of this play-acting, Orlando begins to realize that Ganymede is indeed Rosalind, and the person he has come to know is far deeper and far more complicated, and has very little to do with the imaginary persona of his poems.

Rosalind, for her part, has to face how deeply she is in love.

ROSALIND O coz, coz, coz, my pretty little coz, that thou
    didst know how many fathoms deep I am in love. But
    it cannot be sounded. My affection hath an unknown
    bottom, like the Bay of Portugal.
CELIA Or rather bottomless, that as fast as you pour affection
    in, it runs out.
ROSALIND No, that same wicked bastard of Venus that was
    begot of thought, conceived of spleen, and born of
    madness, that blind rascally boy that abuses everyone's
    eyes because his own are out, let him be judge how deep

I am in love. I'll tell thee, Aliena, I cannot be out of the sight of Orlando. I'll go find a shadow and sigh till he come.

AS YOU LIKE IT (4.1, 145–53)

The "wicked bastard of Venus" is metaphorically and psychologically the source of the creative self, the source of Rosalind, the source of the love between Rosalind and Orlando.

And the only appropriate ceremony to reflect these feelings and connection is to make love: the only human act with transcendence between two separate people. And so we come to the end of the play, where four couples get married: Rosalind and Orlando, Celia and Oliver (who's also had a religious conversion), Phoebe and Silvius (masterminded by Rosalind/Ganymede), and Touchstone and Audrey (court and country). Rosalind reveals herself to her father. The god Hymen descends and blesses the marriages, and everyone dances.

The layers of these love plays are always curled inside one another, going to a center and connecting to the outside world. I think this may be the reason why this heroine and one in *Love's Labour's Lost* are called Rosalind, Rosaline, and Rose. Of course, the rose was the flower of love, particularly the layers of sexual love with spiritual meaning. A guide (Romeo is in love with Rosaline before he and Juliet fall in love with each other—you could say she leads him, prepares him for Juliet). Shakespeare expresses it most directly in a sonnet:

> O never say that I was false of heart,
> Though absence seemed my flame to qualify—
> As easy might I from myself depart
> As from my soul, which in thy breast doth lie.
> That is my home of love. If I have ranged,
> Like him that travels I return again,
> Just to the time, not with the time exchanged,
> So that myself bring water for my stain.
> Never believe, though in my nature reigned
> All frailties that besiege all kinds of blood,
> That it could so preposterously be stained
> To leave for nothing all thy sum of good;

> For nothing this wide universe I call
> Save thou, my rose; in it thou art my all.

SONNET 109

Two things are happening here. First, Shakespeare really was deeply in love with someone. Second, that that love opened the door to so many other journeys and ideas, creative acts and performances, that the depths of feeling were a key to other knowledge. That other knowledge lives on both conscious and unconscious levels; it can be seen and felt, but also acts as a guide, taking us where our lives need to go. It is the rose; its petals fold in on one another, from bud to flower, as it grows to full beauty and dies; it awakens the senses, especially the sense of smell, which is so deeply connected to memory, with briars and branches, which scratch and hurt; they take us down false paths and into thoughtless acts.

The sonnet that immediately follows this opens:

> Alas, 'tis true, I have gone here and there
> And made myself a motley to the view,
> Gored mine own thoughts, sold cheap what is most dear,
> Made old offenses of affections new.

SONNET 110

SCENE 3: Dying to Tell the Truth: Ophelia, Desdemona, Cordelia

Now we come to what for me is the most painful part of the journey: the courageous women who struggle to tell the truth about what they see and hear, and are killed for it. They may run mad; some kill themselves. But all struggle to name things as they really are. They stay in their frocks; they align their perceptions as women not with coquetry or docility but with words that challenge the reality of those in power, and then they die for it. It is a painful truth Shakespeare arrived at: that women speak the truth at their peril.

It went hand in hand with his realization that women are able to understand themselves better on a personal level and survive in the world if they dress in men's clothing, thus living underground, safe, until they are willing to reveal themselves. The presence of women disguising themselves as men dictates that the play be a comedy; women remaining in their frocks, a tragedy. In four great tragedies—*Julius Caesar, Hamlet, Othello,* and *King Lear*—almost all the women die, and five (Portia, Ophelia, Desdemona, Emilia, Cordelia) because they tell the truth or want the truth to be revealed. Their sisters in the comedies—*As You Like It, Measure for Measure, Twelfth Night, All's Well That Ends Well*—find freedom in disguise of one sort or another, and the actions they take contribute to making their world come right!

How much the women have to adhere to the rules and regulations of their environment makes a large difference. Once Rosalind has run away from the court, she has no institutional structures to deal with. Ophelia is surrounded tightly by institutional structures of family, court, and politics; only by going mad can she get out of it all.

At the beginning of the play, Ophelia does what her father tells her: she rejects Hamlet and gives him back the gifts he's given her. In so doing, she's disloyal to herself and Hamlet, displaying none of the bravery of a Desdemona or a Juliet. This violation puts Hamlet into a rage, and he lacerates her and all womankind.

Get thee to a nunnery. Why wouldst thou be a breeder of sinners? I am myself indifferent honest, but yet I could accuse me of such things that it were better my mother had not borne me. . . .

If thou dost marry, I'll give thee this plague for thy dowry: be thou as chaste as ice, as pure as snow, thou shalt not escape calumny. Get thee to a nunnery, go, farewell. . . .

I have heard of your paintings, too, well enough. God hath given you one face, and you make yourself another. You jig, you amble, and you lisp, and nickname God's creatures, and make your wantonness your ignorance. Go to, I'll no more on't. It hath made me mad. I say we will have no more marriages. Those that are married already—all but one—shall live. The rest shall keep as they are. To a nunnery, go.

HAMLET (3.1, 125–27, 136–38, 142–47)

A nunnery, of course, has the double meaning—nunnery and whorehouse. After Hamlet leaves, Ophelia (in true female fashion) tries to work out first what has happened to Hamlet to cause his personality to disintegrate—and only after that does she turn to herself and her own predicament.

> O what a noble mind is here o'erthrown!
> The courtier's, soldier's, scholar's eye, tongue, sword,
> Th'expectancy and rose of the fair state,
> The glass of fashion and the mould of form,
> Th'observed of all observers, quite, quite, down!
>
> HAMLET (3.1, 148–52)

Then she turns to herself—but only for a moment, and only in relation to him.

> And I, of ladies most deject and wretched,
> That sucked the honey of his music vows,
> Now see that noble and most sovereign reason
> Like sweet bells jangled out of tune and harsh;
> That unmatched form and feature of blown youth
> Blasted with ecstasy.
>
> .   HAMLET (3.1, 153–58)

Then the last line and a half of that soliloquy shifts the ground again:

> O woe is me,
> T'have seen what I have seen, see what I see!
>
> HAMLET (3.1, 158–59)

In that last half-line, Ophelia changes tense from past to present—and she sees something she never saw before. She sees Hamlet's "madness," his depicting her as a whore, as a necessary tool. It allows him to accept her disloyalty, and neither of them has to be true to love. She sees, in her father's and the King's spying on Hamlet in her presence, that she is a party to his entrapment. She fails him.

And Hamlet fails her. Earlier, when she did her father's bidding and denied Hamlet's access to her, he came to her room in a parody of the rejected lover.

> He took me by the wrist and held me hard,
> Then goes he to the length of all his arm,
> And with his other hand thus o'er his brow
> He falls to such perusal of my face
> As he would draw it. Long stayed he so.
>
> HAMLET (2.1, 92–96)

And so on. And it frightened her; instead of talking to him, she rushes off and reports to her father; he uses her to demonstrate he's mad.

Either way, she is the pawn—in the middle of a power struggle between her lover and her father and the King.

Hamlet then kills her father in Gertrude's bedroom. We have no idea whether Ophelia knows the circumstances of her father's death; all she knows is that he's dead, and that her lover is being sent to England. But there's no indication that anyone talks to her about it. So she goes mad, using song to tell the truth about what she sees is going on in the court. As Horatio, Hamlet's best friend says:

> She speaks much of her father, says she hears
> There's tricks i'th'world, and hems, and beats her heart,
> Spurns enviously at straws, speaks things in doubt
> That carry but half sense. Her speech is nothing,
> Yet the unshapèd use of it doth move
> The hearers to collection. . . .
>
> HAMLET (4.4, 5–10)

And Ophelia herself says:

> Where is the beauteous majesty of Denmark?
> . . .
> How should I your true love know
>   From another one?

By his cockle hat and staff
And his sandal shoon.

HAMLET (4.4, 22, 24–27)

The cockle and staff have secondary meanings, of course. She sings songs and gives out flowers: observations about people and events in the current state of Denmark.

Gertrude listens to this—and when Ophelia spreads words that incriminate Claudius, she follows Ophelia out of the castle and watches her drown herself. Clearly she could have saved her (she's close enough that she can see the hoar leaves' reflection in the stream), but she doesn't. Ophelia is dangerous—running around the court, spreading rumor, inciting her brother with her lunacy and tales—and she must be stopped. That she takes her own life is a convenience for Gertrude, and not an uncompassionate fate for Ophelia, for no one would marry a cast-off mistress of the Prince, who runs around doing aberrant acts, and whose father died in suspicious circumstances.

We have sympathy for Ophelia, but our hearts don't break for her, as they do for Desdemona: Desdemona, ignoring the convention of how young women should behave, makes choices that demand our admiration for her courage and inventiveness.

She marries Othello without telling her father, knowing that he wouldn't approve. She has fallen in love with Othello because of his life story—and obviously because the chemistry works—and she clearly wants to be part of his adventures.

When her father finds out, he immediately assumes Othello used witchcraft to seduce his daughter: after all, she can't willingly have fallen in love with a black man! He turns to the ruling Council of Venice to right his wrongs. The council is wise—asking that Othello and then Desdemona give an account of their courtship and marriage. This happens at the same time the news arrives that the Turks are invading Cyprus (an island belonging to Venice), and Othello must immediately lead an expeditionary force against them. The council pauses long enough to hear the case against Othello and Desdemona. Once it's clear that Othello and Desdemona love each other and are equally matched, and that she wooed him just as much as he her (if not more), the council gives them their blessing and advises Brabantio to do the same—which he does grudgingly, "dissing" his daughter to Othello as he does so:

> Look to her, Moor, if thou hast eyes to see.
> She has deceived her father, and may thee.
>
> OTHELLO (1.3, 310–11)

The most important thing for Desdemona is that she be allowed to go with Othello in his expedition against the Turks. The council agrees—and so does Othello.

Here we have a relationship between a man and a woman who, convention says, should never be together. They belong to different races. They come from different parts of the world. He's older. She's younger. He has experienced every kind of vicissitude in life. She has experienced none, other than her mother's dying at an early age. She has never left Venice. He's traveled the known world. And they are mad about each other, and determined to be together, even though he has a very manly job—general of the armed forces.

The fleet sets out for Cyprus. The couple are in separate ships, Desdemona attended by Emilia (as you know, I think she was named after Aemilia Lanyer, née Bassano). Emilia is the wife of Iago, Othello's third in command, who was just passed over for a promotion. There's a great storm at sea. The Turkish fleet is all dispersed. Desdemona, Emilia, and Iago come ashore at Cyprus to wait for Othello's ship. Finally, he appears, and his meeting with Desdemona carries the most sublime poetry.

> OTHELLO *(to Desdemona)* O my fair warrior!
> DESDEMONA My dear Othello.
> OTHELLO It gives me wonder great as my content
>   To see you here before me. O my soul's joy!
>   If after every tempest come such calms,
>   May the winds blow till they have wakened death,
>   And let the labouring bark climb hills of seas
>   Olympus-high, and duck again as low
>   As hell's from heaven. If it were now to die
>   'Twere now to be most happy, for I fear

My soul hath her content so absolute
That not another comfort like to this
Succeeds in unknown fate.

OTHELLO (2.1, 185–97)

Once on Cyprus, Othello and Desdemona will finally be able to consummate their marriage.

Except, as Iago has confidentially told the audience, he is going to mess with them, because he hates the Moor and he's in love with Desdemona. It's true he hates Othello, but he's making up that he loves Desdemona—he's incapable of loving anyone, probably incapable of having sex with anyone. Is he obsessed with Othello because he was passed over for promotion? Is it because Othello's black? Or because Othello's slept with his wife? Or is Iago a repressed homosexual? Is it just that he gets a charge out of manipulating everyone and wreaking as much havoc in people's lives as possible, while always appearing to be "honest Iago"? Or is it all of the above?

Iago persuades his wife, Emilia, to steal the handkerchief that Othello gave to Desdemona, a special handkerchief:

I am glad I have found this napkin.
This was her first remembrance from the Moor.
My wayward husband hath a hundred times
Wooed me to steal it. . . .

OTHELLO (3.3, 323–26)

Iago then leaves the handkerchief in the lodgings of Cassio, the man who got the job Iago wanted, hoping that Cassio will carry it with him and take it out in public so Othello will see it.

On their first night in Cyprus—the wedding night, if you will—Iago gets Cassio (who is in charge of the garrison) drunk, and Cassio creates a huge fracas in the town, wounding the governor and rousing Othello from his marriage bed. Furious Othello strips Cassio of his office.

Cassio's shame is overwhelming, and he asks Iago what he should do. Iago counsels him to go to Desdemona and get her to plead with Othello. And that's what happens.

In the meantime, Iago implies, insinuates, hints to Othello that there is something strange going on between Cassio and Desdemona, thus inducing in Othello a state he has never known before: jealousy. When he sees the handkerchief in Cassio's hand, that's all the proof he needs to know that Desdemona is betraying him and sleeping with Cassio.

All this happens over the course of a few days. Desdemona goes from dutiful daughter looking after her father's household, into the men's world of the Senate, the armed forces, the garrison. She has no community of her own. Her only friend is Emilia—who has already betrayed her by stealing the handkerchief in an attempt to get into her husband's good graces.

When Othello accuses her of infidelity, all she can do is tell the truth: No, I love only you. I pleaded for Cassio because he's our friend and I wanted you to restore him. If he has the handkerchief, he found it—I never gave it to him. I will prove I am your faithful wife by being an obedient wife: I will sit still and listen to what you say, I won't scream or run away. I know you love me and in the end our love will be stronger than your power to punish me for the lies you've heard about me. I believe in God, and because I am a Christian my word will save me from your jealousy.

No amount of telling the truth can save Desdemona from her death; in fact, everything she says is used as evidence against her, and she's smothered to death. And when she becomes conscious for a moment before dying properly, she manages to say that she killed herself. Othello is not guilty!

Emilia fares no better. Having tried to bribe her way into her husband's favor by stealing the handkerchief, she is faced with a bigger problem—should she tell Desdemona the truth about the hankie, because she can see the havoc the loss is causing in the marriage, or should she remain silent? She does the latter, perhaps hoping the situation won't escalate. In the scene in which Emilia is helping Desdemona get ready for bed (a scene that is full of unspoken truths, unconscious drives, symbolic sounds—it is worthy of Chekhov some two hundred and fifty years before Chekhov's birth), the one thing Emilia is *not* saying is "I stole the handkerchief and gave it to my husband." Instead, she does her best to get Desdemona to understand what men are like, what the men's world they live in is like, that infidelity and violence are the norm, that the idealized picture of love and goodness Desdemona holds is false, and that she, too, will want revenge for wrongs done to her. Desdemona wants to hear none of it and sends Emilia away—thereby ensuring her own death. It is a brave and honorable action, but not one that is going to save her!

After Desdemona is murdered, and Othello tells the visiting Venetian senators why he did it, Emilia's grief and anger are so great that she, too, decides to tell the truth, exposing her own complicity and her husband's culpability.

> EMILIA 'Twill out, 'twill out. I peace?
>   No, I will speak as liberal as the north.
>   Let heaven, and men, and devils, let 'em all,
>   All, all cry shame against me, yet I'll speak.
> IAGO Be wise and get you home.
> EMILIA I will not.
>   *Iago draws his sword*
> GRAZIANO *(To Iago)* Fie, your sword upon a woman?
> EMILIA O thou dull Moor, that handkerchief thou speak'st of
>   I found by fortune and did give my husband,
>   For often, with a solemn earnestness—
>   More than indeed belonged to such a trifle—
>   He begged of me to steal't.
> IAGO Villainous whore!
> EMILIA She give it Cassio? No, alas, I found it,
>   And I did give't my husband.
>
>   OTHELLO (5.2, 249–63)

So it's out there, the truth, for all to see. And the very next thing that happens to Emilia is—Iago kills her. So two women are dead.

I can still hear the voice of Kristin Wold, the actor who played Emilia in the 2008/2010 production of *Othello* at Shakespeare & Company, as she shook with rage at the injustice visited upon Desdemona and all women. To speak the truth became more important to her than her life itself. And of course her husband (played by Michael Hammond) swiftly and efficiently killed her.

Othello is ineffectual in his attempt to kill Iago, but successful in his attempt to kill himself. His dying words, however, are about the service he has done the state—not what he has done to Desdemona, which in fact he describes as "I loved not wisely, but too well"—so he remains blind to the end. He acknowledges not love but the power structure, where we will never find our truest selves.

The women in *Othello* are never able to escape the institutional structures they live under. Desdemona, with Othello's help, breaks through the rules that govern marriage—they have no permission, no dowry is negotiated, they have no home, they leap over the differences of age, race, citizenship—but thereafter their lives are bound by Othello's job and their own internalized ideas about how men and women should behave. The powerful love that brought them together and was nurtured in secret counts for nothing once it is tested. Othello believes his fellow officer rather than his wife, believes death is suitable punishment for infidelity, and cares more about the state and his status than about the love he destroyed.

It makes me uneasy that we so easily state that *Othello* is a play about race. Race is one of its ingredients, but the most pervasive subject that Shakespeare is tackling is sexism. The two women end up dead. Bianca, the third woman in the play, Cassio's mistress, ends up in jail for something she never did, and nobody bothers to get her out. Iago, the symbol of evil, remains alive among us. Brabantio, Desdemona's father, dies of a broken heart because of his daughter's disobedience. And everyone is very regretful about what has happened. But no one, other than Emilia, has pointed out that there is a terrible double standard, something rotten in the system itself.

> But I do think it is their husbands' faults
> If wives do fall. Say that they slack their duties,
> And pour our treasures into foreign laps,
> Or else break out in peevish jealousies,
> Throwing restraint upon us; or say they strike us,
> Or scant our former having in despite:
> Why, we have galls; and though we have some grace,
> Yet have we some revenge. Let husbands know
> Their wives have sense like them. They see, and smell,
> And have their palates both for sweet and sour,

As husbands have. What is it that they do
When they change us for others? Is it sport?
I think it is. And doth affection breed it?
I think it doth. Is't frailty that thus errs?
It is so, too. And have not we affections,
Desires for sport, and frailty, as men have?
Then let them use us well, else let them know
The ills we do, their ills instruct us so.

OTHELLO (4.3, 89–106)

Women who die to tell the truth make their appearances in other plays, but none build such a strong composite picture as do the women in *Othello*.

Soon after *Othello*, Shakespeare wrote *King Lear*, and, of course, Cordelia is so honest with her father in the first scene that it causes her to lose her inheritance, dowry, and family. In the last scenes, when she has returned to rescue her father from her sisters, she gets killed—Goneril and Regan have always hated her for her truthfulness, and when she returns with an army to right the situation, they have an excuse to execute her—and they do.

Lady Macduff in *Macbeth*, written around the same time, is slaughtered shortly after saying, "I have done no wrong—why should I fear?"

Whither should I fly?
I have done no harm. But I remember now
I am in this earthly world, where to do harm
Is often laudable, to do good sometime
Accounted dangerous folly. Why then, alas,
Do I put up that womanly defence
To say I have done no harm?

MACBETH (4.2, 73–79)

The truth she speaks to the murderers, and the challenge of her little son's words, aggravate the situation, making it easier for them to commit wholesale slaughter on all the children, servants, and Lady Macduff. But the outcome would have been the same, truth or no truth.

Hermione in *The Winter's Tale* is the last woman Shakespeare wrote about who dies because she is simply what she is—truthful, committed, generous, caring. But by the time Shakespeare wrote about Hermione, he had found a way to alter the story and point toward a direction where such atrocities could be exposed for what they were. He found a way of supporting women's ways of doing things. It's one of the shifts into Act 5, that the women can tell the truth and have an impact upon events, and that their story will end in growth and rebirth.

But that doesn't happen until we have gone into the dark night of the soul of Shakespeare's writing life. So into despair and chaos we will go, where greed and ambition dominate, supported by women's voices. But before that happens, Shakespeare writes about a nun and a more conventional spirituality; the strength of the women who live in the south of France, land of the troubadours and the Albigensian movement; and Viola, in *Twelfth Night*, a play in which music is almost as important as the story itself.

SCENE 4: *Measure for Measure*

Isabella is a nun whose habit at least allows her the freedom to go where she wishes and talk with whom she pleases (she's a novice; she wouldn't have the same freedom if she were a fully fledged nun). Nuns had status in the world—which may have been one reason for women to become nuns, rather than a religious calling. They could also have an education, and read and write as much as they liked. So *Measure* reveals a woman who has gone "underground" in a different sort of way.

It is also interesting because it attempts to get to the heart of the Christian Church's teaching about the sexual and the spiritual, the value and the hypocrisy of that teaching.

It's hard now for people in the modern world—unless you live in one of those areas in the States where Evangelical Christianity is the norm of the community, or you are a Mormon living in Utah (but not necessarily Salt Lake City, which is more like the rest of the country), or you live in Iran or Tibet—to imagine religious life in Elizabethan England. Reality existed in the words laid down in the Bible.

There were a few exceptions, such as Sir Walter Raleigh and Christopher Marlowe, but these were exceptions. The accepted norm of the whole country was Christian (whether Protestant or Catholic—that's a different matter). As Rosalind says in *As You Like It,* "The poor world is almost six thousand years old . . . ," and that's what everyone knew to be true. The world had been created as described in the Old Testament, some four and a half thousand years before Jesus Christ came along and redeemed it. And so for some sixteen hundred years almost everyone in the Christian world knew what a state of grace could be—if human beings could live up to it. This was the accepted norm, the basis for all thinking. Also true was that an afterlife existed; you went to either heaven or hell. There was a debate between Protestants and Catholics as to whether there was an in-between world called purgatory, where souls waited to be judged.

And as Dennis Krausnick, director of training for Shakespeare & Company, likes to point out (when training actors to find the power of their voices), in Elizabethan times, when someone put his hand on the Bible and swore to tell the truth, the chance of his lying was negligible—because that would mean his soul would go into perpetual damnation. He wouldn't do it. In our day and age, we look at our politicians in congressional hearings and immediately think they may be lying, *especially* if they've sworn to tell the truth. Presidents do it, judges do it, and police officers do it. In fact, telling the truth is more a matter of calculation today: Can I get away with it? Is it a better strategy to tell the truth, get it over with to stop the gossip? Or is it better to lie? The decision has nothing to do with your eternal soul, only with how you can operate better in this world.

For the Elizabethans, the human voice was the expression of the body and the spirit. The spoken word was the connective tissue between mind, body, and spirit; between this world and the next, a path to knowledge. It was felt in the body.

So the Elizabethans knew their words were who they are. If they disconnected themselves from the truth of what they were saying, they would separate themselves from themselves in this life, and they would pay for those lies in the afterlife. This is a very different relationship to language from the one we have.

We live in a different state of being. We live a large part of our lives disconnected from language (we are the white men with forked tongues); we belong to the chattering classes who expect small consequences from our speech. And we have very little sense of there being consequences to pay if we don't tell the truth to the best of our ability.

All of this is said in preparation for *Measure for Measure,* Shakespeare's attempt to look at man's law and God's law. How does Christian spirituality encounter sexual desire? Is it possible for them to support each other to bring about a larger understanding? Or must they be separated? Are they destructive to each other's growth?

Put another way: is it possible for human beings to know the bliss of the Garden of Eden, and each other, to be on speaking terms with the serpent, to be thrown out of paradise, and still reach heaven? Life-and-death questions for the Elizabethans. Psychologically and politically, on a rational level, they remain important questions for us today.

The play is set in Vienna, part of the Holy Roman Empire for Shakespeare, the worldly power structure, purportedly the upholder of the Catholic Church's spirituality—though it had long since become a counterbalance to the church, often at odds with it. (It was the Holy Roman Emperor who crowned the Pope—so the Emperor could in effect choose or decline the Pope. On the other hand, once crowned, the Pope had ascendency over the Emperor, could excommunicate him and so on.)

Vienna is a mess. The Duke is unable to enforce the laws—and in the play we are particularly looking at the laws regarding sexuality. The city is teeming with brothels, with lowlifes who do as they like, full of petty crime; disease is rampant, language is lewd, everyone thinks about survival on the most basic level. This environment was familiar to Shakespeare: it is Bankside, home to the Globe and the Rose. The theatres stood among the brothels, pubs, gaming houses, and animal-baiting amphitheatres. Shakespeare lived and worked here.

In Vienna, the laws haven't been enforced for years, and the Duke feels incompetent. He has no stomach for it, yet he knows that some kind of law and order needs to be put in place.

He appoints one Angelo (good angel) to run the place, a man much concerned with the letter of the law, especially the state of our souls, an upholder of morality, a supposedly spiritual man, and a lawyer (and the law and the church are one in this place; religious law is the law of the state—no separation of church and state here).

The state of England had some parallels. In England, separation of church law and state law—common law—had evolved over centuries, including the rights inherited from the Magna Carta, but England also had the monarch's laws as head of the church. For instance, everyone had to go to church on Sunday or be fined. Everyone had to use the same Book of Common Prayer. The Puritans were growing in strength, and the most radical of them fervently believed that God's laws should be the country's laws—just as Sharia law is the desire of some Muslims today, or some Evangelicals believe America should institute Christian law.

Anyway, the Duke decides he's going to give this much more stringent version of the law a try. He appoints Angelo, gives him full powers, then disappears, encouraging the idea that he's gone away. In fact, he hasn't. He disguises himself as a friar so he can see how it all works out.

Angelo's first act is to revive an old law, that anyone who has sex before marriage will be executed. (Shakespeare had sex before marriage, and so did many in his audience; this hot issue comes up in several of the plays.) The first person to be prosecuted is Claudio, who is in love with his girlfriend, Juliet. She is heavily pregnant, so although she's locked up she won't be executed. Claudio will, and soon. The young couple is engaged—in fact, would be married, except that some legal technicality has held it up. And as Juliet points out, their sin was mutually committed, so she is as guilty as he is—if guilt and the law are the point.

Claudio is friends with Lucio, a man-about-town, who frequents the brothels, carelessly gets women pregnant, is vain and boastful, and generally an outrageous figure. He and the brothel keeper Mistress Overdone (she's had nine husbands—Overdone by the last, as she tells the judge), together with Pompey the pimp, are at the heart of this underworld; throughout the play, Shakespeare contrasted their antics, ability to survive, and ways of looking after one another with the more abstract and spiritual reasoning of Angelo.

Into this mix comes Isabella, sister of Claudio and novice nun, who has just entered the Order of Saint Clare—one of the strictest in Christendom. Lucio goes to the nunnery to ask Isabella to visit Angelo and plead for her brother. Shakespeare then gives us one of the most psychologically sophisticated portraits of a woman in the canon.

Shakespeare genuinely wanted to know if a rigorous Christianity could lead to a higher knowledge and a more peaceful society; whether sexuality could be transmuted into spirituality; and whether it was possible, by diverting sexuality, to find a higher calling. This is the path that both Isabella and Angelo, in their different ways, are committed to following.

This play demands a close reading of the text, the kind of close reading Isabella and Angelo both practice. Without a close reading there's not a hope in hell of understanding the twists and turns of the medieval/Elizabethan Christian way of thinking; it's a problem in our age of rather sloppy thinking: we are not used to it, and certainly not used to the idea that if we don't understand it properly in this life we will pay for it in the afterlife. Added to which, as actors, we must follow the syntax of the text, the structure of the verse, the clues Shakespeare gives us through the form of his writing. I will touch on them to give you a general idea.

This is not a play that fell easily out of Shakespeare's mind and body. It was a strange world for him, too. He needed to think deeply about it as he wrote it. *Measure for Measure* was his exploration of man-made laws and the institutions men use to harness their deepest urges—the libido reined in. It is also a threshold play; it's after *Measure for Measure* that all the great tragedies came fast and furious. After *Measure for Measure*, Shakespeare let go and wrote *Othello, King Lear, Macbeth, Antony and Cleopatra*.

To get back to Isabella and Angelo: When Lucio first approaches Isabella, she has been talking to one of the old nuns, bemoaning the fact that the Order of Saint Clare is not stricter than it already is—so we know Isabella is keen on having strictures placed upon her to help her find her way more swiftly to God. When Lucio arrives, we learn that, if she was not a novice, she could only speak to a man if she couldn't see him; if she could see him, then she would not be allowed to speak to him. Seeing and speaking would be too much. Too much of what? one is forced to ask. Too much communication? Too many channels open? Too much knowledge passing back and forth? Or is it simply that speaking and seeing can lead to sexual attraction, which is not possible for the Saint Clares—because, of course, they marry

Christ. He will penetrate them. They will receive him. And together they know heaven.

In this first scene with Lucio, we learn several things about Isabella, her life, and her relationship with her brother. When Lucio tells Isabella that Claudio has got someone pregnant, she knows immediately who it is:

> ISABELLA Someone with child by him? My cousin Juliet?
> LUCIO Is she your cousin?
> ISABELLA Adoptedly, as schoolmaids change their names
>   By vain though apt affection.
>   MEASURE FOR MEASURE (1.5, 47–50)

So Juliet is her best friend. Did she know Juliet was pregnant before she went into the convent? She doesn't seem to have known—and yet Juliet is quite far along in her pregnancy.

"Let him marry her," she says.

"This is the point," says Lucio. He can't, because he's in prison and he's going to be executed.

So this background is blurry. Does Isabella's desire to be a nun have anything to do with the fact that her brother and her best friend are lovers? In any case, Isabella agrees to go to Angelo and see if she can save her brother. She can do this because she's a nun. She goes with only Lucio as her escort.

When we see Angelo, he is confidently reinforcing laws, dispensing his version of justice; he seems absolutely secure in his knowledge of right and wrong. Lucio knows him as a cold fish.

> LUCIO . . . They say this Angelo was not made by man and
>   woman, after this downright way of creation. Is it true,
>   think you?
> DUKE *[disguised as a friar]* How should he be made, then?
> LUCIO Some report a sea-maid spawned him, some that he
>   was begot between two stockfishes. But it is certain that
>   when he makes water, his urine is congealed ice; that I
>   know to be true. And he is a motion ungenerative; that's
>   infallible.
>   MEASURE FOR MEASURE (3.1, 326–32)

"Motion ungenerative" means he doesn't move (nor does anything creative come out of him).

Isabella turns up at Angelo's door. He lays out the law to her: no sex before marriage, and a transgression leads to execution. Simple. Clear. Absolute. Infallible. Isabella, who has a brain as good as Angelo's and can speak as well, makes the argument for Christ's law, mercy and forgiveness—even for this sin, which she says she most abhors. Angelo counters with the argument that Claudio's sin has already been committed; therefore, by paying the price for this sin, he can redeem his soul.

> ANGELO Condemn the fault, and not the actor of it?
>   Why, every fault's condemned ere it be done.
>   Mine were the very cipher of a function,
>   To fine the faults whose fine stands in record,
>   And let go by the actor.
> ISABELLA O just but severe law!
>   I had a brother, then. Heaven keep your honour.
>   MEASURE FOR MEASURE (2.2, 50–56)

This argument takes place in scholastic logic—frankly, only understandable by people steeped in the form. They are matching each other equally, both passionate about the ideas they are using; their rhythms find a synchronicity; their breathing responds to each other; they finish each other's iambic lines; and Angelo, seemingly for the first time in his life, falls in love. Isabella can see she has affected him—with her argument, she believes—and will return the next day willingly to continue the debate.

As soon as she leaves, Angelo knows he's in trouble—but is it her fault or his? "The tempter or the tempted who sins most?" And his body, which pissed ice before, is now throbbing and pulsating.

> Why does my blood thus muster to my heart,
> Making both it unable for itself,
> And dispossessing all my other parts
> Of necessary fitness?
>   MEASURE FOR MEASURE (2.4, 20–23)

When she returns the next day, Angelo's formidable intellect and absolute power are used in the service of his sexual desire.

When he had no sexual desire, the world was a simple place. He had a powerful sense of right: This is my interpretation of God's rules; we live in God's image; we must all live under his rules, and he will bless us and take us to heaven. And if you don't live by his rules, you'll be cast into hell.

Once Angelo feels sexual desire, the world is a complicated place— because fulfillment of that desire is overwhelming, and he has no vocabulary, either in words or through intuition, for how to invite Isabella to join with him. He only has language to prove his point, or power to force her into submission. Before she comes, in his soliloquy, he is at war with himself: sex without marriage is a sin in his book, and he's desperate for sexual satisfaction *now*. And she's a nun. The only way he knows to exert his will is through force—physical or psychological. His sexual desire overwhelms all other considerations: if she sleeps with him, he'll let her brother go; if she doesn't, he'll not only kill Claudio but torture him, too. There is one moment in their exchange where a change might be possible. Having used every trick of logic to try and get her to sleep with him, he finally says, "Plainly conceive! I love you." If Isabella could have heard the love and not all the lies that went before, and received it as love, the outcome might have been different. But she doesn't. She slams the door shut, demands he sign a pardon for her brother or she'll "tell the world out loud what man thou art."

Shakespeare really understood the relationship between repressed desire and physical violence—whether it was embedded in the law of the land or stood outside the law. Shakespeare saw no connection between loving, equal meeting with sexual desire, and forced sex. Both Angelo and Isabella are followers of Christ, with his message of universal love, and they both believe they are on the path to spiritual enlightenment, but neither can make the leap from the abstract idea of universal love to the practical everyday action of love.

Shakespeare's use of language to follow the psychological makeup of these two is as sophisticated as any Harley Street shrink's understanding. When Angelo asks Isabella, if she could give her body to save her brother, would she do it, she says she'd rather give her body than her soul. But Angelo doesn't want to talk about the soul, because he reasons that if Isabella did sleep with him she would have been compelled to do it, and therefore it probably would *not* count against her on Judgment Day (an argument Claudio also uses later). No, Angelo wants Isabella to get turned on to his idea of laying down her body to save her brother. Once she realizes what he's suggesting (and we go through quite a few gradations of the argument, all highly charged, juggling words and rhythms backward and forward, until he is forced to spell it out to her), this is her answer:

> . . . were I under the terms of death,
> Th'impression of keen whips I'd wear as rubies,
> And strip myself to death as to a bed
> That longing have been sick for, ere I yield
> My body up to shame.
>
> MEASURE FOR MEASURE (2.4, 104–08)

Now, if that's not the most mixed message you could send someone, I don't know what is. It sounds like something a call girl who specializes in phone sex would say—assuming that her client thinks sex is bad, so has to be chastised for thinking such bad thoughts, while giving a description of what she looks like in bed, naked with gashes and blood dripping off her.

It goes on from there. Isabella decides to tell her brother of Angelo's proposal—so he can redeem himself by choosing death and her chastity, rather than life, Juliet, and the unborn baby.

Of course, it doesn't turn out like that. When Isabella tells Claudio, he, after a bit of an effort to say she shouldn't do it, reverses himself and says, Oh, God, please do it—and if it's a sin, it isn't a very bad one, and you'll be forgiven.

At which point Isabella goes berserk. And this is probably the most psychologically revealing moment of the play, as far as Isabella's journey toward spirituality is concerned.

First she accuses her brother of incest by taking life from his sister's shame. She thinks Claudio can't belong to her father, because he's too great a sinner.

Is't not a kind of incest to take life
From thine own sister's shame? What should I think?
Heaven shield my mother played my father fair,
For such a warpèd slip of wilderness
Ne'er issued from his blood.

MEASURE FOR MEASURE (3.1, 152–56)

Then she says his sin is not accidental but a trade—he didn't just have sex once, he's done nothing but use his sexuality for his own advantage (which is not true). Finally, she says that mercy to him would be wrong, "a bawd," because all he would do with his life here-after would be to have more sex with more people—so she is going to pray for his death, "No word to save thee."

What are we to make of this? It's not a little outburst; it's sixteen lines flying out of her mouth without restraint. And for someone who has been so circumspect, so desirous of God's blessing, so determined to find salvation, it's all the repressed thoughts coming to the surface.

As far as we can tell, Claudio has slept only with Juliet, wants only to marry her; there is absolute mutuality in their relationship, and any reasonable person would think this marriage has a good chance of succeeding. Why does Shakespeare choose this marriage to be the one that Angelo would destroy? Or use to prove that Isabella thinks her chastity is more important than the alliance between her brother and her best friend and the future of their unborn child? If they are interesting questions for us now, can you imagine the impact they might have had on the thinking members of Shakespeare's audience?

Then there's the Duke, disguised as the Friar, who has been watching all this. In fact, before Isabella goes to Claudio to tell him of Angelo's request, he sits Claudio down and gives him a long speech about how we are all nothing, just bundles of little atoms subject to all of our petty emotions; therefore, Claudio should want to give up this vale of suffering and pass on to the next world. This is more or less the argument the church gave to people in the Middle Ages so that they would resign themselves to their lot ("nasty, brutish, and short," as Thomas Hobbes put it) and know that their reward for suffering such poverty in this world would be happiness in the next. For a while, Claudio buys it. But once he has realized there is a chance he can live if Isabella sleeps with Angelo, he gives a terrific argument—much more in line with how many Elizabethans were beginning to feel—that this life on earth can be good, and the delights of the body informative and ecstatic, and actually we don't know where we go after death, and it might be horrible. So he'll take this life on earth, thank you very much.

Measure for Measure is a brilliant play. It's complex in the way our lives are complex: hundreds of competing ideas that don't necessarily add up. Every seeking individual wants to understand the meaning of life, and go on those journeys that will help illuminate that meaning—whether it's following a recognized spiritual discipline, like Isabella, or working to make the laws on earth more effective, like Angelo, or stepping outside of it and saying, I've got the power, but I don't know how to execute it, let me try and study the world as it is, like the Duke. Or there's Mistress Overdone, who takes in the poor children of the city while making money through prostitution; or Pompey or Barnardine (a condemned criminal), who bend the rules to get by. We are all doing the best we can. So why don't any of our efforts work?

I think Shakespeare didn't know the answer—but he had sightings. He realized that our individual histories were all such driving forces that they would come to the surface and must be dealt with. (This was a truly revolutionary insight at the time.) Did Claudio and Isabella have such a close relationship in childhood that she cannot bear his defection? Was it incestuous? Or thought to be? Why is her father overidealized? What on earth did the mother do, that Isabella has joined the Saint Clares?

Why did Angelo never marry Mariana, his fiancée? (Oh, that's where Shakespeare used the bed trick: the Duke persuades Isabella to say yes to Angelo, and then Mariana takes her place and has sex with Angelo in the dark, which supposedly means Angelo will pardon Claudio, but he doesn't, so the Duke arranges for the head of another man executed that day to be sent to Angelo, and the Duke reappears as himself, revises Claudio's death warrant without telling Isabella her brother is saved, and makes a grand reappearance at the city gates; Isabella demands justice in public and puts Angelo on trial, in effect; the Duke makes Angelo marry Mariana, reveals that Claudio still lives, and puts it all right.) Everyone is pardoned, the laws of the land are enforced best they can be, and, frankly, on this earth we haven't got much further along, other than Claudio and Juliet can get married. We haven't advanced enough so that there could be any other positive outcome. Juliet, by the way, is one of those three-line women's parts that are stunning in their wholeness. Every word out of her mouth says it like it is.

Finally, the Duke does something unexpected—and I think points to the way Shakespeare was thinking. (I put *Measure for Measure* half in Act 2, the sexual/spiritual category, and half in Act 3, living underground.) The Duke asks Isabella to marry him. She doesn't answer. What is this about?

I have seen this moment played every which way: Gillian Barge's Isabella at the National Theatre was repulsed and backed out of the room. Melinda Lopez, performing in Boston, was overjoyed and flung herself into the Duke's arms. In 2010, at the Colorado Shakespeare Festival, the director gave the actor playing Isabella permission to change the ending each night, following the impulse that came up in that particular performance.

The only way I could find to solve it was to shift the ground of the play at that point—allow the Duke to be the embodiment of the Higher Power, Isabella the suffering human being trying to reach him—and to symbolize the moment in a tableau like Michelangelo's picture on the ceiling of the Sistine Chapel, of God touching and giving Adam life. Or God giving Christ His Spirit. Or men and women meeting so that together—and with the whole of themselves—they can meet and transform into a larger being which incorporates both the sexual and spiritual.

What we do know about ourselves is that we are teeming with unconscious thoughts and desires, and are unacquainted with many of the reasons behind many conscious thoughts and desires. (It is said by some experts that we are driven 5 percent by conscious thoughts, 95 percent unconscious.) We live in a world where we must look after one another to survive, and the highest expression of ourselves is when we align our language with who we really are. This develops us both as individuals and as social beings. If we know ourselves, the sexual desires we were born with will align with the spiritual desires that guide us—and so we muddle our way to some kind of higher learning.

There isn't a religious recipe that, if we obey it absolutely, will give us the answer. Life's a crap shoot that you maneuver the best you can—and this is true whether you are the Dalai Lama or Nelson Mandela or a Brooklyn Dodger or a Benedictine nun or a mall shopper or a cross-dresser or a mum in Nottingham or a dad from Nebraska. The guide is: how deeply can you ask the questions? If you break the laws of the land (especially if they are repressive laws), are you willing to take the consequences? If you know it is repressive, can you put the law itself on trial? Do you have the inner strength to ask yourself the most difficult questions about your own behavior? Look at the people around you. How are they affected by your behavior? Are they miserable or happy? What are you doing that contributes to their state of mind? How much are you yourself hooked into or dependent upon certain behavior patterns? What is the separation between what you say you are about and what you are actually doing? What is neurotic and what is life-enhancing?

These are fundamental questions. The ability to ask questions (which belongs to the sense anthropologists say matters most in the natural world—the seeking sense) makes us human and constructs human civilization. We all live within limits. Isabella wants to limit herself to the rules of the Order of Saint Clare; Angelo wants the enforcement of the law of the land to be the limit for everyone. They ask questions of each other—questions that are in a way "safe" to ask, because they are within the rules of a certain kind of speech—the art of logic. Then Mother Nature, or the unconscious mind, or the unknown, suddenly thrusts to the fore questions that are unexpected, that can't be controlled; feelings come rushing to the surface which were not recognized before, and chaos of mind and body ensues. Now what?

Isabella could change the world: she has the fervor, an ability with language, her sense of the symbiotic nature of the world, and she could teach the children, not about hellfire, but about the way the world is—and how we can work toward a state of grace, the true Garden of Eden.

SCENE 5: *Twelfth Night*

It's a relief to get to Viola after the complicated repression of the nun Isabella, the despair of Ophelia, the annihilation of Desdemona and Emilia. Though Viola is in mourning for her father and twin brother, she steps out into the world, willing to find new life. Even her name is a joy–Viola–a musical instrument. And, indeed, *Twelfth Night* is called a play with music, and it is steeped in music: the music of Orsino's court, the bawdy songs of Sir Toby and his cohorts, the bittersweet songs of Feste the fool, the sounds of the storm, the music of the verse.

It is subtitled *What You Will.* If we riff on "Will" for a moment, this play is about sexual delight, who has what kind of sexual part: Will is William Shakespeare, willing love into existence after a twin is lost, changing the will of others. It's developing Philip Sidney's precept that music and poetry develop consciousness, are drawn by love and toward love. And as Viola becomes a man/boy called Cesario (little Caesar), she rescues Olivia, also in mourning for her dead brother and father; she straightens out Orsino, moving him from fantasy love to true love; and she finds her own twin, emerging from the "blind waves and surges."

How much Shakespeare was thinking of his twins, Hamnet and Judith, as he wrote it, how much he was collaborating with a musician muse to get the music of the language and the actual music played onstage into alignment with the story of the play, we do not know. But it certainly seems that he must have done both these things. The song of lost childhood and the pain of growing up have never been better expressed. "When that I was a little tiny boy"–the pain of loss and the joy of love are point and counterpoint. *Twelfth Night* is one of the most profound, lighthearted, delicate works of art ever created. Shakespeare begins with music–"If music be the food of love, play on"–then switches to a storm and the loss of a twin, from Illyria to Elysium and back again. Once Viola is disguised as Cesario, she, in essence, becomes her male twin, dressing like him, thinking like him. When she visits Olivia on behalf of Orsino, the substitute courtier who pleads on behalf of a friend, she uses both her male and female selves. She woos as a man, she empathizes as a woman; she understands Olivia's state of mind, her loss of father and brother, and the potential for a free life without them. She asks directly for what she wants—"Good madam, let me see your face"—and Olivia lifts the veil of mourning, lifts her depression, and Viola/Cesario tells her what she sees, without embellishment or apology. She grounds Olivia—and Olivia falls in love with Cesario. Viola is in love with Orsino. Orsino thinks he is in love with Olivia, but he's finding himself more and more attracted to the boy Cesario. I think Shakespeare is gender-neutral in all this: It is more important to love than to love the "right" person. To find your love reciprocated gives it a power that can transform you both.

The third woman in the play, Maria, is a lady-in-waiting who manages to elevate her position to the gentry by serving and then marrying Sir Toby Belch, a drunkard and Olivia's uncle. Malvolio, the steward, who thinks he loves his mistress, Olivia, is cruelly humiliated. Sir Andrew, a vacuous, sad, fun-loving knight, makes the most significant statement in the play: "I was adored once, too." When Kevin Coleman played it in Shakespeare & Company's production at The Mount, the image of the mother who had doted on him when he was little was palpable. And you also knew she was dead now—he had stopped growing emotionally the moment she died. We all deserve to be adored by someone, at least once.

The love complications resolve themselves in the end, because Viola's twin, Sebastian, is rescued from the sea by Antonio, the ship's captain. Antonio is in love with Sebastian. Sebastian loves Antonio but is not in love with him. He falls instantly in love with Olivia when she asks him to marry her (she thinks he's Cesario), and without hesitation he says yes.

At the end of the play, we are sad for those who have not had their love reciprocated—Antonio, Malvolio, Andrew Aguecheek. But suffering for love is its own story, and that can bring new understanding, too. Like the weather, life changes: "With a hey, ho, the wind and the rain . . . For the rain, it raineth every day."

There's no getting around it.

SCENE 6: Descent of Shakespeare's Psyche:
All's Well That Ends Well

All's Well That Ends Well is an odd little play. Shakespeare wrote one of his best heroines ever—Helena, daughter of a first-rate physician. (The date of the play is around 1606, a couple of years before Shakespeare's granddaughter was born—who was also a prominent physician's daughter.) She is in love with a feckless aristocratic youth, Bertram. Helena, with the blessing of Bertram's mother, goes off in pursuit of him to the court of the King of France. The King is very sick, and Helena cures him; in return, the King will grant her a wish. The wish is to marry Bertram, and the King will give her a dowry. Bertram is enraged and outraged (we have some sympathy for him at this point—no one wants to be forced to marry against his or her will), but the King prevails. Once married, Bertram says he'll never acknowledge Helena as his wife unless she's carrying his child, and he's never going to sleep with her, so she'll never be his functioning wife. Bertram storms off to the wars with his best friend, the braggart Parolles. Helena is left behind, realizing she's sent her husband to potential death because he's so repulsed by her and her actions. At this point, Helena seems to give up—she will do penance by becoming a pilgrim and fleeing the court.

The play is really promising in the beginning—it's set in Roussillon, home of the troubadours in the south of France, where women have always been allowed equal rights with men. The actions of the Countess (Bertram's mother) and Helena seem healthy and normal. When I directed it, I made Lavatch, the Countess's resident fool, a worn-out, aging troubadour, a Joe Cocker/Tom Waits kind of guy. And that worked: I could insert songs when the plot weakened. But, ultimately, I think the play isn't rewarding, because Bertram is such an insubstantial, sulky person—he has to be forgiven because of his youth, but he's not really a good match for Helena. You wonder what she sees in him, and it's hard to get excited about their union.

Anyway, Helena becomes a pilgrim (a sort of disguise, I suppose) and goes on her journey. She bumps into her husband and his small army (going to do deeds of daring—the portrait of the Earl of Southampton again?). He falls in lust with a local girl, Diana, and persuades her (he thinks) to sleep with him. But, yet once again, Shakespeare does the bed trick! The women become friends; Helena takes Diana's place and gets pregnant, and all should be well. But the ending is not well, despite the title of the play, because everyone has deceived everyone else. Even at the last moments, Bertram is trying to wriggle out of things he's responsible for. The play has half a dozen false endings. (Did Shakespeare himself get fed up with it after four acts, and so handed over the last act, when all supposedly ends well, to be written by the actors, so each writes a bit where he gets his moment in the sun? It seems like that. I cut the ending to shreds.)

There are some good comic moments in the play, and if it's cast well, especially the outrageous fop Parolles, a message of redemption can be hauled into focus. Helena is *almost* one of Shakespeare's great heroines, but in the end we can't really applaud their marriage or the means by which they come to it! It certainly isn't a sexual/spiritual merging. People do learn something in it, but not a lot.

It is good to see a doctor's daughter make it into the ranks of the nobility—but, then, the nobility have so little nobility, it's hard to get excited about the outcome. A bittersweet comedy, I suppose you'd call it. Several journeys are taken, people learn, the sex is not good, there's a sense of longing for the old chivalric order (which probably never really existed), and some hope for the future and the unborn child.

AN INTERLUDE: Language in the Body

The thoughts about language in this chapter range from Shakespeare's use of language, to the appreciation of the world in general, and to Nigel and myself as actors. It includes how language lives in the body; the language we inherit from our parents, our country, our class; and how we are losing our ability to use language; the commitment to do the plays, *Women of Will*, or any work of art. What are you, the speaker, connecting to, and how important is it to experience what you are saying while you are saying it?

You can probably tell that I think language, and especially the spoken word, is essential to our health, sanity, and poetic mystery. If we don't nurture it, don't actually attend to the voice as an instrument, we will cease to be able to communicate a lot of information about ourselves and one another, cease to have the tools to express the nuance and depth of who we are!

Shakespeare was immersed in a world of language: it allowed him to be the poet and dramatist that he was. It also allowed him to express levels of meaning that those of us who work with his plays sometimes have to ponder, decipher, before we get the full impact of what he is saying. We have already lost some levels of his knowledge and consciousness, so we are forced to re-create them. "To be or not to be: that is the question" is a good example. You can say "Oh, it means to live or to kill yourself"—simple. Yes, it can mean that; but it also can mean to live in a state of being, fully conscious, or to live cut off from yourself and everyone around you. Okay. What happens if it means both those things? How do you connect them, and, more important, how do you speak them so your listeners will get both meanings *and* the connection between them? Now we are dealing with the art of delivery, one of the five sections in the art of rhetoric. Let us suppose you, the actor, deliver the line successfully and the audience or the listener gets it. Recognition happens. That recognition opens a series of images in the mind to connect you to your own life—when you were full of being as a child, say, or a time of despair when you thought no one cared for you and you cut yourself off from yourself because it was just too painful. And each audience member is also experiencing images of his or her life. And the oscillation between being and not being is palpable in the room—and out of that comes the question.

Almost every line in a Shakespeare play has this potential—to connect words and create images. The actors may not be able to see the images inside the imagination of the listener, but the body gives off a deeper knowledge than the words themselves and emits an empathetic understanding. To be a successful communicator, according to the art of rhetoric, the speaker needs to be in touch with three things: logos, ethos, and pathos. Logos obviously is the *sense* of what is being said; ethos, that it is an ethical argument or statement; and pathos, that it holds empathy, feeling, connection to what is being said. Then the listener can "get" someone else's state of being, the other position, and can relate to that position.

There is seemingly no end to the depth and complexity of language, as neuroscientists are revealing daily. We are made up of language in so many ways that I want to pause and ask: what difference does it make?

Taking language into ourselves—having it spark in the brain, reside in memory, touching the cells in our bodies, calling up responses every time a word or phrase or sound or piece of poetry is expressed—means that we are organisms in continuous response and action, creating our very being out of words.

So the language we use sets our life in motion; the language we use with our children gives them the map that they either will use for the rest of their lives or, if it is a destructive map, must identify and dismantle, so they can then create another map, in order to live a healthy life. The words used in the first five years of life enhance or scar us thereafter. But throughout, our language defines us, and can engender vibrant life or send us toward debilitating passivity.

If, as an actor, you memorize Shakespeare's poetry, take it into your body, you are blessed and cursed with the most profound brain waves, passages, and insights ever known to the imagination of man. If two people do this with each other, playing some twelve hours of

Shakespeare's thoughts, feelings, philosophical ideas, and psychological idiosyncrasies (which is what Nigel and I do when we perform all five parts of *Women of Will*), each pouring the sounds and emotions out of his or her own body and into the other's, there is no way, if they are both struggling to be as honest as they can, that they will not deeply know each other—maybe in a way that only people who have spent a lifetime with each other know each other. It is a closeness both terrible and ecstatic, because there is nowhere to hide—or it leads to a desperate but futile attempt to hide.

The concentration needed to ride a great Shakespeare part demands submission: your life is not your own, for it has to be built around the demands of the role. And once you start the ride of playing the role in performance, it will take you where it wants to go, because the power of the embodied words make their marks upon the psyche to reside there ever more.

Nige and I have had this kind of relationship for nine years now—not fifty-two weeks a year, but often for thirty weeks during a year—and we have more to go. To sustain it in generosity, truthfulness, and commitment is a huge demand, the kind of demand Michelangelo put upon himself to paint the ceiling of the Sistine Chapel. And there are two of us; we have to create with all our jagged edges showing, or we will not create the friction, the tension needed for the possibility of great art.

So there comes a point when you ask yourself: Do I want to make this commitment? Do I want the cost to myself and the people around me? Sooner or later, all relationships get ground up in this journey. Are you willing to lose relationships or put them on hold or let them change? Are you willing to put in the hours, are you willing to take on the emotional roller-coaster to bring the piece on home? Are you willing to let other people say or think what they like, knowing that they may be disparaging or indifferent while you are on the journey?

It is a question Shakespeare himself must have asked, as he lived, year after year, away from his wife and children, away from Stratford. When he was touring out on the road, he must have thought, "My body can't take this."

I think I have already answered that question for myself—yes, I'll do whatever it takes. I have already given up the helm of Shakespeare & Company, I rarely live at home, I talk to my husband maybe twice a week, my son once a week. I have given up my income, my autonomy, my institutional support. I am in pain much of the time, but I also have moments of ecstasy. (Not as much pain, I'm sure, as Michelangelo had, lying on his back high on a scaffold week after week.) I don't know how this will come out; at one point, it feels ridiculous; at another, this is the *only* thing to be doing. I often do not know what Nige thinks and feels, but when he's closed off from me I panic. I know I am dependent upon him and his disposition to get our job done.

Being an actor is a balancing act—especially if the actors you are working with inspire you, the roles you are playing are beautifully written, and you really buy into the life situation you are playing. When he was playing Hamlet, Daniel Day-Lewis walked offstage in the middle of the Ghost scene because, so the story goes, he just couldn't take it. Too close to his father. And it is certainly true, when watching his portrayal of Abraham Lincoln, for example, that you cannot see the actor at all—only Lincoln. He is that person. Daniel Day-Lewis takes long breaks between roles (fortunately, he's earned enough money to do that) before choosing what he's going to do next. The extreme sensitivity demanded of the psyche and the body to inhabit ultimately another person's world, and yet allow that person to *be* you, means that the boundaries we all set up for ourselves, the habits we evolve in order to live life, are dissolved, and it is difficult to know who you are or what you are—until you get to the next role. It's a balancing act: you want to invite yourself to play the ultimate game, but then you must step out of it and go back to who you were. Some actors find it more difficult to do that than others. I am one of those.

And yet I know that being an actor has led me to be *present* in almost every situation in my own life, including work that has nothing to do with theatre. When I am aware of this, I bless its influence in my life.

The place, or state of being, where art is made lies in the mystery of things. It is deeply intuitive. The voice, the body, and the questions make up the journey, create the map. In theatre, the audience creates the energy and focus to transform the imagination of all present, actors and onlookers; and this imagination creates a reality that has the power to affect lives. The power emanating from a work of art, whether through voices and bodies or paint on a canvas—that is where the reality will come forth by itself if we (artists and audience) let go of control and allow it to do so. We don't know what it is, we only have crude indicators of how it was made, but once we can sense it, we have to allow it to use us and do its work. It is beyond reality and yet it is reality—and it changes everything around it.

In the end, it is ownership of the words in Shakespeare that aligns me, the actor, to myself. My security, the sense of who I am, is finally anchored in my ability to speak the truth of the character I am playing. And to offer that reality to the audience and my fellow actor. That's when the alignment or harmony comes in. No matter if painful, funny, violent, or loving, the vulnerable offering of inner and outer truth, manifested in words, builds the connection between human beings. It allows a psychic connection of flow—never resting in one place, but building a security in the knowledge that "this is how this is in this moment of time" and allowing us to find the power and joy in that.

Elizabethans *experienced* speech: it was felt in their bodies as they said the words. Thus, the life of a conversation was far more present for them. Our modern habit, by contrast, is to have a thought and then let our mouths report what the brain thought. The only time this habit changes for us is when our bodies are leading an exchange—for example, in a fight or during lovemaking. As actors, we must feel the words in the whole body or they have no power.

Creativity is far more present in embodied speech—using all the organs, knowing what you feel—and consequently having *ownership* of ideas. The art of memory, another facet of the art of rhetoric, feeds into this. The playhouses were built as places to enhance memory. There is a correlation between the proportions of the playhouses and the size of our bodies, a mental alignment between the organs of the body, connecting to the larger world of the cosmos, the depiction of the roof of the "heavens" overlooking the stage, and a grounding of this connection in the body.

Poetry and music, mathematics, astrology, and medicine all use vibration and harmony to understand ever finer levels of perception, intuitively finding where the connections are and manifesting them in words and notes. The *flow* of ideas was one of the great hallmarks of the Elizabethan age, and finding balance between the ideas created the ability to expand, perceive, connect, and go forward. Eventually, the Puritan faction in England wanted words and reason to be the *only* truth. If it was provable, it was true; if it was embellished, it was not true. This led the way for fanatics to take over. Multiplicity of knowledge needs an open mind and body, and many ways of knowing. Not being able to hold the tension of opposing truths can lead to violence. For example, music had been a part of the everyday lives of all Elizabethans. When the Puritans came to power, they suppressed all music except that played in praise of God. This meant that the body had no freedom, no outlet for so many complicated feelings. This built tension, which burst out in other places. The body and the body politic are not aligned, because such repression is unnatural. Frustration will eventually lead to violence, as it did in England in 1642.

We take our learned behavior with us, everywhere we go. The language of our parents constructs the world we grow up in, and guides the way we live our lives. If the parents' world picture is a destructive one, it is hard work to change it—but it must be changed. As Ovid said: "Only he who knows himself will love with wisdom and according to his powers, perform love's work in full."

Nigel and I have made our way through all the plays of Shakespeare's writing life; we have caught sight of his childhood, teen years, and early parenthood. We try to learn from him and one another, but often we clash in violent disagreement about the value of a part, the degree of commitment to an emotion, the difficulty of being this kind of human being, switching into that kind of person.

As we develop *Women of Will,* the question of how the world is going to develop, in which direction it will go, is part of our process and conversation. It probably is for you, too. Indeed, into every home from every part of the world, around the clock, is beamed "the news": can we ever get our minds around all that is happening, let alone influence any outcome? Through what frame can we look at the world so that it makes some sense, reveals a coherence?

By following the women in the canon, it is possible to see how they looked at the world and how Shakespeare's mind developed as he made them more and more his mouthpiece. There is a form here that allows the huge mass of information to make a pattern—a road map. We can follow the plays; we can take the information pouring in from all over the world and apply it to this road map. We can look at our lives and see how they measure up against Shakespeare's. Is this the right road map? We don't know. We'll find out when and if the results come in.

We are facing the same kind of problems the Renaissance academies faced and sought to answer. An answer is not possible without the arts, because it's only in the space of creativity and the visceral desire to experience new states that we can adjust to each other. If we live only in *the mind* (and by that I mean the voice in our heads that gives us instructions), we won't succeed. The mind fights for survival by hanging on to what it knows, and thinks it is being attacked if asked to change; whereas the artist goes into deeper layers and creates contexts in which several things can be true at the same time. Also, the artist's medium is not one thing—one artist works with space and color, another in stone, another with sound, another with words, another with nature, another with her own body—but rhythm is important to all, and rhythm always connects and unites. Cities that were built as conscious works of art—Venice, Vienna, Prague, Florence—are conducive to imaginative thinking. London had great beauty and indescribable squalor.

Shakespeare's mind expanded with his sensitivity to new information—his grammar-school training in the art of rhetoric and his intrinsic talent with language in the body made him a great rhetorician. His work as an actor exercised his empathetic understanding. He developed his "feminine" qualities while observing the "masculine" qualities of his warrior aristocratic friends. His work in the playhouse allowed him to understand poetry and music as deeply as any of the academicians and connected him to the past and the future.

To quote Frances Yates, citing the academician La Boderie in her book *The French Academies of the Sixteenth Century*: ". . . the present reappearance of the sisters Poetry and Music—closely united as in the best of times . . . is the latest phase of the age-long travels of the sisters in the course of which they have dwelt, turn by turn, in Ancient

Gaul, Egypt, Greece, Judea, Rome, Italy. . . . 'mythological' language is really but an expression of the profound truth of the continuity of all human thought and experience."

Above all, Shakespeare knew and developed his study of the human psyche: Why do people think, feel, and react the way they do? Is there a pattern in their thinking, as there is a pattern in music? Does the pattern in thinking lead to joy or depression?

Shakespeare piled up all these different ways of knowing things—for instance, his love and knowledge of nature; his understanding of the law; the music that accompanied the action of the plays; the handling of hawks and hounds; the quality of glove-making—as metaphors to awaken a deeper knowing in the audience. He experimented with the art of playmaking (so different from Ben Jonson, who insisted on classical form, unity of time and space). He ranged across the universe: the court one minute, a battlefield half a world away the next, a grotto on an island, a passage leading to hell. He mixed philosophy with music and dance, raging anger and death with buffoonery and tricks, always showing how these things are connected. How disparate parts are associated was his fascination—what the sinner and the saint have in common, how the "stranger" demands compassion. As More says to the crowd in the fragment of *Sir Thomas More* we have, written in Shakespeare's own hand:

> You'll put down strangers,
> Kill them, cut their throats, possess their houses . . .
> Go you to France or Flanders,
> To any German province, Spain or Portugal,
> Nay, anywhere that not adheres to England;
> Why you must needs be strangers. Would you be pleased
> To find a nation of such barbarous temper
> That, breaking out in hideous violence,
> Would not afford you an abode on earth,
> Whet their detested knives against your throats,
> Spurn you like dogs . . .
> This is the strangers' case,
> And this your mountainish inhumanity.
> SIR THOMAS MORE (SCENE 6, 139–40, 147–55, 159–60)

And the crowd is persuaded. They stop screaming for the death and expulsion of "strangers" in their land and disperse in peace. (Shakespeare lived with "strangers," the refugee Huguenot family the Mountjoys, for eight years in London. So did his friend Richard Field, with the Vautrollier family.)

The actor saying More's words must truly commit himself to living those words. The body and mind must at all times be vulnerable, so the layers of understanding come through, having an impact on both the crowd onstage and the audience off.

One of the most moving moments I have ever had in the theatre was when a group of young inmates (eighteen to twenty-two years old) from the Roslindale lockup were performing *Hamlet,* as part of a program Brent Blair ran for many years under the auspices of Shakespeare & Company. The actor playing Horatio, with the dead Hamlet in his arms, looked out at the audience and said:

> And let me speak to th'yet unknowing world
> How these things come about. So shall you hear
> Of carnal, bloody, and unnatural acts,
> Of accidental judgements, casual slaughters,
> Of deaths put on by cunning and forced cause;
> And, in this upshot, purposes mistook
> Fall'n on th'inventors' heads. All this can I
> Truly deliver.
>
> HAMLET (5.2, 331–38)

And he could. It was true. He knew far more about these things than anyone in the audience. He spoke it very simply. But we all knew that his eighteen-year path in the inner city, in a town that boasts the most universities in the world, had been through repeated death, violence, intentional and unintentional, and finally jail for young violent offenders.

It was powerful. Did it change anything? I don't know. But just saying it in public, at that moment, felt like it changed the world.

I think Will Shakespeare's desire to understand the world never ceased. And the debt he owed to the stories in the playhouse, and to the learning from the academies, never ceased. The academies advo-

cated myth or parable as the best way of telling the highest truths—
and that is exactly what Shakespeare did, with his use of symbolism
and hidden meanings, drawing back the curtain to reveal the truth.

The plays written during the last five years of his writing life—when
he was living mostly in Stratford and only occasionally in London—
are symbolic tales saturated in the rhythms of nature and music,
engendering tales of unity and hope in the aftermath of great tragedy. But now, at the point we have reached in the canon, he was on
Dante's descent into hell; he was going into the darkest places. There
is no symbolic feminine spirit to guide the way out, only submission
to grief, pain, and suffering, a lament holding the extremes of passion
and the despair of mankind: *Macbeth, Lear, Timon of Athens, Coriolanus.* And the door to this hell is opened in *Hamlet*—a play I think
Shakespeare worked on for much of his life.

[ACT 4]

CHAOS IS COME AGAIN:
THE LION EATS THE WOLF

SCENE 1: Overview: *Hamlet* Leading into *Macbeth*

This is what Hamlet says to his mother, rebuking her for having a sex life:

> You cannot call it love, for at your age
> The heyday in the blood is tame. . . .
> HAMLET (3.4, 75–76)

This is what he says about his father:

> He was a man. Take him for all in all,
> I shall not look upon his like again.
> HAMLET (1.2, 188–89)

In the first statement, we see Hamlet's psyche, direct and moral, chastising his mother for impurity. He is the authority; she has to behave the way he deems appropriate. There is no question that this is how Hamlet feels—he's committed and passionate in his words. He expects her to change her behavior and has no empathy or insight for who she is! In the second statement, when Hamlet is talking about his father to his friend, his speech is idealized, romantic, the description of "a man": one that will inspire men for centuries to come.

Hamlet is named for his father. King Hamlet seems to have been loved and admired. Hamlet Junior eulogizes him as a son should. So why does no one think Hamlet Junior should be king? After all, he is, as Ophelia says, "The glass of fashion and the mould of form / Th'observed of all observers. . . ." Yet, when Hamlet Senior dies, the man selected to be king is Claudius, Hamlet's brother. Prince Hamlet is passed over—he's a student, he thinks too much, he's depressed, he doesn't seem too keen on making a proper dynastic marriage by negotiating for another royal, he may be mad, he doesn't behave like a manly man. This Hamlet doesn't seem to possess too many masculine qualities; in fact, he has an awful lot of feminine qualities. He's full of feelings and wants to talk about them; he seems unnaturally obsessed with his mother and wants to talk about her sex life; he contradicts himself all the time; he intuitively knows his uncle has killed his father—but there's absolutely no proof, so how can he be so sure? He'd better talk about it some more.

He sees ghosts and listens to dreams. And when his ghost father tells him that he (Hamlet Senior) was killed by his brother and asks Hamlet Junior to avenge his death, in the right, honorable way, Hamlet says yes, yes, yes, he'll do it.

But somehow he never gets round to it. Not like the other two young men in the play. The Norwegian Prince Fortinbras (strong in arms) has made his life about pursuing the honor that his father lost when Hamlet Senior beat him in single combat. At the beginning of the play, he's about to attack Denmark. Claudius's ambassadors manage to avert that danger—but we all know it's only a matter of time before Fortinbras will reappear, fighting to overcome Denmark and take back what his father lost. Which is exactly what happens in the last scene of the play.

When the lord chamberlain, Polonius, is killed, his son, Laertes, returns to the court immediately, demanding restitution, ready to kill whoever is responsible, ready to raise an army if necessary. So there is no shortage of examples of how young men are expected to and do act in this world where honor demands an eye for an eye, a tooth for a tooth, a life for a life. But Hamlet doesn't do it. Instead, he beats up on his girlfriend and he's cruel to his mother. Now, admittedly, Ophelia did not show much courage when her father told her not to have anything to do with Hamlet. (Can you imagine what Desdemona or Imogen would have to say under the same circumstances?) But you might think Hamlet would take some time to find out the reason for

Ophelia's actions, not just use their rift as an excuse to elaborate on his pretend madness. And then he gives his mother a terrible time. The two things are linked. The relationship with his mother is intimate, close, and when she does something Hamlet cannot deal with, his response tumbles over into his relationship with Ophelia.

Hamlet is enraged with his mother—even before he knows that Claudius has killed his father—because she is in love and seems to be having a terrific time, especially sexually.

Hamlet Senior loved Gertrude in a particular way. He put her on a pedestal.

> . . . so loving to my mother
> That he might not beteem the winds of heaven
> Visit her face too roughly!
>
> HAMLET (1.2, 140–42)

If you are a woman, you know that a pedestal is lonely and drafty. Where you want to be is in a bed, knowing someone is mad about you and you about him. And that is where Gertrude has finally gotten herself, after about twenty-five years of being on the pedestal. Hamlet's description of Claudius and Gertrude's lovemaking is powerfully erotic.

> Nay, but to live
> In the rank sweat of an enseamèd bed,
> Stewed in corruption, honeying and making love
> Over the nasty sty—
>
> HAMLET (3.4, 91–94)

And it goes on from there. Hamlet makes graphic, visual pictures of what they do in bed: he's obsessed. Sex is not the only reason Gertrude is in love with Claudius: he values her judgment and makes her his co-ruler.

> Therefore our sometime sister, now our queen,
> Th'imperial jointress of this warlike state . . .
>
> HAMLET (1.2, 8–9)

He discusses what action they should take and gives her full agency.

So any woman, and it was certainly true for me both times I performed it, knows that Gertrude is finally coming into her own after decades of disenfranchisement.

But it comes at a price. And the price is: she is in love with Claudius, but she does not ask him any questions. Indeed, she doesn't even see the questions! She doesn't yet have any clear idea of her own will (as in will to power—in sexual will, she wants to be with Claudius). Even if she were adept and experienced in exercising her will, she would have to choose between her son and her husband as they become adversaries. She doesn't have the strength to find out what is actually going on and negotiate between the two. Instead, she chooses her husband. At first she promises her son she won't go back to Claudius's bed:

QUEEN GERTRUDE What shall I do?
HAMLET Not this, by no means, that I bid you do:
    Let the bloat king tempt you again to bed,
    Pinch wanton on your cheek, call you his mouse,
    And let him for a pair of reechy kisses,
    Or paddling in your neck with his damn'd fingers,
    Make you to ravel all this matter out. . . .
                HAMLET (3.4, 178–84)

To which she replies:

    Be thou assured, if words be made of breath,
    And breath of life, I have no life to breathe
    What thou hast said to me.
                HAMLET (3.4, 195–97)

But the moment after Hamlet has left her and Claudius appears, she tells him everything—thereby sealing Hamlet's fate and eventually her own.

The structure of power, the inability to challenge it, is endemic in the plays, and Shakespeare shows the consequences. The women in *Richard III* are the opposition to Richard's rise to power, and they all die or are banished except Elizabeth Woodville. In the *Henry IV* plays,

Falstaff exposes the folly of the idea of honor, mocks at legal systems, exploits his position–but he never offers an alternative to the power structure. Primogeniture or "might is right" is the power structure; a hierarchical form of command is its system.

Rosalind/Ganymede and Viola/Cesario offer potent new models of loving and are courageous in standing within their own truths. But, though we learn from them, they don't necessarily stay empowered once they've returned to their frocks–except on a personal level. It's the inability to change the way systems of power operate that forms both the stability and the destructiveness of power.

If Hamlet had been a manly man, he could have defeated his uncle, taken over the kingdom, and challenged Fortinbras. Instead, he talks and, though not a physical coward, uses his considerable mental powers to try and understand both himself and the world. He never understands the women in his life. But Shakespeare does: he now studies women who want the top job–power status, a voice that is heard. And when women want these things, what happens to the world?

The line of women starting with Gertrude and developing with the two elder daughters of King Lear bursts fully formed with Lady Macbeth and then becomes the ultimate nightmare in Volumnia in *Coriolanus*. In some ways, these characters represent certain individual women who have behaved thus for thousands of years. They accept the way power works and determine to exploit it. Their lives are ostensibly bound up in being helpmates to their spouses. Whatever it is the spouse wants, that is what he is going to get. Think of Nancy Reagan's adoring looks, Laura Bush's quiet goodness (proving her husband couldn't be that bad); Hillary Clinton's support of Bill's political agenda when his infidelities hit the media, and her determined silence, standing by her man, even as every moralist and many feminists asked, "How can you?" These women and others like them joined with their husbands' ambition, empowering their men to get further than they could by themselves. And whereas Hillary wanted power for herself separate from Bill, I doubt Nancy Reagan would ever have been capable or happy heading up a serious campaign to stop drug use. Her real job was supporting Ronnie. This model bears itself out in almost any country you care to name–the Philippines,

England (Margaret Thatcher notwithstanding), France, Italy (maybe Ehud Olmert's wife in Israel was an exception).

Are the models of Goneril and Regan, Lady Macbeth, and Volumnia the template for how women have used their power over the past two thousand years? And if so, how does it work and why do women do it?

I want us to look at *Macbeth* in some depth and see what we can learn.

At the top of the play, Macbeth is general of Duncan's army. He's in the heart of the killing fields, repelling the Norwegians and overcoming the Scottish traitor, the Thane of Cawdor.

> For brave Macbeth—well he deserves that name!—
> Disdaining fortune, with his brandished steel
> Which smoked with bloody execution,
> Like valour's minion carved out his passage
> till he faced the slave,
> Which ne'er shook hands nor bade farewell to him
> Till he unseamed him from the nave to th'chops,
> And fixed his head upon our battlements.
>
> MACBETH (1.2, 18–25)

He's an incredible fighter. And so is Macbeth's best friend, Banquo. Without the two of them, it's doubtful Duncan would retain his kingship. He himself doesn't fight, and his two sons, Malcolm and Donalbain, are considered too young to take to the field.

As Macbeth and Banquo ride home after the battle, they are met on the heath by three witches, and the witches make two prophecies: that Macbeth will become king, and that Banquo, though he'll never be a monarch himself, will give birth to a whole line of kings (James I, now sitting on the English throne, being one of them).

Immediately following this, Duncan makes Macbeth Thane of Cawdor. The news shocks and inspires him—and then he gets very, very nervous. He's shaken with insecurities, the opposite of his behavior on the battlefield.

> *(Aside)* This supernatural soliciting
> Cannot be ill, cannot be good. If ill,

Why hath it given me earnest of success
Commencing in a truth? I am Thane of Cawdor.
If good, why do I yield to that suggestion
Whose horrid image doth unfix my hair
And make my seated heart knock at my ribs
Against the use of nature? Present fears
Are less than horrible imaginings.
My thought, whose murder yet is but fantastical,
Shakes so my single state of man
That function is smothered in surmise,
And nothing is but what is not.

MACBETH (1.3, 140–52)

The next thing he does is write to his wife and tell her about it.

So here we have powerful, brute force in the form of Macbeth's skills as a warrior. We have knowledge of the future, which may or may not be accurate but in and of itself is neutral, neither good nor bad—it depends on how you use it. And we have a whole system of male loyalty and friendship that keeps the balance of how succession to power is decided, how hierarchical form is kept in place, and how alliances are kept. And we have Macbeth's "horrible imaginings."

Writing to his wife, his "dearest partner in greatness," starts a train of events that ends in Scotland's destroying itself through fascism, civil insurrection, the slaughter of women and children, and an instability that could go on for generations.

What happens, and how does Shakespeare develop the strands of the play? (And, as a sidebar, why is it, in so many productions of *Macbeth,* that terrible things happen to the cast and crew? More on this later.)

The play lives on several levels. There are the things that happen in it; and then there are the images that haunt the play. These images work on the audience's unconscious minds, so that the most basic drives human beings have—for love, power, nurturing, and coupling—are awakened, and these basic drives forge a knowledge about ourselves that isn't always easy to accept.

I am going to start with the words most often repeated in the play. "Blood" is the first—"blood," "bloody," "bleeding," blood, blood.

The image of blood is present all over the battlefield; the warriors are bathed in it, and their courage is evaluated according to the blood they have shed.

Then we move to the blood of Lady Macbeth—her allusions to giving birth, her wish to make thick her blood to "stop up the access and passage to remorse." Then we move to Duncan's blood. Killing Duncan covers the grooms of the bed chamber with blood; the hands of the Macbeths are drenched in blood. Then the grooms are killed; then Banquo is killed—he reappears at the coronation feast drenched in blood, and it's reported that horses eat one another. Lady Macduff and her children are killed, including the baby; finally, Lady Macbeth dies, and Macbeth decides he's steeped in blood so deep that he'll just keep killing everyone that he can while he's still alive.

The next image is milk—white, warm, intended to nurture, but somehow "I have given suck" turns into "bring forth men-children only," and milk and semen become intermingled, and the children who are made with semen, and suckled with milk, end up as blood. I always think it works even more powerfully if Lady Macduff is still nursing her youngest in her assassination scene. Macduff has had to make the hardest of choices, whether to stay with his wife and children to protect them, or leave them, go to England, and get help—the basic choice every bird has to make when he leaves the nest to get food. And when Macduff hears of their deaths in England, he calls them his chicks:

> All my pretty ones?
> Did you say all? O hell-kite! All?
> What, all my pretty chickens and their dam
> At one fell swoop?
>
> MACBETH (4.3, 249–52)

Likewise Lady Macduff names them before she's slaughtered:

> Poor bird, thou'dst never fear the net nor lime, the pitfall nor the gin.
>
> MACBETH (4.2, 39)

These two very fundamental images of blood and milk/semen are strengthened by the vulnerability of the young—whether it's the child the Macbeths lost; Banquo's son Fleance, who flees his murderers; Macduff's children, who are too young to escape; or Duncan's son Malcolm, who eventually grows up enough to challenge Macbeth.

But Malcolm wavers. He fears himself. If he gets ultimate power, his nightmare is that he won't be able to control himself: he'll screw every woman in sight, take land and goods from everyone below him, find there is no end to his desire for power. Blood, blood, blood, semen, blood.

Pity, compassion, is a newborn babe and has no power against the wolf.

> And pity, like a naked new-born babe,
> Striding the blast, or heaven's cherubin, horsed
> Upon the sightless couriers of the air,
> Shall blow the horrid deed in every eye
> That tears shall drown the wind.
>
> MACBETH (1.7, 21–25)

These images are so potent in the imagination of the actors and audience (whether they realize it or not) because we are being called to our most fundamental selves—the selves that come out of the basic elements of life, the selves that want to be embodied, to feel ourselves in our bodies, that want to survive in *this* world, want to dominate in *this* world, want to unite the blood and semen and milk in *this* world. Not in the next world. Or the hope of the next world.

Lady Macbeth personifies the desire for power in this world. The moment she hears about the witches' prophecy, she knows her course. She will use all her feminine power to call her man to greatness; she will hold him, through his most basic desires, to achieve that kingship. She knows he is too spiritual to do what she decides is necessary to get the top prize. It's extraordinary, if you think about it. Macbeth knows all about killing—yet he has managed to keep his spirituality, his love for his friends, and his loyalty to his king. But there is something amiss in the marriage: something Lady Macbeth thinks will be healed by their becoming king and queen. I think it's the loss of the child. He (and I'm sure it's a he) must have died recently, for Lady Macbeth still has milk in her breasts. Did he die while Macbeth was fighting the wars? Is Lady Macbeth unhinged by the absence of her husband and the loss of her child?

Lady Macbeth may be Macbeth's most basic other half, but she unwittingly destroys their union. She calls upon the darker powers to take away her compassion and humanity, so she can persuade Macbeth to kill Duncan. She truly believes the fulfillment of the prophecy is going to give them unity, closeness, ecstasy: they will be bound to each other forever because they will know something no one else does. And they will make up for the loss of the child.

Of course, none of that happens. Her actions create the opposite effect. Macbeth loses his moral compass. He goes further and further away from her, and she is unable to get him back. The desire for blood builds in him; he doesn't sleep; he prefers the company of the witches; he gets pleasure from exerting his will over other people. And as he takes this journey, she becomes unhinged, unable to connect with him or to herself—and she goes mad. She dies. It's not clear whether she kills herself or simply falls off a high battlement somewhere; Shakespeare doesn't bother to say, because it doesn't matter. And Macbeth doesn't bother to find out.

So, from the first images of life—blood, semen, milk, sexual will, and the will to power—through the destruction of the young, we go to the complete emptiness of life.

> She should have died hereafter.
> There would have been a time for such a word.
> Tomorrow, and tomorrow, and tomorrow
> Creeps in this petty pace from day to day
> To the last syllable of recorded time,
> And all our yesterdays have lighted fools
> The way to dusty death. Out, out, brief candle.
> Life's but a walking shadow, a poor player
> That struts and frets his hour upon the stage,
> And then is heard no more. It is a tale
> Told by an idiot, full of sound and fury,
> Signifying nothing.
>
> MACBETH (5.5, 17–28)

I never feel productions of *Macbeth* work if the woman playing Lady Macbeth is a trophy wife: there's not enough life experience for the images to resonate in depth; the relationship is too shallow to hold the power of the layers of meaning.

Life's meaning comes through our actions, how we value them, and what we give to others: those "feminine" qualities of relationship, tenderness, nurturance. These are the very things Lady Macbeth gives up because she thinks power pre-empts them. She strengthens the competitive part of herself and Macbeth, yet she understands her existence only through him. She is not willing to put herself through the pain of loss; she must have the salve now, and that salve is power: the power of other people acknowledging you as the most important humans on earth. The undercurrents in *Macbeth*, pointing to power we don't understand and yet want to harness—are relevant to our world. In one of my productions, I made the witches white-coated scientists, playing in a nuclear-power station, bursting into *American Idol* song, seductive in its popularity.

It is the classic feminine conundrum, "I want so much to be with him; let me change the way I think and act in order to have this relationship." (Actually, I'm sure this probably works with couples of the same sex as well, but we have had fewer decades of examining same-sex couples, and same-sex couples have not yet been allowed overt supremacy of power—at least not since Greek times, two thousand years ago—so there's not so much evidence.) If you abandon yourself in order to be in a relationship, you cannot be in a relationship. (A position Carol Gilligan reveals cogently in *The Birth of Pleasure*.)

The male power structure was and is the accepted "norm." It is changing, but slowly. The woman wants to be with the man, and to play where the men are. In order to do that, she has to turn a blind eye, or, in the case of Lady Macbeth and Volumnia, actively support the things men do in order to achieve power. So she will suppress her own natural instincts in order to give a man what he wants (he may not even want these things, but he has so bought into the patriarchal structure that it seems as if it's natural to have them, so of course he must want them). She gives up who she is in order to have this relationship. And in doing so, she loses touch with who she is—and ultimately she loses herself as well as him and the relationship.

This in turn points to an even greater problem—the reinforced structure of the institutions that guide us. From the moment the great institutions were created in the Golden Age of Greece—the athletic center, the religious house, the academy, the army, the law, the theatre, the government—they were created by older males who then trained younger males. They all had a strong homoerotic element. (How could they not? They would never have gotten off the ground without it—in fact, building homoeroticism into the center of each was what made it so powerful.) This thereby increased the "rightness" of masculinity, never mind that half the world was feminine. That other half was also interested in philosophy, the arts, the law, religion, and athletics, but they had this other task—bringing children to term and nurturing them through the early years of their lives. And doing it again and again. Not that this gave status to women. On the contrary, the man's seed made the child. A woman was simply the receptacle provided by nature to carry the child until it was ready to come out. And perhaps the only thing women are not so keen on is war, and its fellow traveler "honor," because this means someone will end up dead, and women know the price of bringing someone into life.

Not only did this blotting out of women's voices so many years ago keep men and women in their stereotypical roles, but institutions developed without women, without including women's ways of knowing and doing. Why did no one think that women and men could equally share in the joys and tribulations of family life and the workplace? Were we pregnant all the time?

Now our institutions in the West are doing their best to "accommodate" women, and they are shifting structures to allow families to bring up their children. But there is no serious debate on how the whole structure needs to be rethought, including the economic systems that go along with them and the thinking patterns they produce.

And, of course, it is the two modern "institutions"—namely, the corporation and the media—where competition has become the very center of their reason for being, and now they threaten to be lethal to our health; and where the modern discipline of economics is used to drive competitive tendencies so hard that we could all end up without a planet. (Albeit with some individuals being incredibly wealthy as we stumble into oblivion.)

And yes, I am grateful for modern medicine, most technologies, and the washing machine.

When we see a Lady Macbeth or a Volumnia using all of her considerable powers—intellectual and sexual—to promote the masculine institutions of war and aggressive superiority in government, we know that we are in real trouble. "Had he not resembled / My father as he slept, I had done't," Lady Macbeth tells the audience—pausing for a moment, and then pushing forward again. But if she had stopped herself in that moment, if she had really examined what she was doing and seen how profoundly unconscious desires were driving her, we would have had a different course of events, and a different kind of world. (When we are performing *Women of Will*, Nigel points out that the two eldest daughters of Lear and Lady Macbeth have no idea monarchies are going to be thrust upon them, so when they suddenly have the top job, they model their behavior on what they are used to—the patriarchal system.)

To counteract the ingrained power of the institutions, women and a few good men must use all their energy and perceptions to create alternative forms for those institutions, replacing money as the sole arbiter of success with the possibility of satisfaction on many levels. Otherwise, we end up as Scotland, a destroyed country where no one is safe and there is no hope for the future.

It is Shakespeare's greatness that he saw that men and women had to be absolutely equal in order to know one another deeply and truly. To know yourself—whether you are a man or a woman—is to be in touch with your most primitive self, fundamental self, and your knowledge in the body. And this in turn allows you to be grounded as you expand into your spiritual, creative, elusive, sensitive self, which stretches beyond your body, out to other people, nature, the world, humanity, the essence of life itself.

The story of the Macbeths is the story of what happens when a powerful woman loses herself and plays the patriarchal game—it ends in fascism. And as we go into *Coriolanus* and *Timon of Athens*, Shakespeare explores the despair that a world without the feminine breeds and engenders.

Earlier in this chapter, I asked why so many accidents of "bad" things happen during productions of *Macbeth*. It's because there are forces at work in the play we are not aware of. We only perceive them dimly; they unbalance us, and unless we are careful, they knock us off kilter. The energy is deeply disturbed around *Macbeth*. I think Shakespeare lit candles and said prayers as he worked on it, not wanting to expose himself to its power even as he sought to expose its power.

SCENE 2: Goneril and Regan

The three daughters of Lear are a conundrum. Why do two of them become so cruel and one so forgiving? Why do Goneril and Regan commit acts of violence upon others, whereas Cordelia returns to rescue her father and then share his fate? Did they have different mothers? Were they brought up in different times? Is it just the genes Mother Nature gave them? Or did Lear treat them very differently as they were growing up? Certainly he puts pressure on Goneril to be the eldest, show the way, set the example (examples he deems right and proper). Regan he coddles more, and her responses to him seem to have a secret sexual code in them:

> I profess
> Myself an enemy to all other joys
> Which the most precious square of sense possesses,
> And find I am alone felicitate
> In your dear highness' love.
>
> KING LEAR (1.1, 63–67)

But with Cordelia, there is nothing hidden. He says publicly that she is his favorite—indeed, he's determined to spend the rest of his days in "her kind nursery," reversing the parent/child relationship. What is happening here? And why is there only one mention of a mother in the whole play?

Goneril is as exacting as her father. She copies him and his way of doing things. She is reasonable but assertive. She expects to be obeyed.

Although Lear is still king, he has reduced his power to a hundred knights and no longer has his own home; he's determined to have a good time, with no care or responsibilities of state. So he makes Goneril's palace his play space and behaves like a disruptive teenager. When Goneril tries to rectify the situation, he curses her and her womb—

asking nature to "dry up in her the organs of increase." Given Goneril's none-too-happy relationship with her husband, Albany (Was he her father's choice? She certainly has no affection for him), this curse will probably come true. Except, of course, she falls in love with Edmund, bastard son of the Duke of Gloucester. Out of that passion, new life may spring forth. Goneril's attempts to control her father are as useless as his to control her once she has attained her inheritance and he no longer has any real power or influence over her.

Regan is even worse. Regan shields herself by always having someone else ostensibly at fault; this shields her so she can do horrendous things and everyone will think, "Oh, it's not really her fault, she was led astray." Goneril states how much she loves Lear; Regan says me, too, I say what she says, "only she comes too short." Goneril wants to halve Lear's train; Regan wants to quarter it. Regan turns on Gloucester when he tries to protect Lear (and we are in Gloucester's home), but it is her husband, Cornwall, who orders Lear's man Kent to be put in the stocks, Cornwall who leads the torture of Gloucester, putting out his eyes, goaded on by Regan. Goneril falls in love with Edmund; Regan follows suit, making sure she's the one who is going to get him by publicly giving him her powers (once Cornwall is dead). In the end, Goneril poisons her sister: obviously, a lifetime of knowing how Regan operates leads her simply to obliterate her.

As for Cordelia, she tells her father the truth, in public, when he decides to divvy up his kingdom according to who loves him the best. She refuses to play the game. We notice she's the one who is marrying outside the kingdom (Albany and Cornwall are both peers of the realm; the King of France and the Duke of Burgundy both live across the seas, have much larger territories than either Albany or Cornwall— and Cordelia will be more important than either of her sisters, no matter which one she marries). Is her impending marriage the reason Lear decides to make this a love competition for the inheritance of his kingdom? Does he want to prove to the world and to her potential husbands that she loves him better than she ever could either of them? And is the fact that she won't play his game the event that then pushes him into his ridiculous display of living the superficial, carefree life? His ostensible journey is from sanity to madness, whereas in reality it is madness turning to sanity and compassion. He goes from being a king who is in charge of all his subjects, to being a king who realizes he never took care of his subjects and their welfare.

Shakespeare's own daughters saw little of him as they were growing up. Did they care? Once their brother died, did that mean Susannah, the elder, received more of the estate? Would the daughter who had sons find a special place in Will Shakespeare's heart? In any case, Shakespeare's line, like Lear's line, ended with the daughters. Susannah had a daughter, Elizabeth, but she died without children. Judith's marriage, to the son of an old friend of the family, did not seem stable. In fact, the week of his wedding to Judith, her husband was prosecuted for getting another woman pregnant; both mother and child died. Judith's marriage to Thomas Quiney produced three children, but all of them died before their parents and without issue. Shakespeare made Susannah the executor of his will (not his wife or any of his many close lawyer friends), so he must have trusted her. But the language of the will shows how strongly he wanted a male line to inherit his now considerable fortune. And how he, like Lear, failed.

Lear acts as a bridge between the plays in Act 4, "Chaos is Come Again: The Lion Eats the Wolf" (with Goneril and Regan grabbing for power) and Act 5, "The Maiden Phoenix: The Daughter Redeems the Father" (with Cordelia trying to rescue Lear). The young women who heal their fathers' lives in the later plays are not as richly drawn as the elder daughters in *Lear*; they are somewhat idealized, as Cordelia is. The ferocity and pain of Goneril and Regan bespeak an estrangement between father and daughters which is hard to experience—anguish to break the heart. Cordelia's love heals, Lear's newly found insight heals, but the images that remain in the imagination belong to Goneril and Regan.

SCENE 3: Volumnia

Despite its plunge into despair, and the absence of any hope that mankind will ever change its ways, *Coriolanus* is one of my favorite plays: it is so honest. Without sentiment, *Coriolanus* tells it like it is.

And the wreckage, as Shakespeare tells the story, has its roots in the way a mother brings up her son. The play was written the same year Shakespeare's mother died. Was he (like Hawthorne, who wrote *The Scarlet Letter* immediately after the death of his mother) finally free? Did her death mean he didn't have to answer to her anymore? Could he now actually write what he wanted about mothers and sons? (Mothers and sons don't fare too well in the canon: there's Gertrude and Hamlet, the Countess and Bertram in *All's Well*, Elinor and John, Constance and Arthur in *King John*, the Duchess of York and Richard III. Hmmm.)

Shakespeare used two other events that happened at that time in and around Stratford in the body of the play. The ordinary people were suffering because of the lack of corn (famine for the workers; the rich had enough stored away, but they were not going to share it); and the people refused to ratify the member of Parliament who has been chosen for them. We hadn't got to democratic elections yet in England, but we had got to the stage before: someone was elected to sit in Parliament as a representative of an area—usually chosen from among the officials of the area, landowners, justices of the peace, sheriffs—people the members of the Queen's Privy Council thought they could work with—and the citizens of that area ratified or refused that election. In Stratford they were refusing—it was unusual, but they were! Just as the plebeians refuse to ratify Coriolanus in the play.

So his mother's death, famine, and refusal to ratify were on Shakespeare's mind. Obviously, from our point of view, his mother's death and how that affected his writing in *Coriolanus* is the most interesting influence to explore.

There are three women in *Coriolanus*—Volumnia, the mother; Virgilia, the wife; and Valeria, the Vestal Virgin, now a middle-aged woman, acknowledged as "the Spirit of Rome."

The first time we see the women, Volumnia is in her sitting room, holding forth to Valeria and Virgilia, her son's wife—who never says boo to a goose and has ten lines in the whole play—the silent, acquiescent wife. (Virgilia can't be based on Shakespeare's wife, Anne—surely not?) Volumnia declares that if her son were her husband she'd infinitely prefer him to find honor in battle than to show love in the bed. Quite apart from the unconsciously revealed incest, this also throws up the question: who fathered Caius Martius? Volumnia is silent on the question; so is Caius Martius. However, his own son has been pulling wings off butterflies, torturing them, mammocking them in his teeth, letting them go, capturing them again, mammocking them, and so on. "One of his father's moods," Grandma Volumnia says proudly. She herself sent her own son to war when "he was but tender-bodied"—somewhere between thirteen and sixteen, I guess—because she thought honor would so become him. "But had he died in the business, madam, how then?" asks Virgilia. "Then his good report should have been my son," replies Volumnia.

As Nige has pointed out, Volumnia loves Rome—she loves the idea of Rome, what it stands for—and if she cannot be the ultimate Roman herself, she will make her son the greatest Roman who ever lived. Having come home from his first battle a hero, with wounds to display, he becomes the fearless warrior, usually seeking out Aufidius, general of the Volsci, to fight one on one, to the death. Twelve times, neither has overcome the other. This is the relationship he seeks.

However, right now he's leading the plebeians, the foot soldiers, against the town of Corioli. They storm the gates, but the ordinary soldiers do not enter the town: they run away. Caius Martius alone enters the town, and although it's never explained to us exactly how he does it, the town surrenders to him—so he alone takes Corioli.

This is cause for a huge celebration in Rome. There is a great military parade, with Volumnia and Virgilia in pride of place and the Spirit of Rome leading, and Caius Martius is given the honorific Coriolanus. (It is not a good parallel, but Henry Hunsdon, Shakespeare's patron for many years, crushed the Catholic rebellion of the northern lords in 1570. He never led another army, but cashed in his fame to become one of Elizabeth's servants, lord chamberlain, and he continued to claim his status as a great warrior and held forth on how *other* people should fight battles all his life.) Coriolanus just about manages to tolerate this public display; he is really happy nowhere but on the battlefield. This makes the next task his mother wants him to undertake even more distasteful: she wants him to become consul.

Historically, two consuls were elected each year and then ruled Rome for a year. Shakespeare didn't bother explaining any of that—he concentrated on the sole election of Coriolanus, with no term limit.

His fellow generals and senators have no problem choosing Coriolanus as the person they offer to the tribunes and the people as Rome's consul. The problem lies in the actions Coriolanus has to take in order to win the people's support. He has to expose his body, so the people can see how many wounds he has received in battle (and Coriolanus has received a hell of a lot—thirty-seven in the Battle of Corioli alone), wear the gown of humility (presumably a modest gown that allows them to see the wounds), and then ask them, kindly, gently, with reverence, for their vote. Well, Coriolanus can't do it. He despises them. These are the same people who ran away in front of the gates of Corioli. He thinks they smell. Their parents were slaves, bought and sold for groats. He thinks they are stupid and he wants nothing to do with them.

So this is where Coriolanus and his mother vehemently disagree. She thinks he should pretend. Since "honour and policy" go together in war, she can't see why they shouldn't go together in peace. Coriolanus is really clear that he wants nothing to do with "pretending":

> Must I with my base tongue give to my noble heart
> A lie that it must bear?
>
> CORIOLANUS (3.2, 118–19)

We must admire him: he cannot countenance his heart not being aligned to his speaking. Yet Volumnia persuades him. Then he changes his mind.

> I will not do't,
> Lest I surcease to honour mine own truth,
> And by my body's action teach my mind
> A most inherent baseness.
>
> CORIOLANUS (3.2, 140–43)

If Shakespeare was fed up with the acting profession, we see the clearest example of it here. Volumnia persuades Coriolanus back again. He agrees to return. But when he goes back to them he can't do it. He's a rotten actor; instead, he insults them. So they insult him and decide to banish him from Rome. But he says they can't do that: "I banish you."

He leaves Rome and joins Aufidius. Together they conquer all the surrounding countryside, and they are going to take Rome itself. They are not just going to take it—they are going to burn it to the ground, with all the inhabitants in it, so nothing is left. (As Rome did to Carthage in 146 B.C.; Cromwell did to southern Ireland in 1651; the Nazis did to Lidice in Czechoslovakia in 1941; and the Allies did to Dresden in 1945. And let's not even get into Hiroshima, Vietnam, or what's going on now.)

First Rome sends Coriolanus's fellow generals to plead with him. That fails. Then Menenius, the nearest thing Coriolanus has to a father figure. That fails. Finally, Volumnia, Virgilia, Valeria, and his son go to plead with Coriolanus. Volumnia does all the talking, of course. Her garments are torn; they are clearly suffering; they all kneel; the boy holds up his hands in supplication. (I think that's one of the turning points for Coriolanus: the boy is not much younger than he was when his mother first sent him into battle, maybe a little older than Shakespeare's son, Hamnet, when he died.) Volumnia reminds Coriolanus of how she has loved him and only him, a hen "fond of no second brood" who clucked him to the wars and home again. She tells him she won't wait for Rome to burn but will kill herself first. She says he had a Volscian for a mother, and his son is, like him, "by chance." (What does she mean? He was conceived during a one-night stand? She doesn't know who his father is? What?) Then, at the end, she says something else that is not easy to understand:

> Yet give us our dispatch.
> I am hushed until our city be afire,
> And then I'll speak a little.
>
> CORIOLANUS (5.3, 191–93)

What will she say then? That she's responsible for this mess? That she's not responsible, it's all his arrogance—"Thy valiantness was mine, thou suck'dst it from me; but owe thy pride thyself"?

It is difficult to find any sympathy for Volumnia. She's a snob, full of "right" privilege, unable to allow Coriolanus to be anything but what she wants him to be. Did she even pick his silent wife?

Coriolanus cannot hold out against her. He relents. Rome is saved.

O mother, mother!
What have you done? Behold, the heavens do ope,
The gods look down, and this unnatural scene
They laugh at. O my mother, mother, O!
You have won a happy victory to Rome.

CORIOLANUS (5.3, 194–98)

Of course, though Rome might be saved, Coriolanus knows that his reversal policy is his death sentence: "But let it come." The Volsci surround Coriolanus and stab him to death—an ignominious end, like Hector's at the end of *Troilus and Cressida*. So much for honor. In the end, might is right.

Dan McCleary, the actor who played Coriolanus for two seasons at Shakespeare & Company, comes from the South. (He's now artistic director of the Tennessee Shakespeare Company.) He had no trouble in understanding Coriolanus. He was brought up to believe "honor" was the most important attribute a man can possess and without it he is nothing. Through Dan, I began to understand the code of honor that ruled the South—and the ongoing ignominy of losing the Civil War.

The last thing Coriolanus says to his mother and the women is:

Ladies, you deserve
To have a temple built you. All the swords
In Italy, and her confederate arms,
Could not have made this peace.

CORIOLANUS (5.3, 220–23)

And so I suppose, if there is a glimmer of hope at the end of the play, it is that Rome didn't get burned to the ground; the peace was made by the women kneeling, not men conquering, and everyone but Coriolanus lives to fight another day.

But when you consider *Coriolanus* and *Timon of Athens* together, it feels as if Shakespeare was running out of options. Theatre's function? Not so good. Conquering Rome? Not so good. Unbridled philanthropy? Not so good. Poets and painters? Definitely not so good. Love? None to be seen anywhere.

SCENE 4: *Timon of Athens*

Coriolanus and *Timon of Athens* are the precursors to the late plays. They are the plays of despair, hitting rock bottom. Shakespeare feverously composed *Timon of Athens,* a play that was, essentially, a failure. It was never performed in his lifetime. The two women in it have few lines, and they are there to sell sex, nothing else. I played the whore Phrynia once. (Paul Scofield was Timon. He made this dull man almost interesting.) I got enormous pleasure cursing Timon— "Thy lips rot off"—in response to his statement to Alcibiades, "This fell whore of thine hath in her more destruction than thy sword." Shakespeare was obsessed with syphilis in *Timon* and in his next play, *Pericles.* There is firsthand knowledge in his writing. It seems as if half the population of London had the clap, and brothels surrounded the playhouses on Bankside. Did he just pass by them on his way to work? Or did he inhabit them? Or did he have a financial stake in some of them, as Philip Henslowe, Edward Alleyn, and George Wilkins (his possible collaborator on *Pericles*) did? Where did his disgust come from? But I digress.

Timon is a play that offers no insight into why anybody does anything—it's a play without a soul. It's as if, after the huge insights of the great tragedies—the self-knowledge that finally comes to Macbeth and Lear, the tracing of the women's ability to ameliorate, or provoke and extend destructive aggression—Shakespeare was tired of insight. Insight, after all, doesn't alter the course of events. It's as if he thinks, "Let's take insight out of this." What happens if Timon has no self-knowledge and no women to show him the way? The result is the most depressing play you can imagine.

Timon is rich; he spends all his money doing generous acts for others; then he has no money left. In fact, he's heavily in debt. He asks his friends to return the favors he has done them; they refuse; he leaves Athens, curses the world, and kills himself. A simple, direct story. Watch it and you end up feeling dead, hopeless, and desiring to remove yourself from the theatre. That is why it's hardly ever done— though in recent times its theme of reckless spending, unrepentant greed, obsession with cash and material goods, cynicism, and contempt for others does shine light on our global financial crisis. The *only* moments of redemption in the whole play are not in the characters or the action (all right, Flavius the steward is a decent guy, but he's so ineffective it's painful to watch), but in the verse and prose—what scientist Richard Dawkins calls "poetic magic." There is some sublime writing, and you can actually feel the imagination beginning to come to life, even though the message is depressing.

> If thou wert the lion, the fox would beguile thee. If thou wert the lamb, the fox would eat thee. If thou wert the fox, the lion would suspect thee when peradventure thou wert accused by the ass. If thou wert the ass, thy dullness would torment thee, and still thou livedst but as a breakfast to the wolf.
>
> TIMON OF ATHENS (4.3, 339–43)

He is writing prose whose rhythms etch into the mind. But it doesn't lead anywhere, other than "life is useless, people are stupid and greedy." Similarly, when he leaves Athens he turns back and commands the walls to fall and let the evil spread everywhere.

> Let me look back upon thee. O thou wall
> That girdles in those wolves, dive in the earth,
> And fence not Athens! Matrons, turn incontinent!
> Obedience fail in children! Slaves and fools,
> Pluck the grave wrinkled senate from the bench
> And minister in their steads! To general filths
> Convert o'th'instant, green virginity!
> Do't in your parents eyes. Bankrupts, hold fast!
> Rather than render back, out with your knives,
> And cut your trusters' throats. Bound servants, steal!
> Large-handed robbers your grave masters are,
> And pill by law. Maid, to thy master's bed!
> Thy mistress is o'th'brothel. Son of sixteen,
> Pluck the lined crutch from thy old limping sire;
> With it beat out his brains!
>
> TIMON OF ATHENS (4.1, 1–15)

Is this what Shakespeare thought about London at the time? It bespeaks a tired, angry mind, a resignation about human behavior.

Was this some kind of breaking point for Shakespeare? Did he see that good intentions are no match for the endemic greed of mankind, that, in all the ways our society is set up—with its defense systems, its hierarchies, its competition, its lack of courage to be vulnerable to others—we have created a system in which the "civilizing" institutions in fact give power to the dominant: the institutions may coat or mask naked power but do little to curb, check, or ameliorate it in any way? Might is right—we can receive the message directly, as in *Timon,* or we can make it a little more palatable by pretending that a killer like Coriolanus will risk his life for a higher good and, providing he's on our side, will be deemed honorable.

When Timon finds gold by scrabbling about in the earth, he doesn't return to Athens. He gives it to Alcibiades to pay his soldiers to kill everyone in Athens. (What is this desire to kill everyone?)

We don't really know how Timon dies—it's scarcely relevant. We just know that his last act is to leave a curse on mankind on his tombstone:

> "Here lies a wretched corpse, of wretched soul bereft.
> Seek not my name: a plague consume you wicked
>   caitiffs left!
> Here lie I, Timon, who, alive all living men did hate.
> Pass by and curse thy fill, but pass and stay not here
>   thy gait."

TIMON OF ATHENS (5.4, 80–83)

Shakespeare included a curse in his own epitaph but, fortunately, not as unforgiving as Timon's:

> Good friend for Jesus sake forbeare,
> To dig the dust enclosed heare.
> Blest be the man that spares these stones,
> And curst be he that moves my bones.

Something was happening to Shakespeare. The artists in *Timon* are "venal scum," as Nige puts it. Did Shakespeare also see that he needed to remove himself from the dense activity of London and the playhouses, the ambitions of the court, the desire for patronage, the disgust at man's folly? Perhaps he was sick, too: Syphilis? The palsy that afflicted people who wrote too much? Depression? All of the above? In any case, after *Timon* he took a series of actions.

He left London and went back to Stratford—and in doing so, he became reacquainted with his daughters, whom he hadn't lived with on a daily basis since they were babies. Now they were grown up. He returned to the country. He returned to his wife. And, even more important for our story, he changed the way in which he constructed the plots of the plays. It's a shift as dramatic as the one that separates the early plays from those in Act 2, "The Sexual Merges with the Spiritual." Instead of pursuing paths created by the neuroses of the protagonists (or flaws in character, as the Elizabethans saw it) and the inevitable destruction they cause, he found a way to refigure the outcome. He asked a different question: How can I write so that redemption is possible? What can I write so that both men and women can play parts such that, despite inevitable tragedy, the end result is healing and joy?

The form he now chose was myth (or fairy story or parable—whichever term you like best). It was in fact the advice Philip Sidney gave in *Defence of Poesy,* in 1595. He didn't abandon the psychological development of his characters; he made the canvas and the time frame so large that he and the audience got an overview of how it could turn out if certain mysteries were allowed to take place—if the artist drew a wider picture so that eventually the children, with their openness, love, courage, and vulnerability, could halt the darkness of greed, inadequacy, jealousy, and desire for dominance.

Art is crucial to how the game is changed—whether it's through sculpture or music or poetry, or a poetic mind seeking its salvation! Art is relational; it only exists if it is being perceived or received by someone in addition to the artist; it awakens the audience to a level of understanding that was not recognized before (and yet was always there). It invites contemplation through feeling, so the level of perception increases in resonance and depth, engendering through an aliveness of sensory perception a compassionate understanding and, we must hope, a love for mankind. Art's ability to engender empathy and magic is brought into play on the stage. And in its presence, a sensitivity is manifested which allows the world at large to come alive. We are all part of the human race. It's intuitive—logic and force cannot create art, only filigrees of form and content that align to point to a greater truth.

So, in these late plays, it is women and the feminine spirit, the soul, who are the artists, the revealer as well as the creator of the art form, the mistress who has the power and the knowledge to halt the cycle of violence. She does it not by direct opposition but by infiltrating the structures of power and changing the cellular nature of the components of power; she sees the wound and blesses it.

To go one step further: Is it possible to use what Shakespeare perceived in his last five plays to help counteract the path of destruction our modern world is on? Does he have an ever-important role, as we go global, to say what he sees in every language, every time zone? Could he be the common text that helps us find the way?

AN INTERLUDE: Creativity

I can sing, weave, sew and dance,
With other virtues which I'll keep from boast,
And I will undertake all these to teach.

MARINA IN *PERICLES* (4.5, 193–95)

For me, to be a writer is to acknowledge the secret wounds that
we carry inside us, the wounds so secret that we ourselves are
barely aware of them, and to patiently explore them, know
them, illuminate them, to own these pains and wounds and
to make them a conscious part of our spirits and our writing.

ORHAN PAMUK IN HIS NOBEL PRIZE SPEECH, 2006

Graves at my command
Have waked their sleepers, oped, and let 'em forth
By my so potent art.

PROSPERO IN *THE TEMPEST* (5.1, 53–55)

It's necessary, at this point, that we look at the nature of creativity,
and its links to the "feminine" attributes of intuition, feelings, relationships, and gestation. I do this because this is the stage in his art
where Shakespeare asked consciously about creativity and sought to
reveal its process and its ability to transform a broken life. The broken
lives he sought to heal were those of the male protagonists of his late
plays: Pericles, Cymbeline, Leontes, Prospero, Henry VIII. But, more
important, he was seeking to heal his own life, for with *Coriolanus*
and *Timon of Athens,* we see him sick in mind and body. Despair seeps
out of every scene in both these plays, and there is no healing at the
end of either story, just an abyss of blankness. "Nothing will come
of nothing" says Lear to Cordelia, "speak again." Yet at the end of
Lear something does come: the reconciliation of Lear and Cordelia,

finding a love that withstands imprisonment and death. There is no such love in either *Coriolanus* or *Timon:* only a final surrender to his mother's power for Coriolanus, only rage and hatred of mankind, followed by suicide, in *Timon.*

All that is left in these two narratives is what is underneath them: the creativity of Shakespeare himself. What is creativity? What is the creative process? What does it mean to me? To you? What does it mean for Shakespeare? What does it mean to the actors of Shakespeare? How do all these things mingle and merge?

It is in the late plays—*Pericles, Cymbeline, Winter's Tale, Tempest,* and *Henry VIII*—that Shakespeare illuminated the artistic process itself. Sometimes he wrote about what it means to be an artist, sometimes what the role of artists in society could be, sometimes what part art plays in our lives. Several of the women or the feminine spirits, such as Ariel, in the late plays are artists of one kind or another, and he links creativity, artistic endeavor, and bringing life out of death to the feminine.

Throughout his writing life, Shakespeare pointed out, This is a play. He said it literally in the text of *Taming of the Shrew, Richard II, Twelfth Night,* and *A Midsummer Night's Dream.* But somewhere in every play he pointed to the form of what he was creating, often briefly, or asked us to think about the creative process as it works upon actor and audience. Macbeth's penultimate moment is probably the best known:

> Life's but a walking shadow, a poor player
> > That struts and frets his hour upon the stage,
> And then is heard no more.
>
> MACBETH (5.5, 24–26)

And Coriolanus rails against actors and the way they use language for effect, dividing, he says, a man from himself. If we run many lines together, we see how powerful the condemnation of actors and acting is!

> Must I with my base tongue give to my noble heart
> A lie that it must bear? . . . Well, I must do't.

> Away, my disposition; and possess me
> Some harlot's spirit! My throat of war be turned,
> Which choirèd with my drum, into a pipe
> Small as an eunuch or the virgin voice
> That babies lull asleep! . . . I will not do't,
> Lest I surcease to honour mine own truth,
> And by my body's action teach my mind
> A most inherent baseness. . . . I'll mountebank their loves,
> Cog their hearts from them, and come home beloved
> Of all the trades in Rome.
>
> CORIOLANUS (3.2, 118–19, 130–35, 140–43, 154–56)

Shakespeare may have loathed theatre from time to time, but he was also fascinated by the art of theatre and theatre's power to effect change.

Many artists recoil from analyzing art—feeling it's a mystery, and any attempt to reduce it to explanation of parts reduces its power—and perhaps they are right. When a teenager, I ran away to be with an artist in Paris and lived there for two years, mostly among painters and sculptors; I don't think I ever heard a single conversation about art. Sex, booze, rock and roll, yes—never art. Yet there was always a power unspoken about what they were trying to do; either you responded viscerally to what they had made, and therefore no explanation was necessary, or you didn't, in which case they had failed. But in theatre we talk much more, maybe because we use words to create; as long ago as Shakespeare's day, the first book on acting came out, Thomas Heywood's *An Apology for Actors*.

It is very relevant here. Shakespeare illuminated the parallels between spirituality and art so subtly, he has been a constant guide to me. I am an artist writing about another artist—albeit a much greater one—and my directing and acting are born and bred from the creativity of Shakespeare; both of us come out of the general ferment of the theatre, inspired by other writers and actors who came before us. By being aware of this continuum, I know that art begets both life and art, and I am confident, if I can be honest, that something of use will come forth.

Buildings give a local habitation and a name to a theatre company.

But it is the human beings who inhabit the buildings who build the art form; it's the energy that pours out from all the individuals as they jockey with one another, trying to find out where they connect and where they cut off, where they are able to embrace the audience and when the audience turns away, when this one student is inspired by the teacher's words, when that actor revolts and shoves his fist through the wall because he cannot get out of his skin, when these two people experiment to find ways of expressing an action, a fight, a death, and that knowledge then passes into the techniques of the company. These are the ingredients that make a theatre company work. Of course, for us to have the words of our fellow artist William Shakespeare to lead us forward and inspire us to greater heights is a blessing that cannot be sounded. It "hath an unknown bottom," as Rosalind says of her affection, "like the Bay of Portugal." There is *always* another level to get to, always another truth to seek out, another philosophical idea to understand. So having the sense of the journey, interacting with others so that you learn something from them, always being willing to pass on knowledge—these are essential to keep the sense of purpose in what you are doing.

It is this human interaction, stretching over centuries, performed in buildings constructed by other human beings, that forms a theatre company. The artists gestate in those buildings, and are inspired by those who have gone before.

And for me personally to know that I have been at the center of all this activity in one small corner of the earth fills me with gratitude, a kind of pride in my tenacity, a joy that the interaction still goes on without my being in the center, plus a fear that, now that I have consciously stepped away from that center, I will no longer exist, that having no structural role will mean that I will disappear, too.

And when Shakespeare stepped away from his theatre company and went back to Stratford to live (as he did after writing the great tragedies and before writing the late plays), would he still be able to create plays without Burbage at his side? Heminges and Condell to keep him sane? Would newer voices now living and working in the playhouse drown out the presence of his contribution? If he wasn't conscious of the daily necessity to keep audiences flowing into the playhouse, would he even be able to write? Knowing you have to open a play tomorrow, come what may, is a great taskmaster. Two of Shakespeare's great influences, Montaigne and Seneca, both advocated that, to really know yourself, it is necessary to leave the hurly-burly: that the last level of the spiritual work can only come with quietness, stillness, stepping aside from the social and political life, *not* living in the maelstrom. What does it mean to become a small individual again, after monarchs, aristocrats, fellow artists, and the buzz on the street have all assured you that you have worth? Is it insanity to walk away? If you have already been acknowledged as a great playwright because you wrote *Hamlet, Othello, Lear, Antony and Cleopatra,* and *Macbeth,* can you walk away? Or is walking away the only thing you can do? Well, that's what Shakespeare did. He started to write very different plays when he returned to live in Stratford, plays that have the ways of women and the creative spirit enmeshed in the fabric of the narrative. He was determined to reveal the process and the ingredients of creativity—which is why I have tried to define it for myself, incorporating what I have learned from him.

And if, by writing thirty-two plays, the playwright has been racked to the marrow of his bones, been forced to acknowledge things about human behavior he never wanted to acknowledge, been brought face to face with the depths of human evil; if the artist has felt the desire to be in control, dominate, felt the destruction caused by helpless, human jealousy, known the extremes of revenge that a violated child now grown into an adult will perform, experienced the unending greed for more, and actually felt the ecstasy of sexual love so deep it transcends into the greatest spiritual knowledge—if as an artist your body and psyche have experienced all these things, and you have focused your imagination into structures that can reflect those feelings and sensibilities, and you've written it down and others are performing your works on a regular basis for thousands of people, then what do you do next? Probably be very, very quiet.

But the truth is, I don't know. I only know that the question is there for Shakespeare. I only know what is happening to me now, in a much smaller way, as I attempt to journey away from upholder of the institution into individual artist, actor, writer, fellow traveler. And my only guide is my imagination around Shakespeare's work and life, the few facts we have. I know how I live those things he writes about, and how my own life as a theatre person gives me some instinctive knowledge about his—the life I am living now as I attempt to put together *Women of Will*, write it, perform it, construct it with my fellow artists.

Let me describe part of a working day for me. The morning has been spent struggling with the scene from *Pericles* in which Marina finds a way to bring Pericles back to life. It's been a miserable morning; all three of us (Nige, Eric Tucker, I myself) are aware that this scene needs to reveal the ability of disinterested, compassionate love to bring a comatose man back to life. We can't do it; I can't sing; Nige doesn't believe anything he does; Eric's suggestions make us more grumpy. We find little bits of the scene here and there. Nige likes the idea of throttling me as soon as he wakes up. I say, "If you did know my parentage, you would not do me violence." I have no idea why I invoke my parentage as a reason he should not do me violence. Eric knows that the music of the spheres at the end of the scene means we have ascended to a transcendent state. We know there's a lot of pain in the scene because the text says so, but for whatever reason we are not able to make much headway with our relationship or the action.

We part. I go and sit in the little garden that holds the ashes of Elayne Bernstein, the woman who helped Shakespeare & Company convert an old ice-hockey rink into three rehearsal rooms, a theatre, and tech shops. It has become a building of great functional beauty, of which the founders of the Bauhaus movement would be proud.

I talk to Elayne. The waterfall beside her ashes enthralls the spirit. I sit within the stark lines of the building, filled now with flowers and trees planted by Elayne's husband, Sol. Elayne hears me. Her soul is here.

I walk back into the theatre. I watch a performance about Willem Mengelberg and Gustav Mahler—the Dutch conductor Mengelberg's great love of Mahler, and Mahler's turning the death of his children into one of the most beautiful pieces of music ever written; Mengelberg's forced to make decisions, as the Nazis took over Holland, about how to keep his orchestra together, how far to negotiate with those in power, life-and-death decisions. It's a play by Danny Klein, a Berkshire author.

The art of others is a deep source of inspiration—those who have come before us, offering roads into the unconscious, bringing out a power that can cut through encrusted ideas, long-held opinions, habitual behaviors, unregistered actions. The play works on me.

I leave the theatre, no longer stuck in my own shame and stupidity of the morning, but raw with the pity of it all. It gives me courage. In the distance I see Nige walking with a tall, sophisticated woman. They are laughing. My heart misses a beat. I am jealous. How, when we were so stuck back there in the rehearsal room, can he now be happy? Why isn't he struggling with his script? My unreasonableness makes me more emotional. I have no idea why I am acting like this. I get into my car and start to drive away.

A pain streaks through my body. I watch myself lift my hand from the steering wheel and wave to them as they wave to me. The cars in front of me blur, I have an overwhelming need to pass them and drive off the property as swiftly as I can. I hear the voice in my head telling me to calm down, but it is far away, through a glass darkly.

I recognize this jealousy (and it is jealousy) as something Othello and Leontes feel—and it is created by my imagination. Nige and I have spent hundreds of hours together, playing lovers, married couples, daughter and father, switching genders, knowing each other on levels few people experience. If I know him on this level, why should I care whom he is walking with? Would I feel these things if we had not been on so many Shakespeare journeys together? And would I feel them if I had not just been on an emotional roller-coaster with *Mengelberg and Mahler*? Would I feel them if we hadn't just had a tedious, unrewarding rehearsal? And then the thought crosses my mind: it's easier to feel this jealousy than allow myself to really register the darkness of a Nazi occupation. Personal passion avoids collective guilt. I feel guilt about Shakespeare & Company's getting into debt, jeopardizing our very existence. I feel guilt every time I use a plastic bag, knowing we are choking the planet. I feel guilt about the Nazi invasion of Holland. I want to do something about so many things I know are out of kilter, but if I lived perpetually in that space I would drown. Let me feel, but don't let me feel all the time.

William Faulkner spoke of "the problems of the human heart in conflict with itself which alone can make good writing because only that is worth writing about, worth the agony and the sweat."

What did Shakespeare do when he felt it? "Blood, blood, blood" pounds in my body. Please, please, please, let me turn this pain into something so it doesn't just tear me apart; let me use it in performance, make a poem out of it, alter its energy so it can be constructive, not destructive. Transform it, transmute it, get it into some sort of form so that it can be seen by others, so that the imagination can make it into something else. Let me scrape off the layers. This is not about Nige, or *Mengelberg and Mahler,* or the company; it's about something underneath that, being left, being ignored, not being enough or being too much, feeling helpless.

Ultimately creativity creates a harmony that gives life. But now its shadow is here before me, outside the rehearsal room. The jealousy is triggered by shame; it makes me angry, and I bang the steering wheel. It gives me cause for fear. I get violent images, imagine doing violent things to wipe out the pain. Then I start to laugh.

I breathe deeply, I pull off the road, I am still for a minute or two, and then I start to write. . . .

As jealousy is visceral, so is the moment of creativity.

In the midst of all this stimulus, pain, longing, and above all *seeking,* a moment arrives when a truth appears, small or great, and a gentle relief is experienced in the body. It lasts for as long as it wants to. And a chase begins, and you start to expand, look for harmonies (or disharmonies, which the more show off the harmony), and as "it" builds, the body connects and takes over, doing things that surprise you—you didn't know them before, but when they appear you know you've always known them. Out of this chaos comes beauty, even if it is the savage beauty of pain, as in a Francis Bacon painting, or the gouging out of Gloucester's eyes—beauty that allows the audience to experience the most terrible atrocities as well as the ecstasy of extreme love. And I realize I want Marina to hit Pericles for having abandoned her fifteen years ago, leaving her in Tarsus instead of waiting until she was strong enough to make the journey home. Finally, I see how we project on one another, how we use each other to generate an excitement out of what we can create.

From time immemorial, male artists have sought the female muse to lead them to a higher truth. It can be awakening what is dead, as in Harold Pinter's 2004 poem "To My Wife":

> I was dead and now I live
> You took my hand
>
> I blindly died
> You took my hand
>
> You watched me die
> And found my life
>
> You were my life
> When I was dead
>
> You are my life
> And so I live

Simple. Exquisitely balanced in form and content. It can be a sense of an absence, always present, "Missing," the title of one of Nige's poems.

> Missing is like the weather
> Looping labile
> Perpetual.
> I linger tranquil, until
> Sunlight glances a leaf
> And our trees, our walks, our days
> Fill the light.
> Missing lives in the mouths
> The eyes of others
> In tongues that do not fit,
> In cadences falling flat.
> Seeing most
> When least seen.
> Memories circle like storms and tideswell.
> Grief passes, pain dissolves

But missing endures
Like weather.
Looping, veiled
Perpetual.

Robert Graves, First World War poet, usually had a muse in his life, no matter to whom he was married. He was savage about the relationship between poet and muse in a poem called "Beware, Madam!":

Beware, madam, of the witty devil,
The arch intriguer who walks disguised
In a poet's cloak, his gay tongue oozing evil.

Would you be a Muse? He will so declare you,
Pledging his blind allegiance,
Yet remain secret and uncommitted.

Poets are men: are single-hearted lovers
Who adore and trust beyond all reason,
Who die honourably at the gates of hell.

The Muse alone is licensed to do murder
And to betray: weeping with honest tears
She thrones each victim in her paradise.

But from this Muse the devil borrows an art
That ill becomes a man. Beware, madam:
He plots to strip you bare of woman-pride.

He is capable of seducing your twin-sister
On the same pillow, and neither she nor you
Will suspect the act, so close a glamour he sheds.

Alas, being honourably single-hearted,
You admire and trust beyond all reason,
Being no more a Muse than he a poet.

In my imagination, Shakespeare's Dark Lady was his muse for most of his life. But I also think he was hers and brought her a poetic courage she did not possess before. Their relationship was challenging.

Finally, we are at a point in the evolution of consciousness where women do not have to exist solely as muses—we create in our own right. Women artists don't have muses, says my shrink: they don't need them, they provide within themselves all the nurture and inspiration. They are whole in and of themselves. Nor do they need an abstract idea to propel them forward. Is he right? He's a man. Does he get his idea from Carl Gustav Jung, or does he know for sure? I am tempted to say that in many ways Nige has been my "on-this-earth" muse for the last six years, though really beneath that is Will Shakespeare, and it's the idea of Shakespeare that spurs me on. Somehow, not surprisingly, the two of them are muddled up together in my life.

This is what I think it means to be an artist. We are forever trying to find the truth even though, as Spinoza says, it is impossible to know the whole truth. It's a process of stripping away inhibitions—alone and with others, alone and through others; through sensory perception, and sometimes beyond sensory perception. And this sense of the truth is not stationary; it alters, especially in theatre. If you are an actor, it depends on the words you are saying and to whom you are saying them and how that actor is responding. If you are an actor, your own being, your own voice and body, is your art form—or at least it is the artifact you are inviting the audience to see and hear, both from within and without. Music, too, has a moving truth, depending on the players, the time and place. And dancing. Painting has a little more seeming solidity. Playwrights end up with a script—but it doesn't come to life until the actors get hold of it. A poet can say, "All right, that's it, this poem is complete," and send it out into the world, not knowing how it is going to land. A novelist lives in her world till she's ready to come out, and then, if she's lucky, she'll like the cover, the binding, the printing of her book—but she will not be present at the reading of it. Does that make the angst she experiences when writing easier or more difficult? Virginia Woolf had a nervous breakdown each time she finished a book. To imagine your reader may be a necessity if you are a novelist, but it could be a self-referencing exercise—

which makes me more grateful for the presence of audiences and their instant feedback.

Whatever the art form, it means searching for a revelation among the chaos (chaos is uncomfortable; hence the joy, the pain), and then, once the thread is found, hanging on to it for dear life, like Ariadne's thread in the labyrinth, knowing that following it will lead to the way out. Dead ends, sluggish moments, dull brains, and anxiety often infect the journey, leaving the artist despondent, stupid, and full of shame. I try to walk with my girlfriend at this point, sifting through the grains of seed, like Psyche in her story. There, alone or in company, the unconscious mind once more peeps through to consciousness, the energy suddenly bursts forth, and I/you/we are off again, going wherever it goes.

That Shakespeare knew jealousy is apparent. That this jealousy was inappropriate and lethal is also true. Shakespeare was living in the thick of it when he wrote *Othello*—and had retreated to Stratford by the time he wrote *Winter's Tale*. And with *Winter's Tale* he found a way to get beyond the destruction. He re-created it and could see it. He found a way to make other emotions—compassion, endurance, faith in love—as powerful as jealousy. How did he do that? And can I do it?

Even writing about the chaos and uncertainty feels like a cover for something else. Always layers of the onion. What is it? What is it? I keep looking. There is a longing . . .

> Give me my robe. Put on my crown. I have
> Immortal longings in me.
>
> ANTONY AND CLEOPATRA (5.2, 316–17)

THE MAIDEN PHOENIX:
THE DAUGHTER REDEEMS THE FATHER

SCENE I: Coming Full-Circle

Shakespeare was now at the height of his writing life. He might have been exhausted, but he had never expressed himself better. He might also have been at the height of his acting powers. He had the energy, technical ability, and perspective to take on vast landscapes and not turn away from the worst things human beings are capable of doing to one another. *Macbeth, Lear,* and *Antony and Cleopatra* are apocalyptic visions, all of which on a worldly level turn out badly for everyone.

The protagonists of *Antony and Cleopatra* and *Lear* find that deep love for another human being finally transcends their desire for power. But the price they pay, and the price paid by the countries they once ruled, is beyond reckoning. Lear's Albion has incipient civil war and foreign troops on its soil. There is no clear leadership at the end—only one rather weak son-in-law, backed up by an inexperienced courtier who, however, is determined to "speak what we feel, / Not what we ought to say." So there may be hope. In *Antony and Cleopatra,* the Hellenistic ethos—that blend of once-powerful Greek culture intermingled, strengthened, its attitude toward women counteracted by the Egyptian cult of Isis—is now annihilated by Octavius Caesar. Alexandria, with its love of the arts and learning, gives way to Roman military power. In *Macbeth,* Malcolm finally gets it together enough to overcome Macbeth, but what kind of king he will become is left open to question.

As quoted in the beginning of the preceding chapter, on creativity, Orhan Pamuk—who resided in Istanbul, a city made up of ever-changing cultural influences—said in his Nobel speech: "For me, to be a writer is to acknowledge the secret wounds that we carry inside us."

Shakespeare, the playwright, brought this world of wounds into the playhouse. Richard Burbage, the actor, re-created this world in front of other people. Each tapped into his own life and imagination to make Macbeth and Lear live.

Shakespeare, alone in his lodgings, examined the desire for and protection of power. His own lack of power, his father's loss of power, Essex's and Southampton's challenge and eventual surrender to power, gave him a personal canvas to draw upon. He may have found fame in the theatre, but he had no power in the world at large other than his pen. The position he held in life was closer to the positions of the daughters in *Lear,* or of Lady Macbeth, or of Virgilia in *Corio-lanus,* or of the poet, the painter, and the whores in *Timon,* than it was to that of a monarch. The only actual power over others he had was the power of the supplicant with a potent argument. For a brief period, Lear's daughters and Lady Macbeth acquire power, but it is useless to them, because they don't know how to use it constructively. Shakespeare was bringing out of himself the language to articulate the invisible structures, the accepted prejudices, the "normal" way of enforcing power, which resulted in the greatest horrors. Not only were the wounds explored; he also pointed to even greater miseries that were beyond words:

> The worst is not
> So long as we can say "This is the worst."
>
> KING LEAR (4.1, 31–32)

Or he fell back on

> O horror, horror, horror!
>
> MACBETH (2.3, 59)

and trusted that the vowel sounds would get Burbage to tap into the unspeakable depth of horror by the third "horror."

Will you accept that art seeks to bring coherence into what often seems like an incoherent world, and that that same coherence exists beyond sensory perception even though the path is through sensory perception? By intuitively linking disparate elements, artists create a truth not seen at first by others. They reveal a harmony that exists only as a work of art yet reflects both what has happened and what is happening now. There is an alignment between the psyche's deepest perception of events, registered either consciously or unconsciously, and its reworked artistic manifestation. This play, or symphony, or painting awakens a new understanding about what is going on. It often takes years for the artist to get to such a truth. But, as Orhan Pamuk says, by patiently exploring these pains and wounds, we can make them a conscious part of our spirits and our writing. The wound is our knowledge that all is not whole, and that therefore we must seek to know that wholeness.

And then there is the task of recognizing that the organizational structures we internalize and hold as normal in order to live our lives with others—structures that have given form to human societies for thousands of years—in some ways are good, by providing continuity and historical perspective. Yet those very structures may do the worst damage: they are embedded in our psyches and train us to accept them as "reality," whereas in fact they are man-made; the weight of them implies there is no way out.

In writing *Macbeth, Lear,* and *Coriolanus,* in which not even the women would or could pull back from the carnage, Shakespeare mapped the unending violence of the world. Timon of Athens kills himself because he hates the world. Ophelia kills herself because she has no free will. Cleopatra chooses love, and the result is that the armies of the Caesars march on North Africa, the eastern Mediterranean, and Greece. The playwright and the actor find these realities within themselves. To act or write about life means choosing suffering. The actor embraces life. Joy is the gift. The world of creativity seeks to know the wounds and expose them, then bring some semblance of form and understanding, so that beauty can stand with the pain and new birth can happen.

Shakespeare's image at the end of *Henry VIII* is of the baby Elizabeth as the phoenix. This mythological bird immolates itself, and then a new creature arises from its own ashes. It was popular in Elizabethan times, borrowed from Persian literature. Shakespeare, however, makes Elizabeth not just the phoenix but the *maiden* phoenix. The bird has a gender: female. As far as we know, Shakespeare was the first to give the bird a sex. He drew attention to the phoenix's gender, because it is the very qualities known as "feminine" that give the bird the stamina to endure the fire, lie dormant, nurture the tiny sprigs of inconspicuous growth, let nature take its course, guard the nest, and see the world again, with new eyes. Not only is the phoenix female, but she has all the qualities of the artist. The phoenix is the artist. The artist—and, frankly, it matters nothing whether the artist is male or female—must possess the qualities of spirit to be able to bring about new life: die to the world, know that growth is happening though it can't be seen, nurture the secret, offer the new life to others—and be willing to go through the cycle again and again.

The bravery and honor of the "hero" (on his the great male journey) may be useful, but these qualities are not sufficient to bring about new life. Nor are they sufficient to bring about a work of art. And only in works of art can we see the whole truth about humanity and be brought to perceptions that may slowly bring more consciousness to our daily lives.

And so I would like to point to the events in Shakespeare's life that he was still struggling to make sense of, not just the acts of violence but the effects of that violence: the wounds, some secret and some not so secret, lodged in his psyche, burrowed deep to make coherent, reveal some grace to manifest it in the playhouse for others to witness. In the late plays, the women and the artists (often symbolically and symbiotically tied together) map a path out of the habitual cycle of violence and back into lasting relationship.

Shakespeare's most courageous portraits of violence live in family warfare, and the inherent structures that humans use to inflict pain and claim dominance. They are loaded into *Macbeth, Lear,* and *Coriolanus.* The attacks on sons abound in every page of *Macbeth;* incest lies in the shadows in *Lear* and *Coriolanus;* despair and avarice suffocate all life in *Timon of Athens.* Love is hard-won but triumphant on a personal level in *Antony and Cleopatra.* Collectively, the military power makes sure that the ways of the Caesars are embedded in our ways of doing things for the next few thousand years, for better and for worse. (And, yes, I know Rome eventually fell and its power structures shifted, but our ways of solving problems and organizing economic wealth have all stayed the same—whether it's the Roman Empire or the British or the American or the incoming Chinese who have the upper hand.)

Shakespeare's understanding of daily life under a failed state could not have been expressed more clearly or more accurately in these plays. And his refusal to express any insight into Timon's descent—just rage, rage, rage—surely made the play a kind of whipping boy for his contempt. He could get rid of every inch of bile, and when he had exhausted himself, he would finally turn to the plays that would map out a way, and find the code, to engendering life, to embodying the maiden.

Pericles, Cymbeline, Winter's Tale, Tempest—what do they have in common? What are the wounds that were still unresolved for Shakespeare, that he felt he must face squarely before he finished, and was there any way to forgive or come to some peace about the past? The four late plays (often called the Romances, for some reason that escapes me) and also *Henry VIII,* which follows, were structured in the same format—so we need not only to know what that is, but to ask why.

At the beginning of each of these plays, there is a massive sin or trauma. Something terrible happens. Either it happens then and there onstage, or it is reported—it happened fifteen or sixteen years ago. This sin must be cured, but it cannot be cured immediately—in fact, it takes a generation to heal, and it's the daughters and the artists who offer the way out.

The story has to be told as a myth or fairy tale. The truth is told through parable, as Jesus Christ told stories. There's a mystery.

And, like a pack of Tarot cards, the same signs appear and reappear in the plays, in different ordering, sometimes upside down, but telling an ancient tale. These indicators are for the person in the play to interpret and act upon, but all of us in the audience must also let the signs work upon us. Sons without fathers, or sons who die because of actions by their fathers, abound: Pericles is a son getting into terrible trouble until he finds his father's armor. Cymbeline loses his sons when they are babies. In the same play, Sicilius's sons (and Posthumus's brothers) die fighting the Romans. In *Winter's Tale,* Mamillius dies of a broken heart because of his father's actions, the only person not to come back into life at the end. In *The Tempest,* Prospero is forced into acknowledging that Caliban, "this thing of darkness," is his own, a son he may have had with Sycorax; or that the evil Caliban wished upon Prospero was caused by Prospero's own anger and neglect. Practically the whole plot of *Henry VIII* is about the wife Henry inherited because the rightful heir to the throne died. And Henry is desperate for a son. We meet his baby daughter, who we know will be greater than any son could be. (Of course, in life, Henry eventually had a son, the sickly Edward, who died after a short reign, allowing Elizabeth, the true maiden phoenix, to inherit.)

Incest is out front as a sin of major proportion in *Pericles,* but it lurks in the background in *Cymbeline,* is only glimpsed in *Winter's Tale,* and has strains in *Tempest,* depending on the interpretation of the family tree.

Absent wives, witches, and healers play complicated and constructive roles, forging an associative path toward new life.

None of the plays would see salvation if it were not for best friends and servants of faithfulness, Helicanus and Lychorida, Pisanio, Camillo, Gonzalo.

Storms abound, changing the course of events, for better or worse.

Music and dreams guide us and our protagonists into different modes of perceiving the truth. Masques change realities. Dances root us again to the power of the earth. The artist creates in front of the audience, exposing the mystery of things. Again and again we are exhorted to "tell our story."

The young men, once they experience love, stay true to it in *Tempest, Winter's Tale,* and *Pericles.*

And in these late plays the daughter, the feminine spirit, brings the father back to life, aided by artistic mystery.

Let's be more specific about the events that must be put right, the horrible wounds that may eventually lead to redemption. And then ask: how personal were they to Shakespeare's life?

The "sins" at the top of the plays are:

Pericles: The blindness of wanting to inherit the richest country
   and marry the most beautiful woman in the world without

understanding either. Nor is the incest lying beneath the surface recognized. Naïveté and just wanting more stuff . . . leads to real danger.

Cymbeline: A father distracted by his love for an unsuitable woman, still blind about what happened twenty years before, still blundering over the fate of others; a husband so insecure in the presence of other men that he's making bets on his wife's fidelity.

Winter's Tale: Jealousy, without cause, leading to the death of others, including a son.

Tempest: A man so obsessed with his art form that he neglects his responsibilities as a leader.

Henry VIII: A man who has enormous power almost fritters it away in his search for his soul, allowing Rome to nearly take over his country. Arrogant nobles who care nothing for the good of the country.

Does any of this line up with Shakespeare's own life?

Shakespeare left London and went back to reside in Stratford after two decades. He continued to write plays, but not at breakneck speed.

For the past twenty years, Shakespeare's playwriting and acting had taken precedence over his family life; he had been an absent father. He was determined to earn, invest, create a fortune to stabilize his family and give dignity to his position.

Shakespeare's own son Hamnet had died, at the age of eleven, presumably when Shakespeare was far from home.

Shortly before Shakespeare's own death, Hamnet's twin, Judith, at thirty-one, got married to a man who, in the very week, had a lover die, with child, in childbirth. No matter what the explanation, it was a messy situation. Judith's betrothed was hauled before the magistrates, and Shakespeare changed his will; obviously, much drama was taking place between Judith and Thomas Quiney, and Shakespeare was in the midst of it.

Shakespeare was deeply beloved by his acting family. But there is little evidence of his affection for his wife, or hers for him. They had married when she was pregnant—he eighteen, she twenty-six. He hardly ever mentioned her—and I think we have to conclude that this lack of acknowledgment for her or about her means that, though he accepted her contribution to his life, it hadn't made an impact on him after the first few years.

His plays reveal a visceral knowledge of jealousy, obsession with work, feelings of ingratitude, importance of rank, desire to manipulate other people, and deep love between people who are not married. I suppose these "sins" are no worse than those we all possess by the time we get to the second half of our lives. It really depends on how you think about them: the degree of guilt or shame you hold makes the difference. I don't know that Shakespeare was actively thinking, "What must I make reparations for?" But these things were part of his life, and, like other people who are looking back, he may have had them come to the surface and begun to examine them. He was writing at Stratford, away from the daily maelstrom of running a theatre. Events he may have hardly registered before would now surface, in quiet; these would be questions, if nothing else, questions he might not have asked so honestly if he had been absorbed in meeting the next deadline, making the next court appearance, learning another fight, counting the box office, developing young actors, having a pint in the pub before he went home.

We have to remember what a young country England was, struggling to give itself an heroic history, as America does today. Allegiance to country rather than just a tribe was only a few generations old. The dialectic between being a proud subject of a country, and the desire to revert to the coziness of your own tribe, was in constant oscillation—much as it is today in American politics. And the switching back and forth between Catholicism and Protestantism affected almost every family in the country. Was there blame and guilt in this? Shakespeare's family wasn't the only one to have the strains of both religions flowing freely through it. His theatre company, too, came from both strains: Southampton and Lord Strange were Catholic; Leicester and the Queen, Protestant. Some of his company were Catholic; many others were Protestant, even serving as officials in their local Church of England parishes. The idea of absolute truth dictated by the church was thoroughly undermined, which was probably one of the factors contributing to Shakespeare's greatness as a playwright. This doesn't mean he wasn't disturbed every time a new plot to kill the Queen was discovered, or a new execution took place. Similarly, the shifting of the language happening throughout Shakespeare's life—the mixing of Latin (language of law, international discourse, intellectual discussion) with the people's vernacular (the oral Anglo-Saxon tongue)—gave a richness of vocabulary and expression to the emerging English tongue, the tool that allowed Shakespeare to write plays. The shape of the world was changing; heaven and hell were no longer assured; the printing press altered learning and communication forever.

So, in this world of shifting values, Shakespeare wrote five plays. He anchored each play at the beginning by saying, in effect, "This event did great damage to many people. How can we find what has been lost? And how do we know the damage it did?" He ends each play with reunion, love, and courage for the unknown.

Shakespeare created his own Tarot cards out of the harsh realities of his life; he drew them, played them, and ultimately turned them into beauty that can lift the soul to the vulnerable experience of truly knowing. So let us take these plays one by one, find the schism, and see how the feminine brings it back into life.

SCENE 2: *Pericles*

The story of Pericles, the *first* of the late plays, can stand as the prototype for all the others.

Many scholars think that Shakespeare wrote *Pericles* with someone else, most probably George Wilkins, who published the novel in 1608. When I worked on it, that's not how it felt to me. At first I thought, "This is an early play that Shakespeare returned to later in life." But then, as I got deeper and deeper into it, I thought, "No, this is Shakespeare trying to write in a simpler style, perhaps mimicking his early plays, when he knew less. He's trying to put himself in a primitive place—the place of Poor Tom in *Lear*." But my attitude in this is probably influenced by the fact that George Wilkins was a despicable man, a brothel keeper who beat women; I don't think Shakespeare would have had much to do with him. It's more likely that Wilkins watched the play, stole the story, and wrote his novel from it.

Shakespeare's first move was a bold one: "I'll bring the poet onstage, up front. There is someone who writes these things." The story is told by Gower, the medieval poet who has died some two hundred years earlier. He comes onstage alone, and reappears throughout the play until he brings it to a close, providing commentary and insights for Shakespeare himself, and never letting the audience forget: this is a story. Why do we tell stories? How are we shaped by stories? Whose stories do you listen to? What's your story? Does any of this ring a bell? What can we learn, together and separately, from this story?

Pericles is a young man from a small kingdom. He's a prince, and he'd like to marry well—he wants to get a lot of loot through marrying. He's at the court of one of the richest men in the Mediterranean, Antiochus, and Antiochus has a daughter. Pericles has never actually met her, but he's sure he's in love with her, because, obviously, whoever marries her is going to inherit Antioch as well, as the King has no other children. Small problem: there's a riddle that must be solved to win the hand of this young lady, and if you get it wrong, you sacrifice your life. And there are an awful lot of dead bodies strung up around the court: it seems a hell of a lot of suitors got it wrong! But Pericles is fearless, and he's mad with passionate lust for the girl (even though he doesn't know her), and he's willing to take the risk. He receives the riddle. It's pretty simple:

> I am no viper, yet I feed
> On mother's flesh which did me breed.
> I sought a husband, in which labour
> I found that kindness in a father.
> He's father, son, and husband mild;
> I mother, wife, and yet his child.
> How they may be and yet in two,
> As you will live resolve it you.
>
> PERICLES (1.1, 65–72)

Now, you would need to be unusually dumb not to get the answer to that riddle: *incest*. Father and daughter are in a sexual relationship. Now these dead suitors look ominous—they must have solved the riddle, too, and they were killed because they knew it! Pericles decides to flee; he makes a run for it. He escapes and puts to sea. Thereafter, for the first half of the play, Antiochus is pursuing him, determined to kill him and do damage to the little Kingdom of Tyre.

The "sin" is not just Antiochus and his daughter—it's Pericles, too, that he's more interested in status and money than really knowing the girl, or the circumstances; that he is ignorant about the ways of the world. He upsets a hornets' nest and then can do nothing about it.

There's a great storm at sea. Again, in these late plays there are always great storms at sea. One is even called "The Tempest." They work on the same symbolic level that we have come to understand through Joseph Campbell and the Jungians—transformation is possible, but all the forces of nature (and our psyches) are pitted against one another, and it feels as if we might all die. Pericles is washed up on the shore of a good king this time, one who also has a daughter. This time Pericles is much more cautious: he's learning. Here, too, there are many other suitors at the court, but Pericles is humble. They are knights and courtly in their behavior. Pericles finds his father's rusty old armor and puts it on. He jousts for the lady.

Thaisa sees Pericles and falls in love with him. She woos him as hard as he woos her—in fact, harder, because he's frightened this might be another plot to take his life. But, no, it's genuine, and we have a swift sexual/spiritual merging worthy of *Romeo and Juliet* but in fewer lines.

The gods burn up Antiochus and his daughter; Pericles and Thaisa set sail for Tyre. She's pregnant. There's another great storm at sea. She gives birth to a daughter called Marina and dies. The sailors, who are superstitious, believe the storm will never abate unless the dead body is thrown overboard. Pericles, with great sorrow, agrees. The storm abates.

Next day, before he makes the long journey to Tyre, he puts down at Tarsus and leaves his baby daughter, Marina, there in the care of King Cleon and his wife. Pericles returns to his kingdom. He never remarries but remains faithful to the memory of Thaisa.

Fifteen years pass, and Pericles returns to Tarsus to collect his daughter. When he gets there, he is told she's dead. He leads a scene of lamentation at her grave, and then his heart breaks. The death of his daughter is too much. He won't speak to anyone, won't wash, change his clothes, or cut his hair or nails; he goes comatose. His friends sail desperately around the Mediterranean, trying to find someone to heal him.

Change the scene to Mytilene. It turns out Marina didn't die. Cleon and his wicked wife thought they had killed her, but at the very moment when the man they'd suborned to do the deed drew his knife, a gang of pirates appeared, captured Marina, took her off to Mytilene, and sold her into a brothel.

Marina, though only fifteen, is a person so secure in her inner authority that everyone tends to do as she asks of them—and although the brothel keeper and his wife have sold her virginity many times over at a high price, every john that comes to take his prize is converted by her, happily leaves her alone, and departs as a spiritual person (a complete reversal of the incestuous relationship leading to the death of so many at the beginning of the play). The governor of Mytilene himself comes to take her, but they end up having a long conversation about sex and life, during which he falls in love with her and her mind; he gives her money so she can get away from the brothel—and he becomes a thoroughly decent human being.

Marina uses the money to set up a kind of commune of young women artists. They can sing, sew, dance, and weave (together with other skills), and they heal people through their art.

Along comes a ship from Tyre with this dirty, smelly old man on board. His friends have heard about this young girl who cures people, and they are hoping she'll have a go with him. They bring the boat to the bay, and Marina goes on board. She plays music. She sings. She touches him. When he attacks her, she starts to tell him her story. This gives him pause, and he finally responds to her. She continues to tell her story. He thinks he recognizes his wife—but, then, she's dead—or maybe his daughter—but she's dead, too. At his urging (yes, he starts to speak), she tells as much of her story as she knows, and he realizes, "This is Marina." So the father is healed by the daughter; they are reconciled; he hears the music of the spheres.

But this is not the end. As Pericles sleeps, the goddess Diana comes to him in a dream and tells him to go to her temple and there tell his life story. So the next day Pericles and Marina go to the temple of Diana, and there Pericles tells his story, and as he reaches the end of it, one of Diana's nuns faints. It is Thaisa. She didn't die after all, but was rescued from the sea and death by a great herbalist holy man called Cerimon (by the bye, Susannah, Shakespeare's elder daughter, was married to one of the greatest herbalist healers in England, John Hall). When Thaisa came to life, she decided she would spend the rest of her days as a follower of the goddess Diana.

So Pericles and Thaisa and Marina are all reunited and live happily ever after. Marina marries the governor of Mytilene. The end.

If this is a parable, or holy story, what do we get? In stories like these, the truth lies below the surface, waiting for the active participation of the listeners to interact with it so that, through their searching, they set in motion the influence of the story as it applies in their own minds and bodies.

When does love fail? When does it come alive and create true resonances? What are the roles of power and wealth? How does healing come about? How do we deal with our pain, and who can help us through the morass? What is the soul, and what nurtures it? How do the women in the play guide themselves and others? Would Pericles ever have been able to be a true prince without his wife and daughter? If a baby doesn't have a mother, who will bring her up? Where does storytelling fit into all this? How do you remain a virgin in a brothel? And where does lust without love lead?

SCENE 3: *Cymbeline*

I am only going to deal with *Cymbeline* briefly and then really plunge into *The Winter's Tale*—for *Winter's Tale* is all about women's ways of being in the world and having the power to get it right permanently!

I don't know much about *Cymbeline*. I've never directed it, never acted in it, never taught it. I've occasionally worked on a few scenes from it, have been to about four different productions, and have read it a couple of times. It has always seemed like the play Shakespeare decided to write in order to revisit every theme, trick, and in-joke he ever used in his canon, and as a kind of merry theatrical exercise: to come up with a new play out of themes used heretofore!

That said, let's review what is consistent with themes of the other late plays. The daughter certainly redeems the father. Cymbeline is a silly old king who has married an ambitious woman—and between them they are wrecking the kingdom. It's pre-Christian; the ways of the gods are mysterious and beneficent in the end. At the end of the story, they create a spectacular "event" or mystery to reveal the truth (as a true artist would).

There's a kind of multiple sin/tragedy before the play begins—the king "lost" his two baby sons somehow; and Posthumus's father died of a broken heart when his two other sons were killed in the wars with the Romans, his mother in labor and sorrow while giving birth to Posthumus. These parents were not very good at looking after their children, you might say. Anyway, the king brings up Posthumus in his court, together with his own daughter; the two fall in love and marry secretly, incurring the wrath of Cymbeline and the wicked stepmother he's recently married (who planned to match Imogen with her doltish son Cloten—rhymes with rotten). They've banished Posthumus, who flees to Rome. And the townspeople are all talking about it. Imogen and Posthumus exchanged a ring and a bracelet at parting, never to take them off unless they are dead!

As soon as Posthumus gets to Italy, he's challenged by the "gentlemanly" company about his wife's chastity—and makes a wager with Iachimo that he will not be able to seduce her. Hmmm. Iachimo gets ten thousand ducats of gold and the ring if he succeeds! This is when I start switching off—didn't we leave behind all of this wagering on your wife's behavior back in the early plays, *The Taming of the Shrew* and *The Two Gentlemen of Verona*? Oh God, why did he go back to it?

Well, it might be so he could write about Imogen's bed chamber, and thus invoke half a dozen other plays and poems he wrote. *The Rape of Lucrece, Othello, Titus Andronicus, Antony and Cleopatra,* plus Cupid and Diana bathing, and all the other erotica he previously used during a lifetime of writing. Imogen has a mole under the left breast: Aemilia Bassano had such a mole.

If Shakespeare is pointing to his past creativity, he certainly demonstrates it by using devices from other plays.

This is the list of repeating plot points in *Cymbeline* that come from his previous works:

· A man bets on his wife's behavior *(Taming of the Shrew)*
· A person is put to sleep rather than death by a potion *(Romeo and Juliet)*

- Musicians serenade a would-be wife *(Romeo and Juliet* and *Two Gentlemen of Verona)*
- Woman to be murdered for adultery *(Othello)*
- Woman disguises herself as a man to follow her man to a foreign city *(Two Gentlemen of Verona)*
- Peasant boys realize they are sons of a king *(King John)*
- Disloyal lover is set up to think his beloved is dead and then he'll be sorry *(Much Ado About Nothing)*
- Someone is raped *(Titus Andronicus* and *The Rape of Lucrece)*
- Headless body (reverse of the bodiless head in *Henry VI Part 2* and others)
- Dead father appears in a dream *(Hamlet)*
- Dead family *(Richard III)*
- A god saving the day *(Pericles)*

And that's a quick skim over the surface. In the last scene of the play, revelation is piled on revelation (about eleven in all), creating a veritable farce by the end. Yet the First Folio calls it *The Tragedy of Cymbeline.* I think Shakespeare's making a joke, or he's getting very, very irritable about the categorizing of his plays.

Imogen is a wonderful heroine who, through her actions, cleans up the mess made by her father and her husband. The play itself is a self-conscious act of creativity, and the masque draws attention to the artificiality of gods and happy endings, making it certain that the audience get their money's worth.

And it has one of the most beautiful songs in the canon.

> Fear no more the heat o'th'sun,
>   Nor the furious winter's rages,
> Thou thy worldly task hast done,
>   Home art gone, and ta'en thy wages.
> Golden lads and girls all must,
>   As chimney-sweepers, come to dust.
>
> CYMBELINE (4.2, 323–28)

Break my heart.

Throughout the story, the wily old playwright wove yet another theme from yet another extant play, until all the audience can say is:

We give up, you can't put any more plots in. Yes, you're the master. Give us a break. Let us go home. The daughter is a phoenix. She has redeemed her father. She has redeemed her husband. The wicked Queen is dead. England has acknowledged its debt to Rome. We're tired. You've worn our brains out!

SCENE 4: *The Winter's Tale*

Winter's Tale is about three women and a bear. It's about other things, too, but of all the stories in the canon, this holds Shakespeare's deepest effort to understand how women understand the world, and how it may be possible to live in women's rhythms and resonances, women's perspectives, women's knowledge.

He had been back in Stratford for about two or three years now, back with his wife; one daughter was still at home, the other daughter living down the street with her husband and their daughter. His son, of course, was missing—dead over ten years earlier. Many of Shakespeare's friends from school were still living in Stratford—and Hamnet's friends, whom Shakespeare would see, were all around the same age Shakespeare had been when he first left the town. He'd been back in Stratford long enough now to alter his own rhythms and resonances, long enough to find the power of the countryside again, the seasons, the celebrations of the pre-Christian calendar, the sense that nature itself would regenerate our minds as well as our bodies if we just gave it a chance.

He admired his son-in-law, John Hall, a man deeply respected for his knowledge of plants and their properties, and his ability to heal people. We have some of John Hall's medical diaries, so we can see how far he traveled sometimes to be with a patient, how he treated the poor. He was asked to undertake civic duties, but they vied for time with his medical practice; as a Puritan, he took his obligations with deep seriousness. Shakespeare's baby granddaughter, Elizabeth, promised to have an excessively lively mind.

All the late plays carry a sense of meditation—time passing, the timelessness of the world embodied in present moments, rituals that people have enacted for centuries—yet also a sense that new birth may come anytime now, and then here it is, revealing the huge store of love and joy out of which new growth and new possibilities burst forth! And the new birth comes out of women's bodies and women's minds, aided and abetted by the few good men who stand with them.

So let me tell you briefly the plot of *Winter's Tale*—and of course remember that the plot is composed of events, beneath which what is *really* happening is taking place!

"Only sit tight yourself & *go through the movements of life*," Henry James wrote to Edith Wharton during the darkest days of her divorce:

> That keeps up our connection with life—I mean of the immedi-
> ate & apparent life, behind which, all the while, the deeper &
> darker & unapparent, in which things *really* happen to us,
> learns . . . to stay in its place. . . . Live it all through, every inch
> of it—out of it something valuable will come. . . .
>
> *EDITH WHARTON*, BY HERMIONE LEE (P. 331)

The King of Sicilia has had his best friend and childhood companion, the King of Bohemia, staying with him for nine months. Hermione, Sicilia's Queen, is nine months pregnant and about to give birth. For some reason, Leontes (Sicilia) is desperate for his friend Polixenes (Bohemia) to stay longer. Polixenes understandably thinks it's time for him to be gone. Leontes does everything in his power to persuade him. Polixenes refuses, saying his own wife and child (about eleven years old, the same age as Mamillius, son of Leontes and Hermione) miss him and his kingdom needs him back. He's adamant.

So Leontes turns to Hermione to help persuade him. Hermione obliges and is successful. And in that moment Leontes falls into a jealous rage, convinced that his wife and Polixenes are lovers and the baby she's about to give birth to is Polixenes's, not his! Unlike in *Othello,* Shakespeare is not so interested in why Leontes is jealous, but in the effects of his jealousy. Modern-day psychologists would have a field day with this—and of course, it says a great deal about Shakespeare's insights that he was able to write so accurately about psychology, its symptoms, causes, and outcomes.

Events follow quickly. Leontes bribes his lord chamberlain, Camillo, to poison Polixenes. Camillo agrees, but instead informs

Polixenes of Leontes's psychosis; Camillo and Polixenes flee. That leaves Hermione to face Leontes's rage alone. Deaf to her truth (in fact, the more she tells it, the more he's convinced that she's lying), he throws her into jail, where she gives birth to a daughter.

Enter the Queen's best friend, Paulina, mother to three girls herself and married to one of Leontes's courtiers. Paulina is a strong woman who solves problems by forcefully stating the truth and then staying there, insisting this truth is heard until matters straighten themselves out.

She's convinced that once the King sees the new baby he'll see his own likeness and realize his mistake. So she goes to the prison, collects the baby, and takes it to Leontes. Leontes hasn't slept for days; he's now convinced himself that Polixenes, Camillo, and Hermione were in a treasonous plot together. Even though the two men have escaped, he can at least put Hermione on public trial, so the world can see how he, Leontes, has been wronged, and how his closest friends were all against him and were going to kill him.

When Paulina brings the baby to court, she almost succeeds with her bold plan. The courtiers, somewhat timidly led by her husband, Antigonus, don't throw her out, as ordered by the King; in a dangerous and daring move, she leaves the baby behind in the King's chamber. The baby's vulnerability almost wins the King over–but at the last moment he weakens and orders Antigonus to take her away and leave her on some hillside, to die or to follow whatever fate is in store for her.

Antigonus obeys. He takes the baby to Bohemia (which happens to have a coastline–didn't care much about geography any more than he cared about dates, our Shakespeare).

Before I tell you what happens to the baby and Antigonus, we need to go back to Hermione, Paulina, and Leontes.

Leontes arraigns Hermione. Ostensibly, she's to be judged by others, not by him, but he is never silent in the court; he cannot stop accusing her. As a final backup, to prove that justice will be done, he sends the courtiers Cleomenes and Dion to Delphi, to ask the ultimate judge, the god Apollo, for his ruling. (The people who served and spoke for Apollo at Delphi were women, by the way–again, one wonders, how much did Shakespeare know and think about things like Delphi, Dionysus, and Celtic sacred groves?)

Hermione's indictment is read. She appears—weak, lifeless, having given birth only a few days before, knowing that her baby has been thrown out to die, and not much caring whether she herself lives or dies. But she feels she must clear her name. If people believe that she's lying, her children will inherit her reputation; she's determined to speak the truth, the whole truth, and nothing but the truth, whatever the consequences. (This reminds me a bit of Nelson Mandela's trial in Rivonia way back in 1964, when he and the other eight defendants decided to admit everything they had done, even if it carried the death penalty, deny what they hadn't done, and take the consequences. By explaining why they had done what they did, they put the whole system of apartheid on trial.) So Hermione points out she cannot be found "not guilty," because Leontes has already declared her guilty even though there is no iota of evidence—and her word, her only defense, will not be believed. Nevertheless, she makes the case for herself brilliantly, refuting every point Leontes accuses her of, and then starts piling up the evidence for why her trial is unjust and her imprisonment illegal; finally, she asks that the ultimate power, Apollo, be her judge.

The court justices agree she's allowed to do this, and summon Cleomenes and Dion.

The seals are broken on the Delphic oracle. Hermione is declared innocent and Leontes a jealous tyrant; until "that which is lost" be found, the kingdom will never come right. Then all hell breaks loose. Leontes refuses to believe the oracle; he declares that the sessions will continue. The people and court are terrified. In the midst of this, a messenger comes onstage and declares that young Prince Mamillius is dead. Hermione collapses. The King finally gets it—he has created all of this misery through his own jealous projections. As he asks Apollo's pardon, Paulina, who took away the collapsed Hermione from the court, returns to say she's dead. Paulina is like the avenging angel, raining down thunderbolts of lacerating words on Leontes's head. But when she sees how deeply he's affected, how truly penitent he is, she stops and tries to comfort him.

The scene ends with Leontes asking to be taken to see the dead bodies of his wife and son, swearing that from this day forward he will do penance; he puts himself in Paulina's hands, to be guided in whatever way she thinks fit until the end of his days.

Back to Antigonus. He and the newborn baby are caught in a terrible storm, as his boat is putting ashore in Bohemia. He tells us he had a dream in which Hermione is dead and asks him to call her baby Perdita—which means "that which is lost"—and leave her on the hillside.

Antigonus does so, but Hermione also tells him he'll never see his wife again. And at that point a huge bear comes into sight.

Now, I said *Winter's Tale* is about three women and a bear. The bear comes at the turning point: will the female baby be killed, or will she survive to bring about rebirth?

Bears, because they hibernate, are associated with rebirth. Shakespeare might have known the stories about bears and their associations with the gods, from old German folktales, or Greek myths, or even those Indians who were brought from the New World to England as exhibit pieces. Native Americans, of course, have many connections with bears, which are embedded symbolically in their culture. But I think what Shakespeare was creating, with his infamous stage direction "Exit, pursued by a bear," and then the subsequent detailed description of the bear pulling Antigonus to pieces, is a reversal of what his audience might see any day on Bankside. Bears were ripped to pieces by dogs—or dogs by bears. A little earlier in the play, we have heard the sound of dogs hunting the bear.

So, if Shakespeare's bear is actually played by Sackerson, a famous Bankside bear, and Sackerson every day has to fight for his life with crowds of paying punters screaming for his blood, it would give Shakespeare great satisfaction to reverse the situation by having the screaming human begging for his life. Shakespeare hated cruelty to animals and alone among his contemporaries ascribed emotions to animals. The bear doesn't eat the child—he eats the man—and rebirth can take place.

Two shepherds, one old and one young, discover the baby, the gold that's left with her, and papers explaining her birth. They take her up and adopt her. After intermission, we fast-forward fifteen years.

We are still in Bohemia, at a sheep-shearing festival. Perdita is dressed as the goddess Flora and is Queen of the Feast. She has a young lover who's dressed as a humble swain—but actually he's the son of Polixenes, who, while out with his falcon, met and fell in love with the shepherdess, Perdita, and has been spending all of his time among the country folk ever since. We have many wild dances, including a very primitive and slightly threatening Dance of the Satyrs.

Two strangers at the feast are welcomed by the old shepherd. They are bewitched by the young girl dressed as Flora—and she's certainly able to challenge them, charm them, and even better them in argument. These two are, in fact, Polixenes and Camillo, come to spy on the young man, Florizel, for of late he's been neglecting so many of his duties at court. Now they understand why.

At the height of the feast, Florizel asks the old shepherd to bless his union with his daughter, which the old man is prepared to do. When the stranger asks Florizel if he has a father, Florizel says that he has, but he's not going to invite him to the betrothal. The stranger presses him. Florizel insists the old shepherd go through with the blessing now—at which point Polixenes throws off his disguise and breaks up the promise of the marriage. Then he threatens all the onlookers with death if they disobey him, and Florizel with disinheritance of the kingdom, and rages back to court. Camillo stays behind.

What happens next is of the utmost importance. Instead of following his father, Florizel chooses his love for Perdita over all the power, material goods, and prestige.

FLORIZEL *(to Perdita)*
> Why look you so upon me?
> I am but sorry, not afeard; delayed,
> But nothing altered. What I was, I am,
> More straining on for plucking back, not following
> My leash unwillingly.
> > THE WINTER'S TALE (4.4, 485–89)

Perdita cannot see how this betrothal can go forward, let alone marriage.

FLORIZEL
> It cannot fail but by
> The violation of my faith, and then
> Let nature crush the sides o'th'earth together

And mar the seeds within. Lift up thy looks.
From my succession wipe me, father! I
Am heir to my affection.

THE WINTER'S TALE (4.4, 503–08)

And there you have it. Florizel aligns himself with love, his union with Perdita. Perdita finds strength through his resolution, and they run away together.

Camillo reveals himself and advises them to go to Sicilia—he'll go, too. At Leontes's court, Leontes has been following Paulina's guidance for fifteen years. Courtiers are trying to persuade Leontes to marry again for the good of the kingdom. Paulina's against it—so Leontes won't do it. Camillo and the lovers appear. They tell their story. Leontes swears to help them. Polixenes follows, in a rage. Leontes asks forgiveness for his jealousy and betrayal of Polixenes. Then he pleads for the lovers. How Leontes finds out Perdita is his daughter is not the important scene in the play—as you would think. That gets reported by several servants in a comic manner. Then the shepherds arrive with the secret of Perdita's birth. Shakespeare put his emphasis on the last scene, in which what has really been happening all this time can come true. Stone can turn to life, that which has been lost is found, and the mystery of life can be revealed.

We are in an art gallery, in Paulina's house. We are going to look at a statue of Hermione. Paulina keeps it lonely, apart.

When we get there, Leontes is so moved by the likeness that he is overcome with emotion, wants to touch and kiss her. Paulina says she will make her come to life, but first insists that all present must "awake your faith . . . or those that think it is unlawful business / I am about, let them depart."

She calls for music to awake the statue. "Descend. Be stone no more. . . . Bequeath to death your numbness, for from him / Dear life redeems you."

And so the statue comes to life. Hermione blesses her daughter and begs to know how she has been found.

Love takes over. Leontes asks Polixenes to take Hermione's hand—he'll be jealous no more. He marries Paulina and Camillo. Florizel and Perdita can inherit both the kingdoms. All the shepherds are having a right good time.

The only person who cannot come back to life is Mamillius—the true sacrifice was the young, unformed male spirit.

Why is this a play about three women and a bear? And why is it a story for our time?

First, the women adhere to the ancient archetypes of the mother, the witch, and the virgin—and, *in collaboration,* they are strong enough to ameliorate power structures, redeem even traumas so great it seems they can never be healed; they can bring together the lives of people who live in faraway countries, and they use time, nature, and art as the means of redemption. They move onto the stage when it's their turn and withdraw when it's not. And each one, though very different from the others, contributes her essential quality in order to bring about change.

First Hermione. She is the mother and the lover, the epitome of womanhood, what every man supposedly says or thinks he wants. She is spiritually advanced ("grace" is her favorite word), generous, obedient to her husband under most circumstances, tactful, but no pushover—she can stand up for herself—and she is still very beautiful and sexy, even though she's nine months pregnant. None of this saves her from the wrath of the King or the rules of the patriarchal structure, which allows him almost total power. Once the King thinks he has been shamed, cuckolded, that emotion is more powerful and alive to him than any other consideration: he converts it to "reason" and declares his way of thinking "right" because he can: no one has the authority to challenge him. Almost *because* she is the epitome of womanhood, the King has no defense against his own psychosis. (He can't say, Well, she's just a dumb chick, I didn't want her anyway; or, The people don't like her, they'll be glad I'm getting rid of her.) She is perfect—and her perfection makes the contrast with erring nature absolute. The flesh, if you like, cannot behold its own soul, made of pure love, without some kind of veil to protect it. How a woman uses her body is very personal to the man close to her; he could be deceived into loving another man's child. "Foul toads" may "knot and gender" in her womb, in Othello's expression. A man's perception of himself from the earliest age is bound up with the mother and the lover. His sense of shame if he feels she has abandoned him will destroy all sense of his own worth and, he thinks, his worth in other people's eyes. It is one of the driving forces of the world, but we rarely acknowledge it. What is shame built out of? Where does it come from? Where it goes is obvious—into revenge, violence, annihilation of others, acting out in crime, rape, drugs, a complete disregard for anything other than soothing the sense of shame. Hermione is too perfect, too pure. She needs more flaws, more rough edges for Leontes to bump against. Fortunately, she has a best friend with lots of rough edges.

Enter Paulina, the witch. Why do I call her a witch? Partly because Leontes calls her one, but mostly because of his actions and her choices. She doesn't appear until she's needed. She stands absolutely steady in her knowledge of Hermione's goodness—she doesn't let the legal case or other circumstantial evidence sway her judgment. Camillo and Polixenes fled? There must be some other cause than Hermione conspiring with them. My husband, Antigonus, can't persuade me to behave differently? Of course not—why should he? We both know I'm right. You burn me to death? "It is an heretic that makes the fire, not she which burns in't." But more than anything, Paulina is willing to take actions that she knows can change the narrative. Just as a man might be brave enough to face death and ride into battle to prove his honor, so a woman like Paulina is willing to take an action and tenaciously stick to it no matter how long is necessary, if it has a chance of altering a life-defeating situation. She's resolute. She does not buy into the picture patriarchal men have of women, and she makes no attempt to be anything but who she is. That doesn't mean she isn't a loving wife to her husband or a mother—she's both of those things, but on her own terms, not part of an erroneously crafted construct for women. This gives her great strength. And she backs up that strength by listening to nature and the mysteries of life; there is a rhythm, and a larger truth, beyond our own limited thinking mechanism.

Finally, there is Perdita, the virgin, the young woman who is on the cusp of becoming a mother and a lover—but who is not yet, is still open and vulnerable to the world, and to love. She embraces the love of a man as an adventure, an expanding of herself in which she can find even more of herself. She will travel, cross boundaries, cultures, and class systems.

What none of these women possess is the inside track, the bureaucracies, authority in the mechanisms that make the world work. They can make their stand for what is true, but they will have no automatic backup. Just as a candidate for the presidency hasn't got a hope of winning without having one of the main party machines behind him, so these women have no way of structuring their version of the world unless they find a way of influencing many, many others. Their content, if you will, has no context to support it!

Except that they do find a way—just not an obvious one.

Hermione can say the truth and it'll get her killed. Paulina can back her up, but it'll get her burned at the stake if she doesn't take care. Ultimately, Apollo will back them both up—but that's not enough for Leontes. He'll oppose even the god. And cause more damage. The destruction that comes out of the jealousy, pigheadedness, and shame will permanently kill the young male heir, though courage allows Paulina to start the long process of building a different kind of Sicilia with a different kind of king. It takes fifteen years.

In the case of Perdita, nature has to come to her aid, in the form of good country folk and simple pleasures and a sweet disposition—creating a happy if limited life. But when Polixenes is going to kill her if she doesn't give up his son, she has no defense. To be able to stay true to love, she needs her lover to stand with her—and he does, magnificently honoring love more than kingdoms. And then the lovers need a wise counselor to help them make their next step a constructive one, in which the wheel can come full-circle. Camillo is there, ready to play his part.

But the ingredient needed to get this story to a place where forgiveness can happen and new life can come forth is ART.

Why is art necessary? Or, to put it another way, why did Shakespeare point to art as the vehicle for the divine? Because art is life: the seed of creativity allows something to come of nothing. Art engenders life—and it doesn't need a church or a religious belief to generate its spark. The spark, the life, is in the very fabric of the art form, and if human beings can be in its presence, whether creating or beholding, it in turn awakens sensory perception that will go to a place beyond sensory perception, to the very crucible in which new life is forged. Beauty and truth become one in this place—but it is an experience, not an intellectual perception, which is why a theatre is a good place for it to happen.

Or a gallery—or a gallery in a theatre, which is where it happens in

Winter's Tale. "It is required / You do awake your faith," says Paulina to those who are about to witness this transformation. She's talking to the people in the play *and* the audience. She's not talking about a belief but about open, vulnerable sensitivity, being alive to what is happening. "Music: awake her, strike. / 'Tis time. Descend. Be stone no more. Strike all that look upon with marvel." Love that hurts and is desired; coming face to face with the person you destroyed.

The end of *Winter's Tale,* as Hermione changes from stone to life, is the most magical moment Shakespeare ever wrote. It requires the actors to live it, follow Shakespeare's instructions as they embody it. It creates the indefinable, effervescent space in which Leontes can truly be forgiven. Grace returns to the land; the old turtle (as Paulina calls herself), a bird of love, completes her sixteen-year journey of devotion and steadfastness, and the young woman can be blessed and, with her young man, start the cycle of life again.

When I think of these three women, I know they have the qualities, the ingredients, to make a story, large or small, come back to love. And out of love, new life. The hero story, the one we have been telling for so long and out of which so many of our institutions were born, can never do that. At its best, the hero story brings us face to face with death. And that can mean rebirth—but rebirth for the individual, not for the group. The feminine spirit will stand with the enemy, nurture the perpetrator; the work of art includes the shadow as well as the light. Endurance, the change of seasons, indecipherable growth: it takes a work of art, three women in collaboration, and a good man to make the change the world needs. And let's not forget the bear.

SCENE 5: *The Tempest*

The greatest storm at sea. A ship caught in its eye. On board are all the people of power in Naples and Milan. They know they are about to meet their end. They have been to North Africa, Tunis, to make a power match between the King there and the daughters of the King of Naples. Great rejoicing. Returning home. Great alliance—wealth of Milan, port of Naples, all trade of North Africa, strong shipping routes. Together they can dominate the Mediterranean. But now, because of this storm, all may be lost—they are mortal men at the mercy of the elements.

Except, it turns out, the storm is caused not by Mother Nature but by Master Magician. There's actually a spirit loose who creates thunderbolts, lightning, waves, water everywhere, thunder rolls, the world splitting apart, great shrieks, prayers, cursing, chaos. It's all happening because a magician wants revenge—and perhaps to marry off his daughter at the same time, because she's on the edge of puberty and there's no one on the island where the magician lives for her to marry other than a supposedly deformed native called Caliban.

We've come to the last play—by popular consent—that Shakespeare wrote, *The Tempest*. It actually wasn't the last one he wrote, but it sure feels like it, a "farewell" play (and the things he wrote after this, he may have written with someone else)—and it's a play about what it means to be an artist, to give it up, *not* to take revenge when you want to, how to let your daughter go and start a new life, how to acknowledge the lousy things you've done in your life—and how to start thinking about death.

At the center of the play is the magician Prospero and his relationship with his creative spirit, Ariel—played by either a boy or girl—with a very intimate, sensual, sadomasochistic relationship with Prospero. They love each other in secret. It's this relationship we need to look at to find the power in the themes of the play. Prospero and Ariel interact with everyone else. Prospero exerts his dominance (Ariel does, too, when he/she becomes rebellious: it's easy to see why this play reflects so powerfully the colonialism that followed in the centuries after Shakespeare wrote it). Prospero's wife died soon after Miranda's birth. Prospero, even though Duke of Milan, spent no time thinking about the well-being or organization of the people in his kingdom, but studied esoteric knowledge in order to become a great magician. Inevitably, his brother seized the kingdom. Instead of killing Prospero, he put him and his daughter in a little boat and pushed them out to sea. Prospero managed to take his books with him, so, when he and Miranda landed on a little island (and I always wonder if Prospero knew which island he was heading for and why), he was able to set up shop and again pursue his art form. The island does have an inhabitant—Caliban—who was born there and inherited the island from his mother, Sycorax, a very powerful witch who is now dead, but with whom Prospero used to have some kind of relationship!

So these are the four inhabitants of the island: Prospero; his daughter, Miranda; his creative spirit, Ariel (whom no one but Prospero sees, though others do hear and feel the actions of her/him); and the man Prospero makes his slave, Caliban.

The journey of the relationship between Prospero and Ariel is the first we'll deal with. Prospero was deeply into magic (or playwriting and acting, if you want to think of it as Shakespeare) long before he got to the island, but his "magic" was not powerful enough to prevent his brother from overpowering him, putting him to sea on a boat to perish or get lost. He didn't counteract or understand that kind of worldly force.

Once he got to the island, however, he was able to release Ariel from a tree in which she had been imprisoned by Sycorax, who then grew into a hoop and died (turned in on herself, or became a circle of knowledge?). Once Ariel is free, Prospero can do all kinds of things he couldn't do before—create storms, talk to the nature spirits, bring the spirits of the dead alive, call on goddesses, invoke packs of hounds—there's no end to it! But the power of creating something out of nothing doesn't seem to make him a more generous man. In fact, he seems a rather short-tempered, insecure man.

When Caliban first meets Prospero and Miranda, he loves them and shows them how the island works. In fact, for fourteen years or so they seem to live in comparative harmony. Caliban learns their language, understands how to study the heavens, does the heavy lifting around the household, and is the playfellow for Baby Miranda. All that changes when Miranda hits puberty and Caliban gets sexually interested (not clear whether she does or not—but it would seem likely that she would—nor is it clear how old Caliban is—he must be young, too), at which point Prospero goes ballistic, enslaves Caliban, forces him into labor, and, if he disagrees in any way, shape, or form, gets sprites to punish him physically or just incapacitate him with cramps. A rather one-sided fight.

In the meantime, Ariel, too, would like to become autonomous and stop laboring night and day for what Prospero wants. Prospero has kind of said he will let Ariel be free—but he keeps putting off the release date. He cannot actually do his magic without Ariel, and he has things he wants to put in place before he gives up his power. Is this how Shakespeare felt about leaving the playhouse?

How does Prospero use his creativity? He uses it to keep Caliban, now the household skivvy, in order. He uses it to bring his daughter's potential suitor to a part of the island where he can bring them together so they can fall in love. But most of all, he uses it to create a storm (frightening his daughter, who suspects her father is a monster manipulator) to bring all of his enemies into his power so he can be revenged upon them. Not a very impressive use of power—but not out of line with most governments that wield such power. What changes his course of action? Ariel's compassion. His daughter's joy and terror. And, finally, his own understanding of Caliban, "this thing of darkness I / Acknowledge mine." And actually allowing his daughter to take her own journey.

In the beginning, when she vehemently protests against the storm, he tells his tale of justification, who his enemies are and why they deserve to be punished—and every time she asks questions he doesn't want to answer, he puts her to sleep. Once the lovers meet (and he spies on them), Miranda, like Juliet before her, proposes marriage before Ferdinand does, and binds herself to him. When they are betrothed, they play chess—a sophisticated power game—and she knows he would play her false if power were involved "for a score of kingdoms." Despite this, she willingly begins her journey back to civilization.

Ariel draws all Prospero's enemies together and paralyzes them. Prospero can now take revenge. But Ariel, the creative spirit, pities them.

ARIEL Your charm so strongly works 'em
  that if you now beheld them, your affections
  Would become tender.
PROSPERO Is that so, spirit?
ARIEL Mine would, sir, were I human.
PROSPERO And mine shall. . . . The rarer action is in virtue
  than in vengeance.

         THE TEMPEST (5.1, 19–24, 31–32)

Then Ariel, too, is to be set free—allowing her to go wherever she wants to go, not being "used" by a man who no longer wants revenge.

And what does Prospero mean about Caliban's being "this thing of darkness" as he acknowledges him? Caliban has spent much of the play plotting revenge on Prospero—acting out the kind of oppression forced upon him. Does Prospero see that he has created that violence in Caliban? Could it be that Prospero and Sycorax were actually lovers and Caliban is Prospero's natural son? Is it that Prospero sees that he can use his creativity for new life or for death—and that he was killing Caliban, taking his island, imposing his rules, not letting him propagate?

Whichever it is, the elements of creativity and imagination in the pure feminine spirit are both served in *The Tempest*. The storm, an image in which heaven and ocean meet, becomes calm and still. But in the earth the magic staff is buried, in the ocean the magic book is drowned, and in the heavens the magic music can be called forth. These places hold the deepest secrets, to be unlocked by human beings if they are patient and humble, if they honor rather than exploit.

SCENE 6: *All Is True—Henry VIII*

And so we come to the last play that Shakespeare wrote: *All Is True* or *Henry VIII*—although, dear God, there's a veritable list of plays he may have had to do with at the end of his life: *Two Noble Kinsmen, Edward III, Cardenio.* I'm just not going there. He wrote *All Is True* in 1613, some three years after he wrote *The Tempest*. Many scholars believe that it was written by John Fletcher as well as Shakespeare, but it is included in the First Folio by Heminges and Condell without any reference to Fletcher.

It's an oddball, dramatically. It takes the form of a miracle play—the kind Shakespeare saw in his childhood. It pits good against evil: the King is suffering with his conscience, and there is a fight for his soul.

Shakespeare took known historical events from Henry's reign and deliberately rearranged them, because the theme he was following was this fight for Henry's soul, the soul of England—he was not telling a story of historical record.

On the side of evil are the Church of Rome and its servants Cardinals Wolsey and Campeius. Once Wolsey and Campeius are out of the way, arrogant English nobles become a force for bad. On the side of good are the Duke of Buckingham; Queen Katherine of Aragon, Henry's first wife; and Anne Boleyn, his second. Their fight for good is strengthened by Cranmer, Archbishop in the new Anglican Church, and finally by the baby Elizabeth, Anne's daughter, blessed by Cranmer as "the maiden phoenix."

So both Buckingham and Katherine oppose Wolsey—his taxes, his riches, and his loyalty to Rome. Buckingham is executed. Katherine is put away (Henry should never have married her in the first place), but not until she's pleaded for Buckingham and exposed Wolsey. Wolsey arranges a masque, where Henry dances with and falls in love with Anne Boleyn. Anne says only wonderful things about Katherine. The two women are not in opposition in the play—rather, they are fighting on the same side to rescue Henry's soul. Campeius arrives from Rome to support Wolsey. Katherine falls. Wolsey does not want Henry to marry Anne—she is a Lutheran—but Henry and Anne marry in secret. The King discovers that Wolsey is richer than he is. Wolsey falls. Katherine's soul ascends to heaven. In the last act, just when it looks as if everything is going to come out well, the English nobles arrogantly dismiss Cranmer, humiliating him by forcing him to wait outside the chamber for hours. They are planning to take over England, now that Rome has lost. Fortunately, Cranmer is a true man of God: he is humble and creates no opposition. The King discovers what they are up to and reinstates Cranmer; the baby Elizabeth is brought on, and Cranmer blesses her and the feminine spirit.

It's a parable. Henry's character is almost nonexistent; he's a cipher. Wolsey and Katherine are the good parts; Katherine in this play is not so much wedded to the Church of Rome (as she was in life) as to justice, charity, and spirituality.

Elizabeth, the daughter, became, as everyone knew, the symbol and beacon of the age. The play, with its five masques, was offering competition for the Ben Jonson and Inigo Jones masques at court. But in Shakespeare's case they also remind the audience, throughout the play, that these dramatic displays of power are human constructs, created to keep men in awe, to add ritual and religious significance to political structures.

Shakespeare probably felt that King James's soul and England's soul were also in jeopardy. On the one hand, the King James Bible had been published, a work of beauty and enlightenment; on the other hand, James was bankrupting the country morally and economically with his displays of wealth and promotion of his beautiful boys (called *mignons* in court parlance). Prince Henry, James's son, the Protestant hope of Europe–educated, brave, intelligent, thoughtful– had just died. The play could possibly have been performed at the wedding of his sister, also called Elizabeth, now a potential leader of Europe with her husband, the Elector of Palatine.

The prologue of *Henry VIII* states that the audience "may here find truth, too," and the epilogue says:

> For this play at this time is only in
> The merciful construction of good women,
> For such a one we showed 'em.
>
> HENRY VIII (EPILOGUE, 9–11)

If Fletcher did write this play along with Shakespeare, he obviously felt much the same as Shakespeare did about women. It is, after all, Fletcher who took *The Taming of the Shrew* and writes a follow-up: *The Tamer Tamed*, a play that takes up Petruchio's life after Katherine has died from his ill-treatment of her. Petruchio's new wife takes revenge upon him–she tames the tamer!

And we see how one artist's work infects another's; and rather than thinking of art as separate pieces, think of it as a continuum seeking to give coherence to all the disparate impulses of which mankind is made: in this way we can really perceive the power of art, and the role it plays in our lives.

EPILOGUE

Now that we have followed the women characters in Shakespeare's plays, we have a clear picture of what happens in a world where women's voices are silenced or when women, like Lady Macbeth or Volumnia, adopt the ways of men: how honor and shame triumph over love, how tragedy becomes the dominant story, how we build our addiction to violence, and how it is possible to counteract it. Capulet will throw Juliet out into the street to starve to death if she disobeys him, but by the late plays an Imogen or a Perdita (both having been thrown out of their homes) take a course that redeems the father's violence and brings the world to an understanding of love. There is only one antidote to violence: the courage to love. And if Shakespeare is right, it is millions of acts of love—love for another, love in the service of others (by both women and men)—that will shift the balance away from war and into peace.

In his last statement about a woman, Shakespeare says:

> Good grows with her:
> In her days every man shall eat in safety
> Under his own vine, what he plants; and sing
> The merry songs of peace to all his neighbours:
> God shall be truly known; and those about her
> From her shall read the perfect ways of honour,
> And by those claim their greatness, not by blood.
>
> HENRY VIII (5.4, 36–42)

If we divide human attributes into "masculine" and "feminine" and strengthen only those attributes that "belong" to that sex, we cut off half of ourselves from ourselves as human beings, condemned forever to search for our other half. The world is in desperate need of multilayered human beings with the voices, stamina, and insight to break through our current calcified ways of doing things.

Shakespeare was a white male, but he is not a dead white male. There may be only three or four women in each Shakespeare play but they are the key to how to transform a society. They are the teachers and the leaders in a new way of thinking about relationships, hierarchies, and love. They have the focus and energy to counterbalance the authority of the ten to thirty men who inhabit each play. The patriarchal structures of honor, shame, violence, and might is right, do as much harm to Hamlet, Edgar, Lear, Coriolanus, and Hector as they do to Ophelia, Desdemona, Lady Macduff, Hero and Juliet, Ariel and Miranda.

We learn from the environments we are born into; but as Elizabeth I and Malala Yousafzai, the Pakistani teenager who made a public stand on the education of girls, and nearly all the women in Shakespeare's plays so powerfully demonstrate, it is not impossible to break through those strictures. We do not have to stay in the culture of the country or under the control of the family; or obey the voices that talk to us in our heads or the words we heard in our childhoods. Elizabeth I was three when her father killed her mother, seven when he killed her stepmother. She never married but created a country tough, resilient, and theatre-loving, with an educated middle-class, one that experienced the longest period of peace it had ever known (a few Spanish skirmishes notwithstanding). And she left behind her the idea that peace was an honorable way to conduct the affairs of a state.

The process of the artist is to be fascinated by the psychological intricacy of other human beings, to have feelings, intuitive flights of understanding, a desire to have knowledge of what is happening below the surface, to serve. These are often called "feminine" attributes, and it is true that many of the women in the plays possess them. But they also belong to Kent, Ferdinand, Florizel, Camillo, as well as the women. So they are not "feminine" attributes: they are human attributes. They are the playwright Shakespeare's attributes.

These attributes develop the deep knowledge of the relationships in the plays and the worlds they function in.

The actor Shakespeare could feel in his body the truth; the writer Shakespeare could record what he saw in the outside world and he gave to the women the words to expose the dichotomy between what lay within and what was expected from without. And the only way to bridge the gap, alter it, and bring it to a new relationship is through love. The women acknowledge the love and go on the journey. Creativity? It is the ability to see the world as it is, imagine what it might be, and step out with love.

ACKNOWLEDGMENTS

A Guggenheim Foundation grant allowed me to replace myself as artistic director of Shakespeare & Company for four days a week for six months. During those months, the Bunting Institute of Radcliffe College, under the beautiful leadership of Florence Ladd, gave me a home and an intellectual community. I am forever grateful to my sister fellows, astrophysicists, China specialists, peace activists, artists, and scholars of many disciplines, for the insights of that year. Especially Adrienne Le Blanc and Dorothy Thomas, who remain friends and colleagues. The Van Waverin Foundation paid for early rehearsals and script drafts. Lucy Cavendish College of Cambridge University, under the leadership of Pauline Perry, Baroness of Southwark, gave me a home for several weeks and my first crack at performance before a British audience.

Once I had stepped aside as artistic director of Shakespeare & Company, I wrote this book between performances or while traveling to perform the plays. A rhythm emerged: we would rehearse and perform, then I would remain behind and write more of the book. This happened in England at Colchester Rep under Dee Evans's leadership, Prague Shakespeare in the Czech Republic, Artistic Director Guy Roberts and Producer Jessica Boone. Torrence Harder loaned me his apartment in West Palm Beach, Peter and Helen Randolph sheltered me each time I was in Boston, which was often, especially during our run at the Nora Theatre Company, Artistic Director Mimi Huntington. I stayed with Bonnie MacBird and Alan Kay in Los

Angeles when Lisa Wolpe and the Los Angeles Women's Shakespeare Company gave us a home. We spent two summers in Colorado, thanks to Philip Snead at Colorado Shakespeare and Kevin Landis at the University of Colorado in Colorado Springs.

This traveling and writing was balanced by the steady presence of Sarah Hancock, who not only supported the development of the manuscript with her high-tech expertise, ability to fact-check, and an unending curiosity about the themes in *Women of Will,* but was also the principal producer in New York City, when we ran off-Broadway for four months. Sarah is currently the chair of Shakespeare & Company's board of trustees, which perhaps indicates the range of her skills and commitment.

Victoria Wilson, my editor at Knopf, no slouch herself around theatre, was both patient and insistent. I thank her for her finely balanced care. My agent, Jim Levine, is a Renaissance man who responded to the ideas in the book immediately and guided me into the world of publishing. I could not have remained sane in New York or Prague without the help of Laura Baranek and throughout the whole saga without the ever-present, impish spirit of Catherine Wheeler, reigning from her desk outside the artistic director's office in Lenox, Massachusetts.

The book was read in manuscript form by my friend and colleague in the Shakespeare world, Rebecca Kemper; and by the friend of all my days, from Paris in our youth to Key West in our dotage, the elegant and startlingly original Harry Mathews; and, of course, by my husband, Dennis Krausnick, who patiently pointed out my errors.

I have referred to Carol Gilligan's writing in this book. But perhaps her deepest contribution (besides she and Jim Gilligan giving me a room in their house to write in when I needed to escape the art scene in the Berkshires) was our walks together, often daily, as each of us struggled with things we were seeking to understand and fix in life and art. A true, true friend.

Finally, I want to acknowledge Clive Merrison, who did me the greatest service a friend can probably do. As I went into the final month of writing, under deadline pressure and knowing I must finish, he guarded my door, cooked my meals, made me start and stop on time, and kept me company when I wanted it. All this took place in Suffolk, in a tiny gardener's cottage on the edge of a wood where I'd lived thirty years earlier with my close friend and his wife, the late Gillian Barge. Lorna Heilbron, his current wife and also my friend, occasionally joined us. Through Clive I was able to finally finish saying what I wanted to say and let go.

My debt to the actors, teachers, directors, designers, stage managers, administrators of Shakespeare & Company is unending and ongoing. The Boards of Trustees and Advisors have been steady supporters, linking the inner world of artists to the outer world of practicality. The late Mitch Berenson and Michael Miller have supported me both professionally and personally. The town of Lenox has provided a home for the company, and all our growth.

And to Will Shakespeare and the team of *Women of Will:* thank you.

SOURCES

My knowledge about Shakespeare's women comes from several sources. First of these has been either directing or acting in the plays (often many times) onstage. The only play I have neither directed, performed, nor taught is *Cymbeline*—though I hope to have done that, too, before this book goes to print. So most of my knowledge is experiential, learned in the theatre.

The second source is my fellow actors and directors, both in my own productions and in the productions of others. Working in performance breeds close relationships. Actors and directors who worked on the first versions of *Women of Will* in the 1990s—Jonathan Epstein, Johnny Lee Davenport, Chris Coucill, Michael Hammond, Gary Mitchell, Normi Noel—are still alive in my memory. Things they said to me, bits of staging, the ways they played different parts, have merged into the fabric of the performance of *Women of Will*—though none of the current team ever saw the performances of the past.

I have gained great insights simply watching Shakespeare's plays as an audience member. To this day, I can see the way Barbara Jefford ran across the stage at Stratford when I was on one of my school outings, or the way Mark Rylance asked the audience, "Why did you laugh . . . ?" in his performance of Hamlet at the American Repertory Theater in Cambridge in 1991.

I have read hundreds of books on Shakespeare. At any given time, I usually have one or two academic books on the go. I found it difficult at first to read scholarly books, unless they were real crowd-pleasers such as Jonathan Bate's *The Genius of Shakespeare,* but over the years it's become easier, whether they've lightened up or I've got cleverer. I always try to get an image of the authors, what they look like and sound like, why they write in the style they do and why they are fascinated by their subject matter.

The artistic partnership I have had with actor Nigel Gore and director Eric Tucker as we have put together the material over six years for the performance cycle of *Women of Will* is another source. I refer to them often in this story—and their insights have influenced me in a myriad of ways. With Eric, I usually learn from his unique way of staging events, using icons, music, sound effects from every period, juxtaposing props, scenic pieces (though never scenery), actions, to create a context to tell the story. And, through Eric, I am also indebted to the final team of designers we put together to support all our actions onstage: especially Les Dickert, Daniel Kluger, and Valérie Thérèse Bart.

From Nigel I know something almost inexplicable, which I will now try to explicate. We know each other in ways possible *only* because we are actors on a stage together. I do not wish to exaggerate, but when we go into some of our scenes together we are touched by the gods: a force larger than either of us enters the space, leaps over the normal ways of knowing, and catapults us into a place it is not possible to find through willpower, intelligence, technique, or even talent. It can be found only here, in collaboration on the sacred space of the stage.

Perhaps orchestras go to this place when an overture lifts off the ground, or an opera when the force soars to the heavens. Recently, I watched two actors who were playing in the South African *Mies Julie* transcend hundreds of years of separation and violence as they worked together; they were experiencing the connectedness always there under the enforced political social structures, revealing the possibility of the future. They stood side by side at the curtain call, one so tall, so black, the other so white, so diminutive, both exhausted by what they had been through, yet as artists loving each other and us. The ancient gods, called up in the narrative of the play, they stood with us, too. This experience was palpable.

So this is the energy that visits our space as we work through

Women of Will. Not always, and not necessarily in the same scenes, but it comes. So onstage I know what it is to be raped by Nige, made non-human when he puts his hand over my face, have the life squeezed out of me; I know what it is to be loved into eternity, laughed into oblivion. I know humble gratitude felt toward a fellow human being for doing for me something I cannot do for myself; I know the connection and communication beyond words.

Offstage, it has been a long and somewhat rocky journey: a marriage of sorts, as the months turned into years, as we challenged each other on every level. We worked at it, and every time it felt as though it was falling apart, we sought help from others; finally we have come to a committed understanding that hopefully will allow us to create together way into the future.

Yet another source of my knowledge is simply my imagination. Ideas come to me in performance, when I'm traveling across the country, while reading, and when sitting silently in contemplation. I don't know if they are true. I fact-check them if possible. But often something pops into my head, and if it stays there or reappears, I start adopting it, trying it on for size among all the other ideas. And if it makes sense, I include it in my thinking. All knowledge, it seems to me, is based on what came before; we are constantly testing new hypotheses, which either align with our previous material, shifts it, or blows it up completely, invalidating the original hypothesis.

All this is against the backdrop of my own life, immersed in the theatre as it is. I live in the midst of a functioning theatre, which performs, runs massive amounts of education programs on many levels, and a training program that is the source of both performance and education. My intimate family is part of the theatre company as actors, teachers, directors: my son, Jason Asprey; my husband, Dennis Krausnick; and my comrades who helped me build Shakespeare & Company, especially Kevin Coleman and his work in education, and Kristin Linklater, the greatest voice teacher on earth. B. H. Barry not only taught me how to fight; we have collaborated on literally hundreds of battles, acts of violence, death. Tony Simotes, Puck in the very first *Midsummer Night's Dream* and B.H.'s first American trainee, now fight teacher par excellence, took over the helm of Shakespeare & Company. My sense of dance was first awakened by John

Broome at the Royal Academy, reinspired at the Royal Shakespeare, then brought into Shakespeare & Company: continued now by Susan Dibble. Actors, teachers, directors, designers, writers, administrators, grounds crew, tech staff, and of course the Board of Trustees—thirty-seven years of interaction, all focused on Shakespeare's plays.

When people ask me, "How do you know that?" I often don't know how I know. And the truth is, I could be wrong, but it's what my intuition tells me; I somehow "know" it. That's what living with Will Shakespeare does, using language to imagine stuff that, if you play it exquisitely, becomes the truth—or maybe not!

I love the flow of knowledge: seven or fifteen or forty people come together to make a Shakespeare play. We have Shakespeare's text (not definitive, so that, too, has waves, eddies, absences, debatable points in it, and then there are usually different versions of the texts, whether a play is known through a "quarto" version, or the First Folio, or one of the umpteen editions that followed). Then we have the lives and histories of all the people involved in the production, and how these influence the collective effort. They build a coherent narrative for the audience to listen to—and then the audience responds, and that, too, goes into the storytelling. And the critics review it, the scholars refer to it—it's the circle in the water "which never ceaseth to enlarge itself." I love it all, whether berating my fellow artists for their wrongheadedness (though always admiring their courage), hurling the Sunday newspaper across the room, being turned on by something I never understood before, feeling shy in the face of great talent—I love what we learn, see, feel. I have even loved the struggle of writing this book, forcing me to examine in more depth what adrenaline often does for me onstage.

BIBLIOGRAPHY

Ackroyd, Peter. *Shakespeare: The Biography.* New York: Anchor Books, 2005.

Armstrong, Karen. *Fields of Blood: Religion and the History of Violence.* New York, Alfred A. Knopf, 2014.

Astington, John H. *Actors and Acting in Shakespeare's Time: The Art of Stage Playing.* Cambridge: Cambridge University Press, 2010.

Auguet, Roland. *Cruelty and Civilization: The Roman Games.* Allen and Unwin, 1972.

Bakewell, Sarah. *How to Live: Or, A Life of Montaigne.* London: Chatto & Windus, 2010.

Baldwin, T. W. *William Shakspere's Small Latine and Lesse Greeke.* Two volumes. Champaign: University of Illinois Press, 1944.

Barton, John. *Playing Shakespeare.* London: Methuen Drama, Michelin House, 1989.

Basch, David. *The Hidden Shakespeare: A Rosetta Stone.* West Hartford, Conn.: Revelatory Press, 1994.

Bate, Jonathan. *The Genius of Shakespeare.* London: Picador, 1997.

Bate, Jonathan, and Eric Rasmussen, eds. *Shakespeare: The Complete Works.* Basingstoke, U.K.: Palgrave Macmillan, 2007.

Berleth, Richard. *The Twilight Lords: Elizabeth I and the First Irish Holocaust.* New York: Barnes & Noble, 1994.

Boyce, Charles. *Shakespeare A to Z: The Essential Reference to His Plays, His Poems, His Life and Times, and More.* New York: Dell Publishing, 1990.

Brown, Pamela Allen, and Peter Parolin, eds. *Women Players in England, 1500–1660: Beyond the All-Male Stage.* Burlington, Vt.: Ashgate, 2008.

Carr, Nicholas. *The Shallows: What the Internet Is Doing to Our Brains.* New York: W. W. Norton, 2011.

Duncan-Jones, Katherine. *Shakespeare: Upstart Crow to Sweet Swan 1592–1623.* London: Arden Shakespeare, 2011.

Faludy, George. *Erasmus.* New York: Stein and Day, 1970.

Fripp, Edgar I. *Shakespeare: Man & Artist.* Two volumes. London: Oxford University Press, 1938.

Garber, Marjorie. *Shakespeare After All.* New York: Pantheon, 2004.

Ghyka, Matila. *The Geometry of Art and Life.* New York: Dover Publications, 1977.

Gilligan, Carol. *The Birth of Pleasure.* New York: Alfred A. Knopf, 2002.

———. *In a Different Voice: Psychological Theory and Women's Development.* Cambridge, Mass.: Harvard University Press, 1982.

Gilligan, James. *Violence: Our Deadly Epidemic and Its Causes.* New York: Putnam, 1996.

Girard, René. *Violence and the Sacred.* Translated by Patrick Gregory. Baltimore: Johns Hopkins University Press, 1977.

Goodland, Katherine. *Female Mourning and Tragedy in Medieval and Renaissance English Drama: From the Raising of Lazarus to King Lear.* Burlington, Vt.: Ashgate, 2006.

Green, Martin. *Wriothesley's Roses in Shakespeare's Sonnets, Poems, and Plays.* Clevedon, U.K.: Clevedon Books, 1993.

Greenblatt, Stephen. *Will in the World: How Shakespeare Became Shakespeare.* New York: W. W. Norton, 2004.

Grossman, David A. *On Killing.* New York: Little, Brown, 1995.

Gurr, Andrew. *Playgoing in Shakespeare's London.* Cambridge: Cambridge University Press, 1987.

Harries, Frederick J. *Shakespeare and the Welsh.* London: T. Fisher Unwin, 1919.

Harrison, G. B. *The Life and Death of Robert Devereux, Earl of Essex.* New York: H. Holt, 1937.

Hart, Clive, trans. *Treatise on the Question Do Women Have Souls and Are They Human Beings?* Lewiston, N.Y.: Edwin Mellen Press, 2004.

Hayes, Alan. "Untamed Desire." *Sex in Elizabethan England.* Mechanicsburg, Pa.: Stackpole Books, 1997.

Heywood, Thomas. *An Apology for Actors in Three Books: From the Edition of 1612, Compared with That of W. Cartwright.* London: Elibron Classics, 2005.

Hill, Errol. *Shakespeare in Sable: A History of Black Shakespearean Actors.* Amherst: University of Massachusetts Press, 1984.

Hillman, James. *A Terrible Love of War.* New York: Penguin Books, 2004.

Holst-Warhaft, Gail. *Dangerous Voices: Women's Laments and Greek Literature.* New York: Routledge, 1992.

Honan, Park. *Shakespeare: A Life.* Oxford: Oxford University Press, 1998.

Jardine, Lisa. *Erasmus, Man of Letters: The Construction of Charisma in Print.* Princeton, N.J.: Princeton University Press, 1993.

Lanham, Richard A. *A Handlist of Rhetorical Terms.* Berkeley: University of California Press, 1991.

Lasocki, David, and Roger Prior. *The Bassanos: Venetian Musicians and Instrument Makers in England, 1531–1665.* Brookfield, Vt.: Ashgate, 1995.

Lee, Hermione. *Edith Wharton.* London: Chatto & Windus, 2007.

Lewalski, Barbara Kiefer. *Writing Women in Jacobean England.* Cambridge, Mass.: Harvard University Press, 1993.

Loraux, Nicole. *Tragic Ways of Killing a Woman.* Translated by Anthony Forster. Cambridge, Mass.: Harvard University Press, 1987.

McMillin, Scott, and Sally-Beth MacLean. *The Queen's Men and Their Plays.* Cambridge: Cambridge University Press, 1998.

Miola, Robert S. *Shakespeare's Reading.* Oxford: Oxford University Press, 2000.

Mitchell, C. Martin. *The Shakespeare Circle: A Life of Dr. John Hall.* Birmingham, U.K.: Cornish Brothers Limited, 1947.

Mortimer, Ian. *The Time Traveller's Guide to Elizabethan England.* London: Bodley Head, 2012.

Nicholl, Charles. *The Reckoning: The Murder of Christopher Marlowe.* New York: Harcourt, 1994.

Petersen, Lauren Hackworth, and Patricia Salzman-Mitchell, eds. *Mothering and Motherhood in Ancient Greece and Rome.* Austin: University of Texas Press, 2012.

Plutarch. *The Lives of the Noble Grecians and Romans.* Translated by John Dryden and revised by Arthur Hugh Clough. New York: Modern Library, 2001.

Rowse, A. L. *Sir Walter Raleigh: His Family and Private Life.* New York: Harper, 1962.

Scanlon, Thomas F. *Eros and Greek Athletes.* Oxford: Oxford University Press, 2002.

Schiavone, Aldo. *The End of the Past.* Cambridge, Mass.: Harvard University Press, 2002.

Schiff, Stacy. *Cleopatra: A Life.* New York: Little, Brown, 2010.

Shakespeare, William. *The Sonnets.* London: Barrie & Jenkins, 1988.

Shapiro, James. *Shakespeare and the Jews.* New York: Columbia University Press, 1996.

———. *A Year in the Life of William Shakespeare: 1599.* New York: HarperCollins, 2005.

Shay, Jonathan. *Achilles in Vietnam.* New York: Scribner, 1994.

Soens, Lewis. *Sir Philip Sidney's Defense of Poesy.* Lincoln: University of Nebraska Press, 1970.

Spencer, Theodore. *Shakespeare and the Nature of Man.* New York: Collier Books, 1971.

Stanford, W. B. *Greek Tragedy and the Emotions.* London: Routledge and Kegan Paul, 1983.

Thomson, Peter. *Shakespeare's Professional Career.* Cambridge: Cambridge University Press, 1992.

———. *Shakespeare's Theatre.* New York: Routledge, 1985.

Tillyard, E. M. W. *The Elizabethan World Picture.* Harmondsworth, Middlesex, U.K.: Penguin Books, 1975.

Tobin, J. J. M. *Shakespeare's Favorite Novel: A Study of the "Golden Asse" as Prime Source.* Lanham, Md.: University Press of America, 1984.

Vyvyan, John. *Shakespeare and Platonic Beauty.* London: Chatto & Windus, 1961.

———. *Shakespeare and the Rose of Love.* London: Chatto & Windus, 1960.

———. *The Shakespearean Ethic.* London: Chatto & Windus, 1959.

Walker, Barbara G. *The Woman's Encyclopedia of Myths and Secrets.* San Francisco: Harper & Row, 1983.

Waller, John. *The Dancing Plague: The Strange, True Story of an Extraordinary Illness.* Naperville, Ill.: Sourcebooks, 2009.

Weir, Alison. *The Life of Elizabeth I.* New York: Ballantine Books, 1998.

Weis, René. *Shakespeare Unbound: Decoding a Hidden Life.* New York: Henry Holt, 2007.

Wells, Stanley, and Gary Taylor, eds. *The Oxford Shakespeare: The Complete Works.* Second edition. Oxford: Clarendon Press, 2005.

Wickham, Glynne, Herbert Berry, and William Ingram, eds. *English Professional Theatre 1530–1660.* New York: Cambridge University Press, 2000.

Wilson, Ian. *Shakespeare: The Evidence: Unlocking the Mysteries of the Man and His Work.* London: Headline Book Publishing, 1993.

Woods, Susanne, ed. *The Poems of Aemilia Lanyer.* New York: Oxford University Press, 1993.

Woolf, Virginia. *The Virginia Woolf Reader.* Edited by Mitchell A. Leaska. Orlando, Fla.: Harcourt, 1984.

Yates, Frances A. *The Art of Memory.* Chicago: University of Chicago Press, 1966.

———. *Astraea: The Imperial Theme in the Sixteenth Century.* New York: Penguin Books, 1977.

———. *The French Academies of the Sixteenth Century.* Nendeln, Liechtenstein: Kraus Reprint, 1968.

———. *The Occult Philosophy in the Elizabethan Age.* London: Routledge & Kegan Paul, 1979.

———. *The Rosicrucian Enlightenment.* New York: Routledge & Kegan Paul, 1972.

———. *Theatre of the World.* Chicago: University of Chicago Press, 1969.

Zimmer, Carl. *Soul Made Flesh: The Discovery of the Brain—and How It Changed the World.* New York: Free Press, 2004.

A NOTE ON THE TYPE

This book was set in Garamond, a typeface originally designed by the famous Parisian type cutter Claude Garamond (1480–1561). This version of Garamond was drawn by Günter Gerhard Lange (1921–2008) and released by the Berthold type foundry in 1972. Lange based his Garamond revival on a combination of models found in specimen sheets from both Paris and Antwerp.

Claude Garamond is one of the most famous type designers in printing history. His distinguished romans and italics first appeared in *Opera Ciceronis* in 1543–1544. While delightfully unconventional in design, the Garamond types are clear and open, yet maintain an elegance and precision of line that mark them as French.

Typeset by Scribe, Philadelphia, Pennsylvania

Printed and bound by Berryville Graphics,
Berryville, Virginia

Designed by Betty Lew